Contents

The handbook of dramatherapy

Sue Jennings,
Ann Cattanach,
Steve Mitchell,
Anna Chesner
and Brenda Meldrum

Routledge
Taylor & Francis Group

LONDON AND NEW YORK

First published 1994
by Routledge
27 Church Road, Hove, East Sussex BN3 2FA

Simultaneously published in the USA and Canada
by Routledge
270 Madison Avenue, New York NY 10016

Routledge is an imprint of the Taylor & Francis Group, an Informa business

Reprinted 1995, 2000 and 2007

Transferred to Digital Printing 2010

© 1994 Sue Jennings, Ann Cattanach, Steve Mitchell, Anna Chesner
and Brenda Meldrum

Typeset in Times by LaserScript, Mitcham, Surrey

This publication has been produced with paper manufactured to strict
environmental standards and with pulp derived from sustainable forests.

British Library Cataloguing in Publication Data
A catalogue record for this book is available from the British Library

Library of Congress Cataloguing in Publication Data
A catalogue record for this book is available from the Library of Congress

ISBN 978-0-415-09056-8 (pbk)

Publisher's Note
The publisher has gone to great lengths to ensure the quality of this reprint
but points out that some imperfections in the original may be apparent.

The handbook of dramatherapy

Dramatherapy, first established in the UK in the early 1960s, is being increasingly practised in a range of therapeutic settings and is of growing interest to theatre practitioners and teachers. *The Handbook of Dramatherapy* brings together five authors who are all practising dramatherapists, working in clinical, artistic and educational fields. Their clinical experience includes preventive and community-based work, as well as dramatherapy in long- and short-stay psychiatry, work with elderly people, forensic dramatherapy, work with abused children and adolescents, and children with learning difficulties.

An easy-to-read introduction to the major contrasting models of drama-therapy, the book looks at the developmental approach, the use of role theory, the ideas of 'the theatre of expression' and 'the theatre of healing', and presents an integrated model of dramatherapy. The authors explain the theoretical background of these approaches, show how each works in practice in a particular situation, and suggest how it might be adapted to other settings. They also describe the historical background, explain the difference between dramatherapy and psychodrama, discuss assessment and evaluation techniques, and how to develop more appropriate research methods to address the aims and goals of dramatherapy.

The Handbook of Dramatherapy provides a comprehensive basis for theory and practice, and will be a valuable source of reference for all mental health professionals, as well as students of dramatherapy and theatre.

Sue Jennings is Senior Research Fellow in the Academic Unit of Obstetrics and Gynaecology at the London Hospital Medical College, and Visiting Professor at Tel Hai College, Israel. **Ann Cattanach** is a therapist for Harrow Health Trust, and Course Director of Play Therapy at the Institute of Dramatherapy, Roehampton. **Steve Mitchell** is a dramatherapist for Lancaster Health Trust and Course Director of Dramatherapy at the Institute of Dramatherapy, Roehampton. **Anna Chesner** is a senior dramatherapist for the Mid-Surrey Health Authority and a tutor at the Institute of Dramatherapy. **Brenda Meldrum** is a co-founder and director of Theatre Therapy Partnership, a freelance dramatherapist and a tutor at the Institute of Dramatherapy.

Illustrations

FIGURES

TABLES

Notes on the authors

Sue Jennings is an actress, author and theatre therapist who has pioneered and practised dramatherapy for over thirty years. She is Visiting Professor of Dramatherapy at New York University and Tel Hai Regional College, Israel and retired director of the Institute of Dramatherapy, London. She is currently researching her hypothesis that the mind has a dramatic structure. Her publications include *Dramatherapy Theory and Practice 2*, Routledge, 1992 and *Theatre, Ritual and Transformation: The Senoi Temiar*, Routledge, 1995.

Ann Cattanach is a dramatherapist, play therapist and a lecturer in Communication and Drama. She is currently a therapist for Harrow Health Trust and is running courses in dramatherapy and is Course Director of Play Therapy at the Institute of Dramatherapy, Roehampton.

Steve Mitchell is a dramatherapist for Lancaster Health Trust and Course Director of Dramatherapy at the Institute of Dramatherapy at Roehampton, regularly contributing to courses abroad in Greece, Norway and Israel. As Project Director of Pathfinder Studio in the 1980s he developed the 'Theatre of Self-expression', a form of therapeutic theatre combining theatre art with personal development.

Anna Chesner works in the NHS as a senior dramatherapist. She has been involved in the training of dramatherapists since 1986, and is a tutor at the Institute of Dramatherapy at Roehampton. In her private practice she uses dramatherapy, psychodrama and group analytic psychotherapy, and she is currently researching the relationship between these methods as a therapeutic triad.

Brenda Meldrum is a dramatherapist and a co-founder of Theatre Therapy Partnership, an enterprise which uses theatre structures and techniques for therapeutic purposes. She also writes, directs and performs. She is a tutor at the Institute of Dramatherapy at Roehampton.

Prologue

Sue Jennings

Telemachus You have conjured up too marvellous a vision: I cannot bear to think of it. And I, for one, dare not expect such happiness . . .

(Homer, *The Odyssey*)

Bottom I have had a most rare vision . . .

(Shakespeare, *A Midsummer Night's Dream* IV. i. 203)

Was it a vision, or a waking dream?
Fled is that music:- Do I wake or sleep?

(Keats, 'Ode to a Nightingale')

DRAMA AND THEATRE AS CULTURE

The theatre is a place we visit in order to have a 'vision' – to see how something is or how it was or indeed how it might be. The theatre is able to condense a story in time, space and action in order that we can take it in as a piece; it also expands the story so that we have a new perception or understanding. The theatre, through spectacle, helps us to understand who we are and where we are in the world.

This idea is not new: dramatic ritual which can establish individual and social identity has existed for millennia in some form or other; early theatre forms were very explicit in their visionary and healing function. The theatre is a structured experience within which we respond or interact as an engaged audience, in an enacted story that is being presented for us. It speaks to us and for us as both individuals and groups, and it is unique to the particular audience who are present. Each performance is different from the next one, however well known the story; the actors create a difference every time it is performed, thereby allowing us a privileged vision when we attend. This is what makes theatre different from television or film where the image is formed and the only variation is our response to it; whereas in the theatre, our very responses assist the actors to shape the drama to our expectations and energy, so that indeed we are a part of the performance; an important dimension of the theatre process. As we see below, there are many others who are involved in this process before the actual performance is shown to the audience.

Glynne Wickham (1985: 7) reminds us that:

> every member of an audience (ourselves included) spends a large part of
> every day acting out some chosen role (often an imposed role), giving a daily
> 'performance'. Those people whom we encounter in the course of the days are
> our 'audience'. We wear clothes or 'costume' we consider to be appropriate to
> that role . . .

He suggests that for much of the time we are not aware that we are actors, except
perhaps when we are relaxing and then realise that we have changed our
personas. This phenomenon is of a vital importance in understanding the unique
group experience in dramatic art because:

> it links, through mimetic action, each and every one of us with those rare and
> exceptional individuals whom we label as actors. Yet they, like us, are human
> beings, but the role that they have chosen to play in life consists in putting this
> whole process into reverse. The major difference lies in the subjectivity of the
> role-playing in our own daily lives and the objectivity of a professional actor's
> public theatrical performance.

(Wickham 1985: 8)

An understanding of this process, that all of us are actors for most of our lives,
enables us to look at a rationale for the therapeutic nature of drama and theatre.
Within this rationale we need to consider the capacity of the theatre to para-
doxically both conceal and reveal. In our everyday lives we conceal aspects of
ourselves that we wish to keep private or that are inappropriate for the setting, and
the actor on the stage will conceal aspects of him or herself that might get in the
way of the character being portrayed. This enables us to reveal what is appropriate and, in the case of the actor, also to surprise us and take us unawares; to
create a vision or a spectacle which in turn allows us to understand something
new or in a fresh way.

Theatre and drama engage us at several levels at the same time; it is little use
us having an emotional response to a scene in a play if our thinking self cannot
accept the story's premise. The power of theatre is our engagement with it, with
both of our brain hemispheres; the left hemisphere to appeal to our logic and
intellect and the right hemisphere to engage our intuition, creativity, artistry and
dramatic imagination.

It is interesting to reflect on the number of different artists and craftspeople who
are needed to create a work in the theatre. The director, designer, costumier, tech-
nician, engineer, architect, painter, musician, as well as the actors and actresses; and
this group of people, who may be as diverse as any human group, have to work
together in the service of creating the ensemble to produce the given piece. Indeed,
one dramatherapeutic device is to explore several internal artistes in any client group,
rather than just concentrate on the actor. Many of my groups will consider themselves
as designers of sets and costumes and lighting, as directors and producers, as well as
actors within the 'theatres of healing' that we create.

Whereas, as Wickham says, we engage subjectively in acting in our everyday lives, we can now understand how we can make use of 'objective' acting if our everyday lives are not running as smoothly as we would hope. We may well be familiar with the technique of role-play to explore a situation or to learn new management skills or to develop assertiveness or to re-enact a painful past event. This type of role-play is usually very close to the reality of the everyday world that we inhabit or wish to inhabit. The objective reality of the actor establishes another type of reality – that of 'dramatic reality' – which creates through dramatic distancing, symbolic time, space and action. It is within 'dramatic reality' as contrasted with 'everyday reality' that dramatherapists are able to work therapeutically with a wide variety of client groups.

The theatre is unique in its capacity to integrate several art forms as well as several aspects of the self. In no other structure can art, music, dance, play, story and drama come together in a single entity; we are engaged by the juxtaposition of visual images, sounds, movement, verbal statements at sensory, emotional and thinking levels. It is said by many to be the most dangerous of the arts and was banished by Plato from his ideal Republic and thrown out of the churches in the Middle Ages. Even in the present time, theatres are closing as finance is short, drama teachers are considered a luxury or else subversive, and dramatherapists were formally 'recognised' years after music therapists and art therapists. Theatre and drama still make people anxious, especially when these active forms have not been explained or understood, or when they are equated with magical practice and shamanistic rituals. Recent demands for Shakespeare to be taught in schools has emphasised reading the plays rather than witnessing theatrical performances. Yet Shakespeare himself knew how important dramatic reality was as a means of understanding life itself. He constantly makes use of the metaphor of the actor, the stage and the theatre when discussing the human condition.

> The actors are at hand, and by their show
> You shall know all that you are like to know.
>
> > (*A Midsummer Night's Dream* V. i. 115–16)

> Like a dull actor now
> I have forgot my part and I am out
> Even to a full disgrace.
>
> > (*Coriolanus* V. iii. 40–2)

> an excellent play, well digested in the scenes, set down with as much modesty as cunning.
>
> > (*Hamlet* II. ii. 438–9)

Therefore if the theatre can be understood on the one hand as a separate reality within which we engage and interact with our imaginations, and on the other hand as intimately connected with all of our lives and personal stories, we can begin to reflect on its therapeutic efficacy. The fact that it creates dramatic distance makes it more possible to interact with aspects of one's own life and to understand these aspects which previously were too close to us, for us to see. Therefore dramatherapy is connected with our own lives, because theatre is connected with our lives. Through engagement with theatre we are able to experience a vision of how we are or how we might be.

DRAMA AND THEATRE AS HUMAN DEVELOPMENT

Dramatherapy, however, does not just rest its case on the importance of cultural forms of theatre in societies, it is closely bound up with the development of human beings themselves. Observations of infants from birth demonstrate that they are 'mimetically engaged' with their parents and carers and the world around them from an early age. They 'move and sound' in rhythm, they 'mark-make' with food and saliva, they 'imitate' sounds and facial gestures close to them; these mimetic experiments begin before an infant can walk and develop into 'performance' by about the age of 10 months when a child needs an audience as witness. This 'proto-drama' develops into sensory and dramatic play during pre-school years, and in Western culture makes a transition into drama at about 7 years. This drama developmental paradigm is known as 'embodiment–projection–role' (EPR). The drama and theatre that ensues is influenced by family, school and culture, and whether it is given educational, social or cultural value: does society actually value the capacity to have a vision? (Or is it more concerned with re-vision or super-vision or even tele-vision?) Nevertheless, whatever the value system, it is important to understand that, throughout our human development, there are dramatic rituals which mark the various stages.

DRAMA AND THEATRE AS RITUAL

Dramatic ritual is important at the various stages through which we pass during our life journey; rituals of transition move us through our age stages and changes of status. Whether it is a wedding or a naming or a burial, we dress in different clothes, take on different roles and use different language. We enact these changes in dramatic form in ritual. Ritual also forms a part of religious practice in all belief systems as well as being a part of ceremony and celebration. Many rituals in themselves are meant to produce a visionary state in the participants. This idea causes some anxiety in traditional church people but, nevertheless, we can see that in most religious ritual there is both the aim to change human consciousness as well as the effect of altered states of consciousness. This is brought about by the dramatic ritual itself and the various sensory stimuli that accompany it, such as incense, music, icons, costumes, movement and dance.

Western society has seen a decrease in ritual in the latter half of this century and it is thought that ritual specialists in some cases are being replaced by therapeutic specialists. For example, funerary rituals are less protracted and elaborate but we note there has been the establishment of the role of bereavement counsellors. Drama as ritual and dramatherapy as ritual have an important contribution to make in the re-establishing of secure dramatic structures within which change and transition are possible. Dramatic ritual is linked to the emergence of theatre art, and most writers would agree that more formal theatre grew out of dramatic group rituals in ancient societies, and that early theatre was also linked to belief and therefore to vision. The rituals of any society or social group can be observed in the dramatic play of children. Children's dramatic play reflects the norm of the child's familial and social world.

DRAMA AND DRAMATIC PLAY

We are all familiar with the games and dramas that occupy extended time with young children. Sensory play, toy play, story play, drama games, dramatised or enacted play are central to the life of young children. Western society tends to discourage play once a child enters the serious world of school or else replace the human engagement with both self and others in play, with video and media games; the latter has its own function – like film and television described above – but it does not replace the involvement of the child and the child with its peers in the active and reactive nature of play. Children play out past fears, rehearse current strategies and anticipate new events through various forms of play. Dramatic play is a natural culmination of the developmental drama described above, whereby people have in-built therapeutic mechanisms which help them deal with their day-to-day life and the unexpected; through enactment we are empowered to act – acting helps us 'act'. We learn how to act through involvement in dramatic play where we are able to develop a range of appropriate roles and behaviour. We learn about the outcome of choices, we rehearse those skills we may need in later life, we are able to project into the future and test both our realities and our dreams. The foundations for preventive dramatherapy are laid within the early years of life and we may find that many adults need the opportunity to engage with dramatic play once again to enable self-healing to take place. The roles we play at are an education for our life when a diverse range of roles is required of us, especially living in a complex society. And play itself can allow us both our personal dreams as well as the visions for our future.

DRAMA, THEATRE AND ROLE

In each of the sections above, whether we are describing drama and theatre, drama as development, drama and ritual or drama and dramatic play, we find that the basic concept of 'role' is essential. We cannot begin to consider drama and theatre in any form without role; in the theatre we may refer more often to the character we are playing which in itself has many roles. All of us need a wide repertory of roles and the skills to go with them in order to function as both an individual and a social being. We talk of role-confusion or role-conflict when our roles are doubled – for example when the head teacher is also our parent, or the doctor's receptionist is married to one of our siblings. We have ideas about the appropriateness of dress, language and behaviour in different roles and whether these are prescribed by the institution or whether there is a degree of individual choice.

How do we acquire our roles? As suggested in the section on development we begin to imitate at only a few months old; we learn much from the 'role-modelling' of others, especially in our early life. How our parents and teachers behave towards us shapes our roles and our own role repertoire. If we are not able to move between a wide range of roles then often we get trapped in a single role which can prove to be inappropriate for certain situations. We need time to practise our roles in play and in drama; to test their effect on others and to 'try them on for size'; we need to refine our roles and see subtleties and fine tuning in our responses. This role behaviour becomes internalised as we mature so that much of our 'acting life' in 'everyday reality' no longer needs rehearsal. New situations and major changes will, however, still need some preparation. The theatre itself can inspire us to resolve or change things in our lives or to realise the implications of our behaviour. The more experienced we are in our range of roles, the more we are equipped for survival in a rapidly changing society. However, it is important to bear in mind that our roles are attached to our inner self. They are not just quick changes of clothes. Our inner life motivates our roles and projects them into our social interactions. If we wish to change our role behaviour then it needs to be done through active involvement in the new role; insight alone is often not enough to bring about lasting change.

DRAMA AND THEATRE AND DRAMATHERAPY

In the foregoing sections we have discussed various models of dramatherapy and the way it can be viewed from different perspectives. The heart of this book on dramatherapy is to illustrate the myriad of variations of the dramatic act and therefore the dramatherapeutic act. Any one of the above can be held constant as a model for a dramatherapy group or individual practice. The choice about which model, or whether it should be a combination of several, is dictated by the needs of the client(s) and the skills and experience of the dramatherapist. Drama and theatre are such vast topics that it is easy to get lost in the plethora of possible formulations. Can this be simplified? The various authors in this book demonstrate the rich canvas of dramatherapy practice but what is common to all of them is the explicit or implicit assumption that dramatherapy enables the creation of dramatic reality and therefore dramatic distancing. Therefore everyone will work with a greater or lesser dramatic distance through the medium of dramatic enactment or role-play, which calls upon the dramatic imagination. This engages us both in the outer space of the theatre or dramatherapy room, and the inner space of the imagined world, together with the corporeal space of the inner and outer body.

THE DRAMATHERAPEUTIC SPACE

The dramatherapeutic space is an actual concrete or 'concrete' place where it is appropriate and safe to establish dramatic reality. It may be a room which is in multiple use and therefore needs special attention to ritualise its change into the dramatherapeutic space. It may be a specially designated space which can be developed dramatherapeutically in a variety of ways. I asked two practising dramatherapists their view on space to work in:

> I have to overcome an initial thoughtless reaction: 'somewhere big enough to hold about a dozen people'. Certainly I would want this, but it may not be the most important thing. First of all it should be a space that outsiders or non-group members will not easily invade. It should be big enough in width, breadth and height in order to create a series of spaces. It should be quiet enough. I believe that the tendency to create 'a room that is a womb' in order to encourage new life is not necessarily helpful and that the most 'unsuitable room' can in fact produce significant experiences. The space should be better at asking questions than producing answers; a space that the group uses and not one that uses the group. Above all it should be a space that 'gives rise to character'.
>
> (Roger Grainger)

Here the practitioner is immediately concerned with the symbolic possibilities of the space. The following is a quite contrasting response which deals with the practicalities:

> The following is put together with my own client group in mind – people with multiple physical and mental handicap.
> The Studio: needs to be private but not isolated, with a key so that it can be locked. The dramatherapist needs to have identified a space that is not a thoroughfare or a hall or somewhere used for lots of other things. I prefer a carpeted floor for warmth, large enough for eight people to move around; not cluttered and seats which can fold away; shelves and cupboards for equipment. Curtains or blinds at the windows and a heater one can operate oneself.
> The Equipment: needs to be simple and flexible: large blocks (hard and soft) that can be transformed into different things; soft mats; cassette player which also records; music and blank tapes; sensory objects for sense play; simple costumes: hats, cloaks, masks, glasses; pieces of different textured material; mirrors; elastic rope and tow rope; boxes and bags; cushions and blankets; small toys; finger paints and brush paints; clay and/or plasticine; water jug and cups; tissues; cloth and towel; possibly bean bags. If possible a camera for recording work and a polaroid for giving instant feedback to clients.
>
> (Becky Wilde)

Equipment is very personal to the individual dramatherapist and is usually built up over a period of time; equipment should be new as well as well used without being 'tacky' or others' rubbish! I would add my own predilection for a set of nesting dolls, sufficient mask-making materials of different kinds, and sufficient storage so that clients are not overwhelmed by all the equipment having to be on show. Dramatherapists need to negotiate a budget for setting up their practice as well as for adding to the equipment and replacing consumables.

WHERE DO DRAMATHERAPISTS WORK?

In the ensuing chapters various dramatherapists talk about their practice in relation to different client groups and a clear idea emerges of the variety of remits and applications. Many dramatherapists work in hospitals – specifically in medical settings – as well as in the community and for education, prisons and social services. Dramatherapists work with adults, including elderly people as well as children. Dramatherapists usually find it more fruitful to be part of a therapeutic team which may include medical and paramedical staff, social workers and other arts therapists. Dramatherapists find that time spent in networking other staff and institutions will be helpful in getting support for their own practice. A possible hand-out to describe dramatherapy in brief is included in Appendix 1. It is important to remember that, whereas many professionals may do short or long courses in dramatherapy and integrate the approach into their existing practice, those people who wish to become dramatherapists and registered as such have to complete a postgraduate training at one of the training establishments which are recognised by the Department of Health and validated by the British Association for Dramatherapists (BADTh, see Appendix 3). Dramatherapists have to adhere to professional Codes of Practice and Ethics (see Appendix 2) and are recommended to join BADTh (see Appendix 4).

THE INSTITUTE OF DRAMATHERAPY

All the contributors to this *Handbook of Dramatherapy* have either trained with, or contributed to the teaching in a significant way of, the Institute of Dramatherapy (IDT). It is a unique organisation in that it enables people to train over a longer period of time in a modular system which makes it possible for people to attend both from overseas and the further reaches of the UK. It has expanded rapidly in recent years, actually doubling student intakes in 1992 and 1993 with various combinations of dramatherapy and play therapy. This year sees IDT move to the Roehampton Institute (University of Surrey) as a separate organisation within the wider framework of Roehampton. This will mean a greater access to a flourishing drama and theatre department, as well as music therapy, dance-movement therapy, art and play with children. An integrated centre of excellence in therapeutic play and artistic therapies will emerge in the next few years, and the following chapters illustrate the range of expertise.

THE HANDBOOK OF DRAMATHERAPY

In Chapter 1, Brenda Meldrum traces the history of the profession in Britain and examines its present position. In defining 'dramatherapy', she attempts a synthesis of the two concepts of 'drama' and 'therapy' and describes four theoretical models which underpin the discipline: a theatre model; a model from therapeutic drama; a model based on role theory; and an anthropological model. This chapter gives the reader a flavour of the diversity of dramatherapy practice.

In Chapter 2, Ann Cattanach explores the creative life of the client as part of their whole life journey. She emphasises the importance of working and re-working the life stages of individuals and groups and the struggle to integrate conflicting elements of experience. She describes this process as 'restoring life through art' and draws upon theories of dramatic play, developmental psychology and social psychology to illustrate this model. Cattanach identifies the processes as 'Living in and out of time', 'Dramatic fiction' and 'Playfulness'.

Chapter 3, by Steve Mitchell, describes in detail how he applies theatre structures as a therapeutic modality when working with different client populations. Drawing on his extensive experience in the professional theatre as well as his clinical work as a dramatherapist, Mitchell offers the reader useful processes which can be employed with clients and patients whether as individuals or in groups, that come from his experience of acute treatment, rehabilitations, elderly populations and out-patients.

Chapter 4, by Anna Chesner, attempts to put dramatherapy in the context of the large institution and in the context of the particular needs of people with learning disabilities. Chesner stresses that it is important to see the total person rather than focus on the disability. Dramatherapy is described as a tool of empowerment, wherever possible within a group: the group becomes the therapeutic agency which fosters greater self-esteem and greater appreciation of the peer group. Clinical examples of this work are included and explanations of the development of the dramatherapy, both within a single session and over time, which illustrates the movement from the ritualised and the concrete towards increasing imaginative involvement, and towards greater autonomy of the group.

Meldrum moves the debate forward again in Chapter 5. She presents a definition of 'role' as used by leading American dramatherapist, Robert Landy, and traces the development of his theory through the social psychological writings of Erving Goffman. She examines the role model in the light of philosopher Bruce Wilshire's critique of the claim that, as social beings, we play roles in 'real life' in the same way as actors play characters on the stage. Meldrum presents an alternative way of looking at role through the theory of symbolic interactionism of social psychologist G.H. Mead and the constructivist position of personality theorist Sarah Hampson.

In Chapter 6 I take a contrasting pathway and consider the expansion of human experience and perspective through engagement with the dramatic and theatrical structure. Drawing on inspiration from Artaud, in particular, as well as contemporary anthropology, I suggest that ritual is an important and necessary part of the healing process. The metaphysical model is seen as often working from the 'outside in', through larger-than-life masks and effigies.

Many people reading this book will want to ask the question, 'What is the difference between psychodrama and dramatherapy?' Anna Chesner addresses this question in Chapter 7. She explores the importance of the centrality of the drama (see Cattanach below) to both methodologies, which is what they share in common. The differences are explored through fictionalised case history sessions, with observations of method, philosophy and technique. She suggests that psychodrama is a more defined technique whereas dramatherapy can draw upon any structure or method in drama and theatre. She contrasts the direct, protagonist-centred approach of psychodrama with what she describes as the oblique, metaphorical, group-centred approach of dramatherapy.

Ann Cattanach, in Chapter 8, provides the links and synthesis between these two fields that are often seen as disconnected. She discusses the prime focus of the play therapist and the dramatherapist. Play therapy is seen as the integration of the part that is 'me' and the disengaging from the parts that are 'not me', whereas the dramatherapist is more concerned with the issues of life and death and a place in the world outside. She emphasises how the play and the drama are *central* to the therapy rather than a stimulus for talking or interpretation. Cattanach illustrates with clinical material how the play and the drama can ebb and flow within a single session, thereby emphasising the importance of practitioners understanding the wider view.

In Chapter 9, Steve Mitchell describes an innovatory piece of practice known as 'The Dramatherapy Venture Project'. This chapter is a detailed case study of a residential group working in dramatherapy on the edges of Dartmoor. It demonstrates how the dramatherapist can set up and prepare a time-intensive project which can encompass working both indoors and outdoors. Mitchell works in this project within a para-theatrical rationale of dramatherapy and uses ritual processes to generate healing images. This chapter continues his own exploration of the interface between theatre, therapy and healing.

Chapter 10 is rather different from the others in that I employ a series of interviews with well-known practitioners and ask them the question 'What is dramatherapy?' The various people – Gordon Wiseman, Robert Landy, Mooli Lahad and Pamela Mond – talk freely of the areas that they come from, the journeys they have made through drama, theatre and dramatherapy, and openly acknowledge the areas where there are still question marks. They all reflect on the fact that dramatherapy still needs a lot of research and investigation and will no doubt continue to need it in the future – such is the complexity of its process.

The final chapter, by Brenda Meldrum, looks at the way that dramatherapists assess and evaluate their practice. She first discusses the work of dramatherapists who use story-making and second, the assessments of dramatherapists working within the National Health Service. There is not a large number of research publications in the literature, but research into dramatherapy practice is growing. Meldrum describes five very different published research programmes and examines current research and evaluation with groups and individuals. She then looks briefly at some research programmes that are now in their planning stage. While arguing that dramatherapy is not, nor should it become, 'scientific', Meldrum believes that dramatherapists, the majority of whom work in the National Health Service, will have to come to terms with demands of managers to budget, evaluate and assess their practice. She urges debate within the profession to find a truly dramatherapeutic way of approaching these demands.

Finally there is a brief Epilogue which looks forward, and echoes Meldrum's emphasis on encouraging greater expansion of the diversity of dramatherapy method and application. I believe we are approaching a renaissance in dramatherapy with the very rapid expansion of trainees and practice which could provide a potent force for change in the future.

The Appendices include a brief résumé of 'What is dramatherapy?', the Codes of Practice and Ethics of the Institute of Dramatherapy, and a useful list of addresses of professional bodies and training programmes.

The authors hope that this book will move the reader forward too, with ideas and imagination, but wish to emphasise that the written word here is no substitute for active engagement in the process.

REFERENCE

Wickham, G. (1985) *A History of the Theatre*, Oxford, Phaidon.

Chapter 1

Historical background and overview of dramatherapy

Brenda Meldrum

INTRODUCTION

This introduction to what dramatherapy is, where it comes from, who does it, where and why they do it, is a somewhat breathless dash through the current state of dramatherapy practice. I hope that it will show the complexities of the profession, born of its different approaches, influences and models. I shall begin with a very brief history of its origins; I shall then proceed to give some definitions of dramatherapy and the status of the profession in the early 1990s; finally, I shall consider some of the models underlying practice.

A BRIEF HISTORY OF DRAMATHERAPY

The profession of dramatherapy is new and evolved in Britain in the 1960s from drama in education, theatre in education and remedial drama. This chapter is concerned mainly with the development of the profession in Britain.

During the early 1960s, when so much of the establishment, including the certainties of psychiatry, was under attack by the newly liberated young, arts therapy groups began to be formed in Britain and in Continental Europe. They were influenced by the optimism of the times, when it seemed that new ideas and radical approaches to learning and the arts would really change society.

Peter Slade, a gentle man with a mind of flexible steel, was encouraging children to express themselves through drama, but his message to adults – parents and teachers – was that they should listen to their children. We adults, he said, usually spoil our children's absorption in their tasks and deny their creativity by our attempts to control their actions. Listen to children? It was a radical message in the 1960s!

At the same time, Peter Brook, the great international theatre director, was experimenting with different theatrical forms such as Artaud's 'theatre of cruelty', culminating in theatrical productions like Peter Weiss's *Marat-Sade*, which had a much greater influence on theatre practice in Britain than the whinings of Jimmy Porter around the mythical kitchen sink.

In Poland, Jerzey Grotowski's experiments with his laboratory theatre were producing extraordinary actors who were trained to think of themselves and their work as 'a paradigm of human kind' – a new role, indeed, for the actor used to playing 'as cast'! In the laboratory theatre, the process for the actors was a form of analysis, of therapy for them and for the spectator.

In education, Dorothy Heathcote brought drama into the realm of the pursuit of knowledge; Heathcote's approach was truly child-centred: 'unlike the kind of progressive teacher who abandons the child to its own resources, she accepts that teaching is an act of benign interference in the lives of children' (Johnson and O'Neill 1984: 12). Heathcote's innovation was that, instead of directing the children and keeping her distance as a teacher, she entered the drama by taking a role herself.

> The encounter with the role may be intense and absorbing for her pupils, but it will also be objective and reflective, since experience alone without reflection will not lead to learning.
>
> (Johnson and O'Neill 1984: 12)

In 1982, O'Neill and Lambert, two of her many disciples, wrote:

> The most significant kind of learning which is attributable to experience in drama is the growth in the pupils' understanding about human behaviour, themselves and the world they live in. This growth of understanding, which will involve changes in customary ways of thinking and feeling, is likely to be the primary aim of drama teaching.
>
> (p. 13)

Alas, this radical message frightens the establishment. They do not want children to think in new ways. Drama, perhaps because it is so subversive, is not even included in the core curriculum and instead of looking at different ways of experiencing, we are encouraged to return to what is loosely termed and never defined 'traditional values'. Teachers are prevented, sometimes by law, from giving their pupils the opportunity of learning about alternative religious experiences and different family and sexual relations.

In the early 1960s these radical approaches in drama and education influenced Sue Jennings (the co-ordinating editor of this volume) who formed the Remedial Drama Group which used drama techniques developed in education in clinical areas. The Group developed into the Remedial Drama Centre in Holloway Road in London, and became the first centre specialising in the training and the practice of creative and expressive drama with adults and children with special needs. In 1970, the Centre called itself the 'Dramatherapy Centre', and by 1972 it had expanded into a private consultancy offering training and group work with adults and children. In parallel, Billy Lindqvist began the Sesame organisation which eventually opened a full-time training programme in Drama and Movement at Kingsway College.

By 1977, dramatherapy was becoming known in the arts therapy world as an alternative to psychodrama, and the Hertfordshire College of Art and Design decided to expand the work of their Art and Psychology division by taking its first group of dramatherapy students. In the following year, a research fellow in dramatherapy was employed by the College of Ripon and York St John and a course in dramatherapy was begun. By 1980, a third diploma course was initiated in the South Devon Technical College.

Out of Dramatherapy Consultants came the Institute of Dramatherapy in 1988, with a theatrically-based diploma in dramatherapy. There are now five post-graduate training courses in Britain, which are discussed in greater detail below.

WHAT IS THE DEFINITION OF 'DRAMATHERAPY'?

To state the obvious, 'dramatherapy' is the synthesis of two massive processes: that of 'drama' with 'therapy'. I shall begin by defining what 'drama' is and what 'therapy' is and then turn to the definition of 'dramatherapy' itself.

What is drama?

The *Shorter Oxford Dictionary* defines drama as:

> A composition in prose or verse, adapted to be acted on the stage, in which a story is related by means of dialogue and action and is represented with accompanying gesture, costume and scenery, as in real life.

Drama does not, however, need a stage, nor does it need costume, props and scenery. What drama does need is an individual or a group of people who use themselves – their bodies and their minds – through action and often through speech to tell a story.

'Drama' in ancient Greek meant something that is acted out, or lived through. I may talk about the story of my life, or the drama of my life which, although I am focusing on myself, is set in a social context of my interaction with others. Drama is 'essentially social and involves contact, communication and the nego-tiation of meaning. The group nature of the work imposes certain pressures on the participant, but also brings considerable rewards' (O'Neill and Lambert 1982).

Very young children take an empty beaker and 'pretend' to drink; before they can speak they imitate sounds – not randomly, but in a context: the soothing noises mother makes when her child is crying are imitated by him as he plays with a toy. The child is developing an essential requirement for human beings – the ability to take the role of the other. Humans recognise the emotional res-ponses of other people, because they feel what the other person feels. Dramatic activity is 'the direct result of the ability to role-play – to want to know how it feels to be in someone else's shoes' (Heathcote, in Johnson and O'Neill 1984).

Drama is thus a separation of the self and the non-self within a particular time and space. The child who is 'pretending' to give her teddy-bear a drink from a plastic beaker is operating in a dramatic reality. What she is doing is in real time but also in imaginary time. It may be the middle of the morning, but she is pretending it's tea-time. She may be sitting in the garden, but she is pretending she is at Buckingham Palace having tea with the Queen. Dramatic distance allows the person, whether as actor or as spectator, a passage back and forth between two planes: the subjective and the objective.

This experience is most obvious in the theatre. 'Theatre is a direct experience that is shared when people imagine and behave as if they were other than themselves in some other place at another time' (Neelands 1990: 4).

As audience in the theatre we allow actors to stand in for us, but we still maintain our own separation or distance. When we identify with the characters the actors are playing: 'We accept our kinship with monsters: we enlarge the domain of our being' (Wilshire 1982: 10). The actors do not become the characters they are playing, but they bring themselves and their own experience to their interpretations of the roles in the text. The actors, too, are experiencing both the subjective and the objective reality through the aesthetic distance of the drama.

So drama is a social encounter in a special place and in a special time. The actors and the spectators move between real time and imaginary time, from existential reality to dramatic reality.

What is therapy?

The word 'therapy' is derived from the Greek, meaning 'healing'. So a 'psychotherapy' is the healing of the mind and 'dramatherapy' is healing through drama. 'Dramatherapy' is not simply the use of drama techniques in psychotherapy: dramatherapy is a discipline in its own right with its own professional body and research. It would be useful at this point to look at some definitions of psychotherapy and see how they relate to dramatherapy.

Cox (1986: 45) defines 'psychotherapy' as:

A process in which the patient [sic] is enabled to do for himself what he cannot do on his own. The therapist does not do it for him, but he cannot do it without the therapist.

The role of the therapist, then, is one of a facilitator, helping the client to act. Hence, the therapist/client relationship is a dynamic one.

Holmes and Lindley (1991: 7) quoted by Doktor (1992: 9) define psychotherapy as:

The systematic use of a relationship between therapist and patient – as opposed to pharmacological or social methods – to produce changes in cognition, feelings and behaviour.

This definition states that the relationship between the therapist and her client is in itself the therapeutic medium.

Yalom (1985) encourages therapists and clients to speak freely, to shed all internal censors and filters save one – the filter of responsibility: 'In the therapy group, freedom becomes possible and constructive only when it is coupled with responsibility' (Yalom 1985: 225). The therapist's responsibility is to the client and to the task of therapy. The therapist sets a therapeutic process in motion and his or her responsibility is to this process and not to put him or herself in the central position. The role of the therapist is that of the responsible facilitator, concerned with the process of the client's journey and not of his or her own.

The initial goal of therapy is the relief of suffering. Therapy is of its nature interpersonal, whether it be work with one client or work with a group. The therapist's first relationship with the client is to help relieve suffering and mental distress; then the goals of the therapy change 'from wanting relief from anxiety or depression to wanting to learn to communicate with others, to be more trusting with others, to learn to love' (Yalom 1991: 7).

Therapy is not merely emotional catharsis. It is both an emotional and cognitive experience. The client feels something strongly; he or she tries to understand the implication of the experience and the emotions attached to the experience and this process has a direct relevance to his or her existential experience in the here-and-now.

Yalom (1985) provides clear research evidence that what distinguishes a successful experience of psychotherapy is the cognitive component which is at the core of the therapeutic process. Thus insight and understanding are essential for therapeutic change. The client assumes responsibility for her or his life predicament: 'As long as one believes that one's problems are caused by some force or agency outside oneself there is no leverage in therapy' (Yalom 1991: 8). Then the problem becomes one of moving from an intellectual appreciation of a truth about oneself to some emotional experience of it. 'It is only when therapy enlists deep emotions that it becomes a powerful force for change' (Yalom 1991: 35).

Thus, therapy concerns strong emotions, insight, intellectual appreciation and change. Central to therapy is a relationship with the therapist or relationships with the therapist and the group, which helps individuals to do what they have not been able to do for themselves alone. They are empowered to experience life as it is happening now.

What is dramatherapy?

Definitions of what dramatherapy is stress the influence of the creative and expressive in contrast with, say, psychoanalytic psychotherapy, whose stress is on the relationship between therapist and client and the working through of conflicts and tension within that relationship. These processes are labelled 'transference' and 'counter-transference'. Enhancing the client's creativity and expressive ability using drama structures is allowing non-verbal and symbolic expression of emotion, which is in contrast with the talking psychotherapies. Of course, dramatherapists encourage verbal emotional disclosure, but may do so through the drama itself, not necessarily directly.

In 1979, the British Association for Dramatherapists (BADth) defined dramatherapy as:

The means of helping to understand and alleviate social and psychological problems, mental illness and handicap; and of facilitating symbolic expression, through which man may get in touch with himself, both as individual and group, through creative structures involving vocal and physical communication.

Nowadays terms such as 'mental illness' and 'mental handicap' do not have the clarity that they seemed to in the 1970s and are seen, rightly, to be negatively value-laden.

The current (1991) 'outline' definition from the BADth is somewhat tentative: 'Dramatherapy is the intentional (planned) use of the healing aspects of drama in the therapeutic process.' This definition begs many questions, not least 'What are the healing aspects of drama?' and 'Are there aspects of the drama that are harmful?'

Jennings's definition of dramatherapy is: 'The specific application of theatre structures and drama processes with a declared intention that is therapy' (Jennings 1992b: 229). Here we are faced with the phrase 'theatre structures' which reflects Jennings's theatrical model of dramatherapy. She sees drama-therapists not as 'psycho'-therapists, but as creative artists, and dramatherapy as a profession whose roots are set firmly in theatre art. For her, dramatherapy is an art form constantly renewing the creativity of the therapist and the client.

Jenkyns and Barham (1991: 3), while admitting that it is hard to encapsulate the complex processes of dramatherapy within the confines of a precise definition, quote Read Johnson's (1982) formulation as the one most frequently used by professionals:

Dramatherapy, like the other creative arts therapies (art, music and dance), is the application of a creative medium to psychotherapy. Specifically, drama-therapy refers to those activities in which there is an established therapeutic understanding between client and therapist and where the therapeutic goals are primary and not incidental to the ongoing activity.

One infers that this definition sees dramatherapy as a creative psychotherapy.

Dr Robert Landy, a renowned American dramatherapist, sidesteps the task of definition by expressing the aims of dramatherapists:

[they] aim to reach goals that are essentially dramatic in nature. A general goal might be to help others increase their repertory of roles and their ability to play a single role more effectively. Specific goals are very much dependent upon the nature and needs of the client. Although therapeutic in nature, the goals often bear resemblance to educational and recreational drama goals. Further, drama therapy relates in some ways to many major psychotherapeutic theories, viewing the client as embodying a confluence of conscious and unconscious processes of mind, body, feeling and intuition.

(Landy 1986: 59)

This statement defends an eclecticism which is reflected in practice and carries with it a danger of being imprecise; it does not defend dramatherapy as a discipline with its own language based on theatre and drama. As Jones (1991: 8) says:

What needs to happen is for dramatherapy to have its own clear orientation concerning its processes, its own way of describing and defining what actually can occur within a dramatherapy group.

Landy, whose model of the person is based on role theory, nevertheless finds it both necessary and important to stress that dramatherapy relates 'in some ways' to many major psychotherapeutic theories because of the debate, sometimes acrimonious, within the profession between those who see dramatherapy as drama-based and others who see dramatherapy as a psychotherapy.

Professional agonising over dichotomies is not peculiar to dramatherapy. Reviewing the effects of eclecticism in the psychotherapies in Britain, David Pilgrim (1990) explores the dilemma of the different disciplines in deciding whether they are psychological practices or medical treatments. He examines the boundary disputes between the humanistic psychotherapies and the traditional biologically based mechanistic and reductive theories of humanity in medicine and behaviourally-based psychology:

> [if there is] an eventual eclectic integration of psychotherapy into the main-stream workings of the British mental health industry, I fear it can no longer claim the role of the radical humanistic conscience of that industry. This is the result of the energy dissipated in intra- and inter-professional disputes about ownership and regulation and in the obsessive desire to acquire the trappings of professional accreditation.
>
> (Pilgrim 1990: 15)

This debate has raged through dramatherapy and other psycho- and arts therapies and is not resolved. Some want dramatherapy to declare itself as a therapy based on theatre art; others wish to declare dramatherapy to be a form of psychotherapy. For example, the dramatherapist Dorothy Langley (1989: 74) contrasts

> the psychotherapeutic model where the therapist and client or client group communicate verbally with the approach of the arts therapist who may com-municate non-verbally and whose client group may include those without speech for whatever reason and where verbal therapy is inappropriate.

Langley sees dramatherapy as inherently different from psychotherapies where the process is language-based, because dramatherapy is able to treat clients who are unable to speak. Drama is mime, sound, gesture, body language and speech.

Yet the Humanistic and Integrative Group of the United Kingdom Standing Con-ference on Psychotherapy, in the person of John Rowan (1992), when asked to com-ment on his view as to whether dramatherapy was a form of psychotherapy, said:

> By a form of psychotherapy, we simply mean that it takes a client from beginning to end of a problem – usually but not always a significant and fairly central life problem – staying with the client through difficulties and hind-rances which may arise in the process of psychotherapy itself.
>
> (p. 6)

This definition does not mention communication through language; it is the nature of the psychotherapeutic relationship that is important. It would seem that Rowan's definition of what psychotherapy means in practice does not exclude dramatherapy, since many dramatherapists are indeed taking clients through a therapeutic process, using drama as the healing medium. However, this debate is still very much alive in the profession and at the time of writing, has not been resolved. The majority of dramatherapists welcome the freedom of eclecticism and while using a broad drama base, take from other disciplines what they feel is appropriate for their client groups and individuals.

Perhaps at this point it might be wise to make the important distinction between what is therapy and what is therapeutic. Going to the theatre is often said to be a therapeutic experience, when we are deeply emotionally moved by a performance which gives us insight into our own relationships and conflicts. Irwin (1979) defines a 'therapeutic experience' as 'any experience which helps an individual to feel a greater sense of competence'. She defines 'therapy', on the other hand, as 'a specific form of intervention to bring about intra-psychic, interpersonal and behavioural change'. And this distinction is important within dramatherapy, where the dramatherapist uses drama structures with the specific intention of assisting clients to experience the emotions they may have blocked from consciousness, to gain insight into their motivations and to see how their own processes affect their interactions with others and the others' reactions to them in their lives in the here-and-now.

To make a synthesis of the definitions of 'drama' and 'therapy' that I have given above, I define 'dramatherapy' itself as:

> healing through drama allowing the client, with the use of dramatic structures, to receive insights and explore emotions in a special place in real and imaginary time, within a social encounter.

THE PRESENT PROFESSIONAL POSITION OF DRAMATHERAPY

The British Association for Dramatherapists (BADth) is the professional body among whose aims are:

- To promote mental and physical health in every way, but especially by the use of drama.
- To protect and promote the interests of its members.
- To uphold the Equal Opportunities policies of the Association.
- To encourage suitable persons to enter the profession and to promote and monitor courses of training for such persons and to see that proper standards of professional competence are maintained.

There are four degrees of membership of the Association: Full, Associate, Student and Library. Full members are those who have a qualification and experience recognised by the Association. Associate members are those who are interested in the furtherance of the objects of the Association; these may be arts therapists, psychologists, educators and other people interested in dramatherapy. Student members are those who attend one of the courses approved by the Association which will qualify them for eventual full membership.

The Association is managed by an Executive Committee elected by the Full members at the Annual General Meeting and consists of a Chairperson, a Vice-, Chairperson, a Treasurer and ten members, eight of whom are elected from the Full membership and two from the Associate membership. The Association's legal status is that of a non-profit-making company, limited by guarantee; it regulates the training of dramatherapists and has established a register of qualified members, representing their interests to the various employing authorities and other professional bodies in the UK.

The Association supports various sub-committees: Supervision, Training, Equal Opportunities and Fund-raising. The Association sends representatives to committees relevant to dramatherapy such as the Arts Therapies in Education Committee, the Standing Committee for Arts Therapies Professionals and the Arts Therapies Research Committee.

In 1990, dramatherapists within the National Health Service joined arts therapists and music therapists as members of professions recognised by the Whitley Council, under the Professional and Technical 'A' Committee. The Whitley Council agreed the following definition of what a dramatherapist is:

> A person who is responsible for organising appropriate programmes of drama activities of a therapeutic application with patients, individually or in groups, and possesses a degree or qualification considered equivalent for entry to an accepted postgraduate training course and also a qualification in dramatherapy following the completion of an accepted course at a recognised institution for higher or further education.
>
> (DHSS PAM/[PTA] 2/89 App. B, quoted in Jenkyns and Barham 1991)

In June 1991, the Association applied to join the Council for Professions Supplementary to Medicine and the Board have accepted the application, which will be submitted, in tandem with the Arts Therapists and Music Therapists to the Privy Council.

Postgraduate training in dramatherapy

There are currently five postgraduate/post-professional training courses in dramatherapy in the UK (see Appendix 3 for addresses). These are at The University of Hertfordshire, St Albans; College of Ripon and York St John, York; South Devon College, Torquay; The Institute of Dramatherapy, London, recognised by The Roehampton Institute (University of Surrey); and the Central School of Speech and Drama (Sesame). Each course is recognised by the Department of Health. Successful candidates are awarded a postgraduate Diploma in Dramatherapy. A new Diploma course is now being negotiated in Manchester.

Following a period of work, it is now possible for dramatherapists to under-take a one-year part-time advanced training in dramatherapy and a two-year part-time MA in Dramatherapy at the University of Hertfordshire. These two courses are designed to promote further enquiry and research and to give students a basis to proceed to MPhil or DPhil level.

The Association has adopted additional supervision requirements for those who have received their diplomas and when they begin clinical practice. All qualified dramatherapists who wish to retain their full membership are expected to attend forty mandatory sessions of supervision within three years of com-pleting their training; in addition, the Association recommends that all drama-therapists should continue supervision throughout their working life.

Dramatherapists and the workplace

The membership list, published by the BADth and dated April 1991, gives details of 127 Full Members, 78 Associates, 76 Students and 31 Library members. Of the Full Members, 40 per cent are employed in the medical services; 28 per cent describe themselves as 'freelance'; 25 per cent are in education; and 7 per cent work in prisons, the theatre or in psychotherapeutic centres.

What do dramatherapists do?

Dramatherapists work with individuals and groups; they are involved in consulta-tion, both to individuals and organisations, looking at difficulties in the workplace and in overcoming stress. They are involved in management training; they run staff support groups and training groups. They run courses and they conduct long-term and short-term therapy groups with a range of clients from those diagnosed suffering from schizophrenia to primary school children.

The dramatherapy session is geared to the needs of the client or group.

Dramatherapy refers to those activities in which there is an established thera-peutic understanding between client and therapist and where the therapeutic goals are primary and not incidental to the ongoing activity.

(Jenkyns and Barham 1991: 3)

Furthermore:

Clients are treated through drama, in part, because through their play and past dramatisations they have created a dysfunctional image of themselves in the world. In dramatherapy, they re-create that image so that it can be reviewed, recognised, and integrated, allowing a more functional self to emerge. The dialectical nature of drama as moving between fictional and actual context provides a way of looking at not only the conceptual basis of dramatherapy, but also the practical.

(Landy 1986: 47)

As with the psychotherapies, a contract is drawn between the client and the drama-therapist, whose aim and goal is to help the client heal him or herself, through the intentional use of drama structures and activities. Dramatherapists may use a wide range of theatrical and dramatic properties such as masks, puppets, make-up and costume; they may use the client's own story as the drama or incorporate myths and legends, but all within the therapeutic aims of the contract.

FOUR THEORETICAL MODELS OF DRAMATHERAPY

The theoretical base of dramatherapy lies in theatre, in therapeutic drama, in psychology and in anthropology. It is not possible to do justice to the wide variety of different approaches, but the following paragraphs will, I hope, illuminate some aspects of practice.

Theatre models of dramatherapy

Theatre is a direct experience, where groups of people agree to encounter each other in a set space at a given time, where some of those people will be behaving as if they were someone or something other than themselves. These actors take different characters and different roles, while the spectators suspend their dis-belief and accept that, in that space and in that time, the actors are the characters they are playing, in a make believe place in an imaginary time. Thus, a theatre model of dramatherapy would expect to have the following ingredients: an actor/client, or a group of actors/clients; a director/therapist; a set space; an agreed period of time and a common goal.

The principal exponent of the theatre model is Sue Jennings (see Jennings 1990, 1992a, b, Chapter 6 this volume). Jennings sees dramatherapists not as psychotherapists but as creative artists and dramatherapy as a system whose roots are set firmly within theatre and drama. Over the years, Jennings has developed a 'true' dramatherapy model, based on the understanding of the healing properties of drama itself. Within this 'true' model there may be different models of practice, depending on the client group and the context, such as a creative-expressive model, a task-centred model and a psychotherapeutic model. The main process involved in theatre and hence in dramatherapy is that of dramatic or aesthetic distance, which paradoxically allows us to experience reality at a deeper level. In psychodrama, by contrast, clients work directly with their own material; in dramatherapy the story, the myth, the drama itself becomes everybody's story and the client's drama is not interpreted. This allows him or her to travel rapidly between objective and subjective reality, from the microcosm to the macrocosm.

'What is essential for the therapeutic effect of dramatherapy is another person and a special place' (Jennings 1990). Jennings stresses the need for what she calls 'a special ritual place; a space set apart' (1990). Metaphor is the medium of theatre, drama and dramatherapy and rituals are played out in the empty space.

The role of the therapist in the theatre model is that of the facilitative director. Steve Mitchell (1990 and Chapters 3 and 9 this volume), another dramatherapist imbued in the theatre model, compared and contrasted the roles of dramatherapist and of theatre director, exemplified by Peter Brook. Brook sees the role of the director as a facilitator – one who helps the actor do what he needs to do to find the character and play the part in interaction with the ensemble and, ultimately, with the audience. Mitchell's theatre model of dramatherapy is a model of healing. The dramatherapist helps the client shift the everyday problems of life into a theatrical reality, to capture the appropriate image and make it both emotional and cognitive. He then facilitates the client's return to everyday reality.

Meldrum (1993 and Chapter 5 this volume) proposes a theatrical model of dramatherapy which sees the dramatherapist as the empathic director who takes the role of the responsible facilitator, helping clients or group members take responsibility for their own lives through the use of theatrical metaphors. The core of the model is that the dramatherapy sessions may be structured like a theatrical production. The rehearsal or session is structured to allow the clients/ actors to use their physicality, to develop their characterisations in role and to engage their intellect. Through projective techniques clients are assisted to express their selves and to give voice to their own feelings and desires, through the drama. The therapist and other group members take the role both of audience member and actor to become what Boal (1992) calls 'spectactors' – both spectators and actors. As the spectactors watch the drama of others they see in their stories multiple mirrors of themselves.

Theatre models of dramatherapy, then, take inspiration and structure from theatre drama.

Therapeutic drama and dramatherapy

Therapeutic drama frequently makes use of the client's story as well as myths, legends and folktales. Chief among dramatherapists who use stories and myths in therapy are Mooli Lahad and Alida Gersie, while Marina Jenkyns uses texts from Shakespeare and Berkoff as dramatic structures in group dramatherapy. (See Chapters 10 and 11 this volume for more on Lahad's methods, and Chapter 11 for more on Gersie.)

For Gersie (1991) a form of transmission is encoded in the traditional story. Working with familiar stories, memories and images are evoked. Mooli Lahad (1992) uses the story to discover what sort of language the client is using and what sort of coping mechanisms he or she uses in response to stress. The client tells his or her story and the therapist looks at the overtone of the story, the method in which it works. Lahad's multi-modal approach stems from the six dimensions that, in his experience, underlie the coping style of the client: beliefs and values; affect (emotion); social; imaginative; cognitive; and physical – what he calls the BASIC Ph. These elements are combined in the unique coping style of each person.

Both Gersie and Lahad use story-making as a therapeutic technique for clients to project their own stories based on the elements contained in fairytales or myths. Gersie's basic story-making structure contains a landscape, a dwelling place, the main character, an obstacle, the helpmate and the resolution. Lahad's structure contains a main character, who has a mission or task, a helper, an obstacle in the way of the character, the coping strategies applied by the character and a resolution. The client or group draws, enacts or tells the story and the therapist listens or observes on several levels to the tone in which the story is told; the content of the story and its message or theme; and the way the character copes. The coping strategies are of greatest interest to Lahad while Gersie considers the nature of the helpmate as the most likely area of healing for the client. The therapist may observe that the helpmate is not being utilised and will then assist clients to help themselves to solve their problems.

Marina Jenkyns's psychodynamic approach to text is a form of therapeutic dramatherapy of a different kind. Jenkyns will take a text such as Shakespeare's *The Tempest* and will use the text itself as a projective or metaphorical technique for the group members to explore their own personal journeys. Since Shakespeare's language is itself imbued with metaphorical images, clients use the text as a play within a play; a play of their journeys in the therapy group within the play of the text, which contains within itself multiple players of experience. Group members, like actors, bring aspects of themselves to the characters and, using the voices of the roles, they express themselves within the group, structured by the dramatic theme.

Therapeutic drama within dramatherapy can take many forms but what is common is the embodiment of a role within a dramatic structure and form.

Role theory models of dramatherapy

The role model is discussed later in this volume in more depth (see Chapter 5). The role model of dramatherapy sees the individual as one who plays a number of biological, familial, occupational and social roles, which he or she plays in real life and in the dramatherapy session.

In this model, the therapeutic goals of the dramatherapist are to help clients increase the number of roles they have, not to be engulfed or stuck on one or two roles and to be flexible in their ability to move from one role to another. The role theory model is not concerned with self-actualisation as such, but in the quality of the social roles the person plays. Therapists may enter roles with their clients and are thus expected to be able to explore many different roles themselves. Role theory invites the dramatherapist to look at the healing aspects of the clients rather than their psychopathology. A resolution is successful 'when the client has recognised the existence and significance of the healing part of himself and has acted towards himself as the therapist has acted toward him' (Landy 1992: 103).

The clients, through the dramatherapy process, have brought into the light their internal cast of characters and roles and become themselves 'consummate actors', and because they have worked through these roles in thought and action, they are able to be skilled performers in their everyday lives (Landy 1992).

David Read Johnson (1992) sees the dramatherapist as playing three major roles: as a transference figure for the client, such as a parent; as a character or role in the client's drama; and also the role of the therapist. Read Johnson uses a concept he calls 'the playspace' – an interpersonal and imaginary realm jointly shared by therapist and client. This playspace is an illusion, an alternative reality brought into the dramatherapy session. The therapist acts as a guide to the client in his inner landscape and effects changes through a variety of techniques and levels of participation within the playspace.

The role theory model, while more popular in the States than in Britain, is becoming increasingly influential through the number and quality of its publications.

The anthropological approach to dramatherapy

The great Polish director, Jerzey Grotowski, sees the actor as a shaman, a spirit-inspired priest and he is preoccupied with recreating ritual in theatre 'as a way of healing the many splits both within an individual and between people' (Kumiega 1987: 129).

Thus, through his image of the actor as sorcerer or magician, Grotowski sees the shaman/actor leading those who witness or participate into unknown territory. Some dramatherapists are now examining the role of the dramatherapist as shaman, influenced, as was Grotowski, by religous practices emanating from the Indian sub-continent, Africa and native American cultures. Sue Jennings (1992a) links the role of priest shaman with that of the traditonal healer, for in many cultures, she says, they are combined. The shaman goes into a trance state during the seance, he and the client change roles and 'there is a symbolic enactment of the malady and its roots' (p. 235). Read Johnson (1992) claims that the dramatherapist should be comfortable in the role of shaman, which, he says, is the most intimate of the role relationships between therapist and client, where the therapist as actor/shaman enacts the images in the drama while the clients watch as audience.

Some dramatherapists, however, are critical of this development; they do not think it appropriate that the therapist play the role of the actor and the client that of the spectator; the therapeutic alliance, as they see it, requires that the client's embodiment of her story is central to the therapeutic intervention. However, this new area for dramatherapy is of great interest and will no doubt be developed further.

These dramatherapy models from the theatre, drama, role theory and anthropology and ritual are only four among others used in a practice which is eclectic and wide ranging. Unlike psychodrama and Gestalt psychotherapy, with which it has much in common, dramatherapy does not have an agreed theoretical base and clearly defined structures underpinning training and practice. Dramatherapy practice ranges from an intellectual pursuit of metaphor in Shakespearean text and its meaning for the individual, to the use of touch and simple mime with the severely brain-damaged person.

CONCLUSION

In this chapter I hope I have conveyed a sense of the creativity, complexity and eclecticism of the profession, which, from a developmental point of view, has taken its first steps and is now almost ready to run.

REFERENCES

Boal, A. (1992) *Games for Actors and Non-Actors*, translated by Adrian Jackson, London, Routledge.
British Association for Dramatherapists (1991) Membership List and Code of Practice, BADth.
Cox, Murray (1986) *Coding the Therapeutic Process: Emblems of Encounter*, London, Pergamon Press.
Doktor, Ditty (1992) 'Dramatherapy a psychotherapy?', *Dramatherapy*, 14(2): 9–11.
Gersie, Alida (1991) *Storymaking in Bereavement: Dragons Fight in the Meadow*, London, Jessica Kingsley.
Holmes, J. and Lindley, R. (1991) *The Values of Psychotherapy*, Oxford, Oxford University Press.
Irwin, Eleanor C. (1979) 'Drama therapy with handicapped', in Ann Shaw and C.J. Stevens (eds) *Drama, Theatre and the Handicapped*, Washington, DC, American Theatre Association.
Jenkyns, Marina and Barham, Michael (1991) *BADth Application to Join the Council for Professions Supplementary to Medicine on behalf of the Profession of Dramatherapy*, BADth.
Jennings, Sue (1990) 'Dramatherapy', public seminar at the Institute of Dramatherapy, 6 March.
Jennings, Sue (1992a) (ed.) *Dramatherapy Theory and Practice 2*, London, Routledge.
Jennings, Sue (1992b) 'The nature and scope of dramatherapy: theatre of healing', in Murray Cox (ed.) *Shakespeare Comes to Broadmoor*, London, Jessica Kingsley.
Johnson, Liz and O'Neill, Cicely (eds) (1984) *Dorothy Heathcote: Collected Writings on Education and Drama*, London, Hutchinson.
Jones, Phil (1991) 'Dramatherapy: five core processes', *Dramatherapy*, 14(1).
Kumiega, Jennifer (1987) *The Theatre of Grotowski*, London and New York, Methuen.
Lahad, Mooli (1992) 'Storymaking: an assessment method for coping with stress. Six-piece storymaking and the BASIC Ph', in Sue Jennings (ed.) *Dramatherapy Theory and Practice 2*, London, Routledge.
Landy, Robert (1986) *Drama Therapy: Concepts and Practices*, Springfield, IL, Charles C. Thomas.
Landy, Robert (1992) 'One-on-one: the role of the dramatherapist working with individuals', in Sue Jennings (ed.) *Dramatherapy Theory and Practice 2*, London, Routledge.
Langley, Dorothy (1989) 'The relationship between psychodrama and dramatherapy', in Phil Jones (ed.) *Dramatherapy: State of the Art*, Papers presented at the conference held by the Division of Arts and Psychology, Hertfordshire College of Art and Design.
Meldrum, Brenda (1993) 'A theatrical model of dramatherapy', *Dramatherapy*, 14(2): 10–13.
Mitchell, Steve (1990) 'The theatre of Peter Brook as a model for dramatherapy', *Dramatherapy*, 13(1).
Neelands, Jonothan (1990) *Structuring Drama Work: a Handbook of Available Forms in Theatre and Drama*, Tony Goode (ed.) Cambridge, Cambridge University Press.

O'Neill, Cecily and Lambert, Alan (1982) *Drama Structures*, London, Hutchinson.
Pilgrim, David (1990) 'British psychotherapy in context', in Windy Dryden (ed.) *Individual Therapy*, Milton Keynes, Open University Press.
Read Johnson, David (1982) 'Developmental approaches in drama', *The Arts in Psychotherapy*, 9, 183–90.
Read Johnson, David (1992) 'The dramatherapist "in-role"', in Sue Jennings (ed.) *Dramatherapy Theory and Practice 2*, London, Routledge.
Wilshire, Bruce (1982) *Role Playing and Identity: the Limits of Theater as Metaphor*, Bloomington, IN, Indiana University Press.
Yalom, Irvin (1985) *The Theory and Practice of Group Psychotherapy*, 3rd edn, New York, Basic Books.
Yalom, Irvin (1991) *Love's Executioner*, London, Penguin Books.

Chapter 2

The developmental model of dramatherapy

Ann Cattanach

As foolish as monkeys 'til twenty or more
As bold as lions till forty and four
As cunning as foxes 'til three score and ten
Then they become asses or something – not men

(Traditional)

At ten a child; at twenty wild;
At thirty fame if ever;
At forty wise; at fifty rich;
At sixty good, or never.

(Traditional)

A DEFINITION

The developmental model of dramatherapy explores the creative life of the clients as part of their whole life journey. The theme of this model is the working and re-working of the life stages and changes of individuals and groups. This kind of working would include the change, flux and transformations experienced through social, cultural and psychological aspects of life: how we struggle to integrate the conflicted elements of experience. When that struggle is explored symbolically through the fictions we create in dramatherapy then the healing process could be described as restoring life through art.

This personal struggle to be authentic means we are constantly exploring the fractured aspects of the self, the buried self, the dislocated self, the self that is not in conjunction with the self that we wish to be and that we never arrive at. Through drama processes we can explore back and forth along this life-line finding images, symbols, stories, texts to discover who we are or what we might have been. We can create fictional lives, perhaps a childhood we would like to have lived or one we are thankful we didn't live.

I remember the struggle of Jane and Tom, two children from different backgrounds placed in the same family at different times. Tom was there first and lived with the family for two years until Jane came along. Both Tom and Jane were 4 when they went to their adoptive family. They fought like cat and dog, hated each other and were jealous of any attention the other received. Tom's strategy in the family was to be 'good', Jane's strategy was to be 'bad', but together they just fought.

In dramatherapy together, they created a fiction, a sort of Hansel and Gretel brother and sister. They enacted a childhood as natural brother and sister, making up stories of what they might have done together if they had the same parents from birth. They re-invented another childhood, full of fighting, fun, terror and danger but a shared experience. This alliance which they did not share in their reality life was learnt in their fictional story.

In reality they continued to fight, continued to have individual difficulties due to their separate experiences of abuse from their natural families, but they began to form an alliance with each other. They began to support each other and establish a sort of sibling relationship with less jealousy and pride in the other's achievements.

These children's early life experiences meant they were stuck in negative and distorted ideas about the value of self and together they mirrored each other's self-negation. In dramatic play they joined forces to struggle against these negative aspects and tentatively to find positive value for themselves and each other. Confusion, clarity, distress, pleasure, malfunction, integration, are part of an unfolding life-story in the developmental perspective. In this approach distress is seen as a blockage or halt in the process: a stage in our journey where we stopped and got stuck.

David Read Johnson (1982) says that while other paradigms suggest human dysfunction is due to something missing or out of balance, requiring things to be put right, the developmental perspective sees human disorder as a blockage or a halt in development. Treatment first involves an assessment of where in the developmental sequence the person has stopped him or herself, and then starting the journey again with the therapist as companion and guide.

Tom and Jane re-started their journey from birth and in all their dramatic enactments they played with dummies in their mouths: a symbolic reminder of the infant experience they wanted.

Read Johnson states that the developmental approach works with processes and sequences not lists of games and techniques with the therapist aware of the way the clients move to advance or retreat through a developmental sequence.

Developmental sequences cover the whole of the lifespan, not just returning to childhood events. Development continues through adulthood; we are living in time. Phillida Salmon (1985) suggests that our experience of time is far more complex and delicate than we usually allow, that we all carry within us something of the people we have been and will become, and it is only when we can encompass rather than deny all the phases of our lives that we will be able to give full meaning to the personal destinies we are engaged in creating.

CREATIVE DEVELOPMENT BEGINS WITH PLAY

Sue Jennings (1990) describes the play of children as evolving through three developmental stages from early infant sensation through to the dramatic play of young children. She describes these stages in this developmental process as embodiment play, projective play and role-play.

Embodiment play

Embodiment play includes the pre-verbal explorations the young baby makes of the immediate sensory world. All that pleasure in smearing the face with cereal, banging the spoon on the plate, touching faeces!

As the young child begins to sit up, crawl and walk, then the environment widens and the sensory world enlarges. These initial experiences of the sensory world lay the foundation of our sense of self and our pleasure in the physical world.

Projective play

The world expands for the child who begins to explore objects in his or her environment. Winnicott (1980) described the first special possession adopted by the infant as having a particular importance as the first 'not me' possession. This first object, that smelly bit of blanket or in my son's case an entire shawl, is taken everywhere. It is special because it is not 'not me' and not 'me' but exists in the area of illusion as the transitional object.

There is a direct development from the transitional object into play activities. The child begins to explore toys and objects outside itself and starts to play out experiences through the use of this external media. This is the beginning of symbolic play for the child when for the first time the child realises that one object can represent another.

Piaget's (1962) description of symbolic play states that for children it is indispensable to their affective and intellectual equilibrium that they have available to them an area of activity whose motive is not adaptation to reality but assimilation of reality to the self without coercion or sanctions. Such an area is play, which transforms reality by assimilation to the needs of the self.

Role-play

Children begin 'make-believe' play with activities in which the role taken is one of self-representation then gradually through playing with other children and with toys and other objects children learn to pretend to be someone else. This role-taking of young children is not just imitation because, while still being themselves, children identify completely with those whose role they are taking. Children develop more sophisticated role-playing and by 4 years of age the child can combine role-play with the make-believe play of other children. At this stage each child is absorbed in their own role but there is a sense of playing together and playing separately. As children learn negotiating skills and some of the complex rules of social interaction then their play develops into dramatic play with all the complexity of dramatic exchange.

THE DRAMATIC METAPHOR

While these three stages of play are part of the child's developing awareness and skill maturation, they also seem to be part of the development of any dramatic activity of a group of people who are making drama. A really exciting session of drama exploration will contain elements of body awareness, projected play and role-taking.

Sue Jennings (1990; see also Chapter 6 this volume) states that the metaphor that is embodied, projected and enacted enables profound change to take place.

This developmental process is described by Bruno Bettelheim (1978) using the metaphor of the fairy tale. He states that the fairy tale begins when the child is at a time in his life where, without the help of the story, he would remain stuck, feeling neglected, rejected, degraded. Then using the thought processes which are his own – contrary to adult rationality though these may be – the story opens glorious vistas which permit the child to overcome momentary feelings of utter hopelessness.

Phillida Salmon (1985) says that if we are to do full justice to the exploration of our own developmental psychology, we shall need to enter the ground of metaphor, that in the end it is through the metaphorical interpretations we place upon the life cycle that we come to experience the deepest meanings of our lives.

DEVELOPMENTAL PSYCHOLOGY

The developmental psychologists use the concept of living in time as a way to understand human development. Their exploration is of life stages and the mechanisms and processes of human development. Individual theorists put forward developmental schemes which emphasise a variety of aspects of the self. These theories are useful guides for the dramatherapist helping clients explore the metaphor of life as a journey. The theories of Piaget (1962) and Erikson (1965) offer ideas about the cognitive and emotional stages of development and have many connections with the processes explored in a developmental drama-therapy group.

THEORIES OF DEVELOPMENTAL STAGES

Jean Piaget: a theory of cognitive stages

Piaget stated that from the beginning of life we build up a working model of the world around us, a model of a world of persisting and moving objects and recurring happenings set in a framework of space and time and showing a regular order.

Human development is the gradual unfolding of the individual's ability to construct this internal model.

Sensory-motor stage (0–2)
Action patterns are the key to this period since it is through the combination of sensation and movement that the infant builds a permanent picture of the world. Piaget called these action patterns 'schemas', and as the child develops he or she learns to assimilate new objects to the schemas and accommodate to new situations. As the baby acts on the world he or she assimilates objects and events to the schemas.
Preconceptual thought (2–5)
The beginnings of representational thought emerge and the infant is able to make a distinction between the self and the world through symbolic means.

Through imaginative play and exploring, experimenting, questioning, listening and talking infants expand and enrich their working models of the world.
Intuitive thought (5–7)
This stage is marked by the development of language and social relations, though thought is still tied to action and perception. Reasoning is still somewhat egocentric but the child is able to evoke an object or event in his or her mind which is not present in reality.
Concrete operations (7–11)
At the stage of concrete operations from 7 to 11 years, children's thinking is logical and mathematical. This is characterised by the child's ability to take into account several aspects of a situation at the same time, the ability to reason in a chronological fashion and to classify objects into groups. Children become interested in more formal games and play.
Formal operations (11+)
Finally there is the stage of formal operations which marks the beginning of theoretical thinking, the capacity to anticipate the future and choose a value system, and to assimilate viewpoints that differ from those of the child's immediate social environment.

Piaget's developmental model is a cognitive one and is important as it places the development of play, symbolic processes and representation in the context of human development.

Erik Erikson: a theory of emotional stages

Erik Erikson's theory of emotional stages defines 'eight stages of man'. Each stage is marked by a struggle between contrary elements of the psyche, an interesting notion for the dramatherapist.

Basic trust v. basic mistrust
The baby's trust is created through maternal care and leads to a sense of identity. With mistrust the emotional model is to enjoy hurt whenever there is a loss.
Autonomy v. shame and doubt
Between 3 and 4 years old muscular maturation leads to experimentation with

feelings of 'holding on' and 'letting go'. To hold on can become a destructive and cruel retaining or restraining, and it can become a pattern of care – to have and to hold. To let go can turn into the letting loose of destructive forces or the relaxed 'let it be'.

Initiation v. guilt
Between 5 and 7 years the child now takes the initiative and is able to undertake the planning and 'attacking' of a task. The danger of this stage is a sense of guilt if 'attacking' a task becomes aggressive coercion. The resulting guilt brings jealousy and rivalry.

Industry v. inferiority
By school age the child takes pleasure in finishing work through diligence. The danger at this stage is in emotions of inadequacy and inferiority.

Identity v. role confusion
The emotions of adolescents are primarily concerned with what they appear to be in the eyes of others as compared with what they feel they are. The danger of this stage is role confusion, if they cannot settle to their own identity they identify with the heroes of cliques and crowds.

Intimacy v. isolation
The young adult emerging from the search for identity is eager and willing to fuse his identity with that of others. The avoidance of such experiences because of a fear of ego-loss may lead to isolation and self-absorption.

Generativity v. stagnation
Generativity is the concern in establishing and guiding the next generation but where such enrichment fails altogether individuals begin to indulge themselves as if they were their own – or one another's – one and only child.

Ego integration v. despair
With older people there is, at best, a feeling of one's life-cycle having meaning but if this life-cycle is not accepted then disgust, hiding despair, signifies the fear of death.

Piaget's model, with its emphasis on the symbolic nature of cognitive development, is of use to the dramatherapist who works in the symbolic processes through metaphor and fiction.

Erikson's model, with its emphasis on conflict, mimics the very nature of dramatic conflict and those acts of 'hubris' which lead to loss and despair: the very life of the theatre.

PROCESSES ENCOUNTERED IN THE DEVELOPMENTAL MODEL OF DRAMATHERAPY

The therapeutic journey is a process to find our own way and the job of the therapist is to make a safe enough place and a safe enough way for the journey to happen. There are some operational concepts inherent in the dramatherapy process which can provide a degree of safety and protection as the client works with the therapist.

Living in and out of time

Richard Courtney (1985) stated that dramatic action creates a fictional present out of both past and future and enables us to face life experiences at a functional and symbolic level. When we explore the fictional present created in drama we engage in problem-solving in a deep and personal way.

The fictional present is not our reality life so we can explore safely distanced from everyday experience. We can learn to adjust to time by playing 'out of time' in the transitional space of the dramatherapy group where we can explore part of a life journey through the 'as if' of the imagination.

The dramatherapist who uses a developmental approach works with this concept of living in time and the fictions created by the group can move back and forward through a variety of developmental structures exploring the paradoxes of each life stage. The paradoxes and struggles inherent in this construction are basic to dramatic literature. Robert Landy (1986) states that in exploring the contraries of human existence the dramatherapist works with the notion of struggle – the individual against internal and external forces – finding dramatic forms in which to stage the great existential battles. (For more on Robert Landy see Chapters 5 and 10 this volume.)

Richard Courtney (1985) says that when the child at play uses imaginative thought and dramatic action to make choices from the evidence, he or she relates the inner world to the environment. Knowledge, in other words, is not an object but a process, a relationship, a dramatic dynamic.

Dramatic fiction

When we work with drama in therapy we are making a dramatic reality; we create a world, a space set apart. Susan Langer (1953) in her book *Feeling and Form* describes this aesthetic illusion in the arts as an otherness from reality, a detachment from actuality.

Elsewhere (Cattanach 1992b) I have described the function in therapy of this abstraction from the real world as a way to be able to examine our fictional world free from the constraints of real circumstances and anxiety. There are no chance accidents or irrelevancies to obscure the logic of our fictional world so we can develop new meanings for ourselves uncluttered by the constraints of our own reality. We can escape from being the victims of our real circumstances.

Sue Jennings (1992; see also Chapter 6 this volume) says that there is a transition from everyday reality into dramatic or theatrical reality. Dramatic distance has been established from everyday experience which enables a move from the actual to the symbolic, from the concrete to the metaphoric. It is because we can move from everyday reality to dramatic or theatrical reality that transformation of our experience becomes possible.

For example, Mary was a 24-year-old woman who frequently responded to stress by cutting her arms with a knife. Mary wanted to understand her own feelings when she cut herself but couldn't find a way to express it. She found it impossible to explore as direct personal theatre. Eventually Mary wrote a short scene between a girl and an audience. The process of writing and then presenting the material gave Mary enough distance from her own reality to make the experience safe. The manifest content of her drama was about the act of cutting but the latent content was about self-loathing. The act of writing and performing gave Mary immense satisfaction and raised her self-esteem. Repeated performance of her scene helped Mary find a voice for herself and a way to reflect and transform experience.

This is what Mary wrote:

Girl	I want to tell you something about myself. I cut my arms.
Audience	Why?
Girl	Imagine yourself with burning in your chest until it hurts very bad. What would you do?
Audience	Don't know.
Girl	Let me tell you. You've got all this pain in your chest, and it feels tight. In your brain you are thinking of blood and you see black, you are feeling so uptight that all your muscles are knotted together and you have to release this tension, you roll the sleeve up on one of your arms, then go for a knife, you take it by the handle, you don't think how deep you are going to cut. Then you put the blade of the knife near your arm and give one quick pull, you have to do it hard, so you could make the cut wide. Sometimes when you do it you can cut until you reach the bone, then the blood pours out of your arm onto the floor. Inside you feel relief from this bad sensation, because you can see the blood which is a lovely feeling.
Audience	What about the arm?
Girl	Oh, you don't worry about that, it gets stitched up and the same thing happens again.
Audience	It's stupid.
Girl	I'm standing up here to explain how I feel and what it feels like.
Audience	You could always find something else to do.
Girl	But I can't 'cos the feeling is inside, and I have to get rid of it by cutting myself.
Audience	You must be mad.
Girl	Oh sod you bastards, nobody understands.

Playfulness

Mary made her play and created other stories about people, animals and objects. It was important for her to be able to 'play' in this kind of way, stopping and starting her stories, keeping within the boundaries of her own anxiety. Her stories about wolves and scarecrows were after all 'only stories', she was safe in this playful world. Mary enjoyed being given permission to play and having that activity validated; she had not played much as a child so being playful was a regressive activity which nurtured her, but also a complex creative act of story-telling with rules and structures to make a good story.

Huizinga (1955) considered playfulness an important feature of our cultural life. He described play as a stepping out of 'real' life into a temporary sphere of activity. At the same time there was an intensity and absorption in play which transcended the immediate needs of life and imparted meaning to the action. He suggested that play assumed a fixed form as a cultural phenomenon. What was played endured as a new-found creation of the mind retained by the memory.

Mary wrote one story about a scarecrow which has many resonances from her own life-story but she felt safe in her story because after all it's 'only playing'.

> Once upon a time in Lancashire, there was a carrot field, in which stood a scarecrow. Every day the birds came but Charlie couldn't do anything, his arms and legs won't move, he was tied to his post, and he wished he could be free.
>
> So one cold night there was a terrible storm with a strong wind blowing, the wind was so strong that it knocked Charlie down. He was happy because he was free, so he got himself loose, he went to the barn to find a hammer and some nails, he couldn't walk properly he was wobbling all the time. He found the equipment and went back to the field. First he got the longest piece of wood and stuck it in the ground and nailed the other piece of wood so it acted like a windmill. Then Charlie wobbled over to the other end of the field. When the birds came Charlie tried to run and chase them away but he wobbled so much that he fell down. He sat in the field and cried because he couldn't get rid of the birds and the windmill didn't work. As he was sitting there he was thinking to himself 'I have got to get will power.' So he got up from the ground and kept on saying 'I can run, I can run.' He was running up and down the field, now and again he fell down but he didn't let it bother him, he kept getting back up and trying to do it again.
>
> So one summer's day the birds came again and Charlie ran to them and the birds flew away then Charlie looked at this field and saw that the carrots were well grown. He felt very pleased with himself because he knew if he didn't have a strong will, the field would have been in a mess.

Mary played with images of a scarecrow and a werewolf as two creatures struggling with being fierce and unloveable, scaring off people yet searching for attachments but always trying to go on with the struggle. They were like her but were not her, just fictions she had created.

Structure

The developmental psychologist describes the infant's early dependence on the external structures both physical and emotional which will facilitate growth.

Read Johnson (1982) states that a stable, clear and nurturing environment provides infants with the safety they need to order the world adaptively rather than in response to their anxieties. Unstable, conflictual, and confusing care-taking prevents children from developing stable representations of the world and self, increasing their vulnerability to future psychological dysfunction. Thus, to the extent that one lacks internal organisation, an external organising environment is necessary to support one's adaptive functioning.

In the dramatherapy group when the theme is to explore life stages, there can be a fictional return to those early infant stages. Initially the therapist needs to offer an external environment which is safe enough for the group to get in touch with that early vulnerability to the external world. This means that the therapist is responsible initially for the negotiation and establishment of the codes of behaviour which will help and guide the processes in the group. The therapist must deal with basic practical organisational matters: issues like selection of group membership, and the setting for the group. There should be ground rules which define the boundaries and limitations to determine a code of acceptable behaviour. The choice of drama material should help focus the group and there should be a continuity in the structure of each individual drama session.

It is important to mirror developmental stages in the group so some drama work should be individual, some in pairs and some with the whole group. I worked with groups of autistic adolescents and with one group the co-leader and I worked with the whole group the entire time because everyone was involved in their personal embodied space. Although the whole group worked together they all worked individually with no social interaction with anyone else. However, like very young children the group members enjoyed the company of the others but were unable to contact them in play.

The other group had developed social interaction and worked mainly in pairs. The social interaction was at a transitional stage and the conflict was considerable. They were not able to work socially with the whole group but could cope working in pairs. When the whole group worked together they regressed to the stage of individual embodied play in the company of the rest of the group with no interaction.

PROCESS IN A DRAMATHERAPY SESSION

There are three phases in a dramatherapy session: the warm-up, the developmental phase and closure. This structure is needed to help the group function in the language of dramatic action, to hold the group together and to create a mood and environment which can stimulate creative work.

The warm-up

The warm-up is preparation time and sets the mood, themes and focus for the rest of the session. Marina Jenkyns (1992) says that the warm-up is crafted so that it prepares the group not just for the work, or as an introduction to each other, but also to introduce the drama tools they will require in that session or in future sessions. This is the time that the therapist can observe the group dynamics and become sensitised to the themes and feelings which create a focus for the drama. The safety of the group is reinforced by the therapist at this stage: ground rules are reinforced, limits and boundaries stated and permission is given for the group to play.

From this warm-up the group proceed to the next stage which is the central core of the dramatic action. The phases of the process should follow seamlessly and this can be facilitated by the therapist who can help keep the focus clear for everyone in the group.

Development phase

This is the phase of creative explorations and enactments. Themes are explored through appropriate drama forms. If the warm-up has stimulated the group to dramatic activity and reinforced the safety of the group then this phase becomes absorbing. It is important for the therapist to find the drama form which can hold the stimulus for the group. If the form cannot contain the material, then absorption falls away. The artistic skill of the therapist can be critical and if he or she can offer ways of authenticating the fictions created by the group through the use of appropriate dramatic media then the material is transformed to the satisfaction of all.

Closure

This stage is the final resolution of the drama as the group choose to express it. I have stated elsewhere (Cattanach 1992b) that if the balance between the structure and the stimulus has been achieved, the stimulus held and centred in the dramatic action, then the group will have experienced the process of using drama to express feeling. The group can finish with reflection on the whole experience and their own form of ending.

In the early stages of a developmental dramatherapy group these stages in the process can be very tightly structured by the group. Beginnings and endings can be set rituals or play and games which are repeated each time the group meet. For many groups these rituals are sacrosanct and are never changed, but other groups move to keep the forms but change the material as the group progresses.

I worked with a group of day-patients in a psychiatric hospital day-centre and they always wanted to keep the same beginnings and endings to stave off anxiety. The security of that sameness helped them to dare to be very adventurous in the developmental phase because they knew their beginnings and endings were predictable. Their endings were rather like those goodnight phrases that keep children safe: 'Night, night, sleep tight, don't let the bugs bite. See you in the morning.' Back to embodied play.

TRANSITIONS

The trouble with life stages is having to make the transition from one stage to another. Perhaps the major task of the therapist is to help with these transitions by observing what is happening to individuals and the group and by facilitating the developmental flow. This flow should appear seamless as the group move along the developmental continuum in each individual dramatherapy session and through the process as a whole.

Van Gennep (1960) stated that the life of an individual in any society is a series of passages from one age to another and from one occupation to another. Progression from one group to the next is accompanied by special acts. Transitions from group to group and from one social situation to the next are looked on as implicit in the very act of existence so that a person's life comes to be made up of a succession of stages with similar ends and beginnings. He used the term *rites de passage* to describe the type of rituals which accompany these transitions which can be times of upheaval sometimes full of chaotic feelings.

Sue Jennings (1986; see also Chapter 6 this volume) says that the therapist can be seen as a consultant in transitions, a liminal specialist who can be a resource for the client during these changes.

THE JOURNEY

The therapist accompanies the client on their journey through life stages and changes. It is the client's journey, hopefully made safe enough by the therapist. Phillida Salmon says that to create a life-story which is credible, which allows development as well as continuity, which tells a tale worth telling – this is the task that, as human beings, we must attempt. It is a task which essentially demands imagination. It is only through our imaginative construction that we shall be able to own the full heritage of the experience we have acquired through living in time.

The therapist can offer a safe place for the exploration of the story. A celebration of the craftsman in *Awakening Osiris* (Ellis 1988), a full translation of what the Ancient Egyptians called the 'Book of Coming Forth by Day', now called the 'Egyptian Book of the Dead', seems to describe that creative process through which the therapist and client journey together:

> What can be named can be known, what cannot be named must be lived, believed. I speak of the creator and the creation, the ordinary life lived extraordinarily. I work for the sake of working. The joy of creating is the joy of forgetting everything else. I lean into life. My tongue is fire. My breath is wind. The spirit spits from my mouth. I speak of a chain of events where making leads to making, action to action, love to love, where the beginning began so long ago we find ourselves always in the midst of it.

REFERENCES

Bettelheim, B. (1978) *The Uses of Enchantment*, Harmondsworth, Penguin.

Cattanach, A. (1992a) *Play Therapy with Abused Children*, London, Jessica Kingsley.

Cattanach, A. (1992b) *Drama for People with Special Needs*, London, A. & C. Black.

Courtney, R. (1985) 'The dramatic metaphor and learning', in J. Kase-Polisini (ed.) *Creative Drama in a Developmental Context*, Lanham, University Press of America.

Ellis, N. (trans.) (1988) *Awakening Osiris*, Grand Rapids, Phanes Press.

Erikson, E. (1965) *Childhood and Society*, Harmondsworth, Penguin.

Huizinga, J. (1955) *Homo Ludens*, Boston, Beacon Press.

Jenkyns, M. (1992) 'The warm-up', Teaching notes, Dramatherapy Course, St Albans.

Jennings, S. (1986) 'The loneliness of the long distance therapist', Paper from *The Annual Forum*, Axbridge, The Champernowne Trust.

Jennings, S. (1990) *Dramatherapy with Families, Groups and Individuals*, London and New York, Jessica Kingsley.

Jennings, S. (1992) 'The nature and scope of dramatherapy: theatre of healing', in M. Cox (ed.) *Shakespeare Comes to Broadmoor*, London, Jessica Kingsley.

Landy, R. (1986) *Drama Therapy: Concepts and Practices*, Springfield, IL, Charles C. Thomas.

Langer, S. (1953) *Feeling and Form*, London, Routledge & Kegan Paul.

Piaget, J. (1962) *Play, Dreams and Imitation in Childhood*, New York, Norton.

Read Johnson, D. (1982) 'Developmental approaches in drama', *Arts in Psychotherapy*, 9, 183–90.

Salmon, P. (1985) *Living in Time*, London, Dent.

Van Gennep, A. (1960) *The Rites of Passage*, London, Routledge & Kegan Paul.

Winnicott, D.W. (1980) *Playing and Reality*, London, Penguin.

Chapter 3

The theatre of self-expression
A 'therapeutic theatre' model of dramatherapy

Steve Mitchell

There has been one thread along the way that has been an ongoing aspect of this journey: an attempt to find a process that unites personal growth with artistic growth, life and art, one aspect feeding off the other and continuously coming together in new ways.

(Halprin 1973)

Life is sacred. Life is art. Life is sacred art. The art of sacred living means being a holy actor, acting from the soul rather than from the ego. The soul is out of space and time and hence always available, an ever-present potential of our being. It is up to each of us to celebrate and to actualize our being. . . . The soul is our artistic self, our capacity for transforming every dimension of our lives into art and theater.

(Roth 1989: 147)

PROLOGUE

This chapter is concerned with using theatre processes in clinical dramatherapy. It is a form of a 'cookbook' of recipes in three acts; each act is divided into scenes which focus on dramatherapy practice with particular in-patient or out-patient populations. It derives from two areas of practical study: first, my theatre work with Pathfinder Studio and second from my work as a full-time dramatherapist at Lancaster Moor Hospital. The result of this research is a form of therapeutic theatre I call the *theatre of self-expression*. The work with Pathfinder Studio took place in the late 1970s and early 1980s. It involved practical research into creating a theatre form where members of the public could engage in their personal development using the arts of theatre. This work was influenced by my contact with Peter Brook (see Mitchell 1990), Grotowski's Laboratory Theatre (see Mitchell 1991), Anna Halprin's Dancers' Workshop (see Roose-Evans 1989),[1] Gabrielle Roth (see Roth 1989) and Paul Rebillot (Rebillot 1993).

The philosophical orientation of this model gives primacy to two important notions: first, the need for the expression of our 'inner life' and the need to do this in a creative way; second, the healing qualities which are engaged when we live in the 'present' rather than experiencing the world through screens of past perceptions or future expectations. For those who wish to pursue these assumptions from a theoretical stance I would particularly recommend the work of Abraham Maslow (1970, 1971), Irving Yalom (1985, 1989, 1990), Silvano Arieti (1976) and George Kelly (1955; see also Fransella and Dalton 1990) from the world of psychology, and the ideas of Gurdjieff (Ouspensky 1977; Wilson 1986) and Alan Watts (1973a, b, 1976a, b) from Eastern philosophy.

This model also reflects my own theatre background, dramatherapy training, experience of various forms of experiential therapies, clinical supervision and the inner chaos of simply staying with the process of the client or group at the various levels they provide.[2]

ACT ONE

Scene one: dramatherapy with elderly day-patients

I worked twice a week with two different groups of elderly day-patients. These are clients who attend Lancaster and Morecambe Day Hospitals. My contract with both staff and the clients is to provide 'supportive' dramatherapy groups. The groups involve eight to ten clients and each session lasts an hour; each group will last for ten months. The 'therapeutic theatre' model in this context has much in common with creative drama in education. However, I place more emphasis on the expression of feelings than a drama teacher might be inclined to do. The experience of the dramatic process was far more important than any product a group might produce, although I have discovered that it helps the process of the dramatherapy task if the group have a product to aim for. This might be a radio play, recorded on a cassette, a video, a photographic record, stills from the action of scenes you might see outside a theatre, or a script each client can take home. For the clients this gives both a sense of direction and inspires them to engage with the 'supportive' therapeutic factors the dramatic process involves.

The process of creation starts with the *story*. This gives a particular structure and sets a theme for the group to examine. I have sometimes chosen the story and used it as a springboard for them to invent their own. At the present time of writing the Morecambe group is creating their own version of *Romeo and Juliet* and the Lancaster group is devising their own play from the wish to explore 'marital rows'.

The first stage of the process concerns telling the story. For example, a year ago I took into the Lancaster group the story of 'The Good Samaritan'. The first few sessions involved sitting around a table and, by using various 'projective' and 'story-telling' methods, getting to know the story. The group then began to create their own tale of a man who was robbed on Dartmoor – choosing to cut out most religious overtones and to create an inn that was also a brothel! (This was most important dramatherapeutically, where through the distance of the characters they could share their views about sexual behaviour.) During the early phase of the group I acted as both scribe and catalyst, focusing attention on where, when, how, who and what, as well as bringing out and facilitating discussion around emotional subjects such as sex, anger, guilt, love, jealousy, violence, etc., all of which are issues related to the group members' everyday world.

Once their story had been created – this took about twelve weeks – the group then set about scripting the dialogue between the characters. The play was cast and we set up each scene using improvisation as our main tool, slowly working through the scene discovering what was said, what sub-text there might be and what actually happened or, as my gifted writing tutor, Peter Hulton, from Dartington College of Arts, would ask in our 'Writing for Performance' seminars: 'Where's the action?' meaning the action of the characters' thought processes, not simply physical action. In this way the group wrote, or as John Arden would say 'wrought', their play. As this project was to be a radio play, the next stage was to record each scene.

To avoid stilted play-reading I had previously agreed with the group that we would improvise from the script, recording and pausing from moment to moment. Therapeutically this is an important part of the task, as it means that the group members have to inhabit their roles and become their characters – a process that challenges each client in different ways. To foster this, we would go through the scene extracting the next piece of speech, rehearse it, and then as in film make a number of recordings. Once the whole play had been recorded the final phase of the group involved editing what had been recorded, selecting from each 'take' and editing this on to a master tape – this took ten weeks. The group closed with a party for staff and the clients' friends, where they shared the work of the Dramatherapy Group and were presented with their own personal cassette of the play.

Scene two: dramatherapy with elderly in-patients

When I came to Lancaster a major programme of resettlement was under way and many patients who could live in the community had already moved out of the hospital. The patients who attended the Littledale Centre were those who were either too ill, too institutionalised or who had refused to leave the hospital. It was part of my contract to put one session a week into the Littledale Centre and for the first year I really didn't know where to begin. It started with basics: drama games, concentration exercises and various activities detailed in Dorothy Langley's book *Dramatherapy and Psychiatry* (Langley and Langley 1983) but I was not happy with what I was doing. In my second year I set about changing the way I was working and now I run a *story-telling* group with the long-stay in-patients.

The group involves either my telling a story or the group making up their own from a dramatic starting point I introduce into the session. In the former process I will choose a story, legend, myth or play. (The Greek Myths, the plays of Shakespeare – see Lamb's *Tales of Shakespeare* – the works of Dickens and Alida Gersie's anthologies (Gersie and King 1991; Gersie 1991, 1992) have been major resources.) In the telling of the story I enact it to them using the group as other characters in the story. In this way I can involve them in a *seated drama* without them being threatened. I can also choose who I might address a certain part of the story to, so that if someone appears to be on the edge of losing concentration I can directly include them in the story. After the story has been told we close the group with a tea-ritual. This is a very important part of the group; over tea the group reflects on those parts of the story that meant something to them and it is often at this point that sharing or important reminiscence takes place.

When the group creates its own story the session will start with the examination of an object or artifact I bring in to act as the catalyst or focus around which the group will weave its own story. Once the group has examined the object or artifact I will then ask them to help me make up a story about it. The next part of the session proceeds through question and answer and in asking a consensus from the group for each story development. An example might help to make this clear: in one session I was going to use the synopsis from Jennings's *Creative Drama in Groupwork* (1986) where in the late evening someone is settling down for a cup of tea when there is an unexpected knock on the door. I started this session by dramatically knocking on a door, then by using a piano stool that was in our room and had a padded top. I asked each member of the group to knock as if someone was knocking on a front door. After everyone had had a go, I asked them to choose one as the sound we would use in our story. And so it began. When I make up a story with a group, the questions I ask are both the playwright's and actors' questions: where does the scene take place; what time is the scene set; what is the geography of the location; next, to whom and where are they in the location, are they seated or standing, close or distant; what are their moods and what are their attitudes to one another; what happens between them, what is the next action; finally, why does it happen and what are the consequences of what happens to the characters in their story? As I question the group on each of these points, it enables them to create the story from the inside. Once the story has all but been created I bring the tale to a conclusion in one of two ways: either my assistant and I enact the final scene with the group watching and providing us with the necessary dialogue, or I direct different members of the group in dramatising the final scene. Then, as usual, we have our tea-ritual to end the session.

Scene three: dramatherapy rehabilitation groups

The patients who make up my rehabilitation groups are for the most part day-patients who, after many years as in-patients, have now been resettled into the community. They are termed as a 'schizophrenic population' maintained outside the hospital on depot injections and other medications. As part of their maintenance they return to the Occupational Therapy Department on a daily basis. The work with these groups, like the above in-patient group, is 'supportive therapy', as the clients have no wish to 'work through' the reasons they are ill, yet they are often quite 'role-bound' and suffer from chronic institutionalisation. In some cases clients who attend these groups have only just been discharged after twenty to thirty years as in-patients.

I use the 'therapeutic theatre' model of dramatherapy to address indirectly the ways of expanding roles, to examine issues of interpersonal communication and to enable them to experiment in character with new emotions. I have often described these groups to staff as an 'experience' where, in the process of drama, the clients will have their rigid values gently challenged. By working with particular stories and developing specific characters, rehearsing them and playing them to one another, role rehearsal takes place. The stages of work develop the form employed with my elderly in-patient group further into the dramatic process yet the work begins in a similar way. I will choose a story such as Shakespeare's *The Merchant of Venice* and in the first session tell them the story by enacting it to them. In the second session, using projective figurers, I will ask them to re-tell the story, or those elements they particularly remember. The third session will involve making a drawing of any moment in the entire story that particularly stayed with them and we will close this session by each client acting as 'director' and setting up a sculpt of their moment in the play. The remainder of the sessions will expand this process, by setting up the different 'photographic stills' or sculpts and asking the clients to animate the sculpt in any way they choose. Here they act as both playwright and director. When the scene has developed I ask them to take over a key character that is important to them in the scene and I take over the role of 'director' helping them to express the emotions the character experiences in their scene. This procedure first gives them the opportunity to select a scene and projectively set it up, using other members of the group in various roles, and then enter the scene and explore the dynamics of the character. At the point they enter the scene we will also use costume and props that the group will make or collect as part of the group experience. These groups will last for three months, meeting once a week for an hour and thirty minutes.

ACT TWO

Scene one: dramatherapy groups with acute in-patients

For two years I ran a group on a weekly *one-off* basis for the Ridge Lea Hospital acute admission wards. The group was called 'The Next Step'. Its rationale was to prepare in-patients for either day-leave, extended leave or discharge, and to look at general issues concerning leaving hospital after an acute illness. The normal practice was for patients to attend for about three sessions; their attendance began once their 'illness' had been stabilised through the usual medical treatments, and then might continue until their discharge. The group was completely voluntary; there was no formal referral system. This meant that I never knew who was going to be there, how many would be in the group and what their mental state on that particular day might be. I was very dependent on the nursing staff on duty and the size of the group would often depend on my relationship with the nurses on duty. Sometimes I had ten patients, on certain occasions only one!

Briefly the format of the group was as follows. At the start of each session I would give a short introduction. The patients would then be asked if they would like to stay. If they said 'yes' this was an agreement to stay for the duration of the group – an hour and a half – and to participate. If patients had been herded by staff into the group this gave them an opportunity to leave without losing face – this was an agreement I had with both medical and ward staff.

The first phase of the group began with simple introductions such as going round sharing names, getting into pairs with someone they didn't know, again sharing names and where they lived and finding out if they were intending to go on leave that week. They were then asked to find yet another partner and once again share names, but then to share something they would miss in the hospital when they went home (like the food!). Finally they were asked to think about something at home that was precious to them, something that was positive for them. (Often they would choose a pet, an armchair or picture; one client chose his motorbike.) This warm-up employed two different pairing exercises because I found it helped to nurture interactive sharing later in the group. After these pairing exercises they returned to the large group and shared round the group their precious object at home and what their partner had said they would miss about the hospital when they returned home.

This was followed by a brief relaxation exercise that led into a short guided fantasy. They were asked to imagine their journey home from the hospital up to the arrival at the front door, then to think about what was behind the door, what they would first do when they opened it and entered, and if there was any particular time or part of their leave or period of discharge that particularly concerned them. I also asked them if there was anything that they particularly wanted to achieve while on leave, any goal they had set themselves or if there was something they would like to do now. To close the guided fantasy I returned to the relaxation, the rhythm of their breath and the sounds of the hospital.

The main task of the group was to share verbally the various elements of the guided fantasy and this inevitably led to focusing on each member of the group in turn. In a 'one-off' acute group there is not enough time to warm-up to dramatic action in physical terms. Instead we would discuss their immediate dramas and explore them using metaphors such as imagining that you are seeing what you are describing in your life on television and you were the 'writer' of the episode, how would you write the scene? Once the distance had been achieved then we would return back to the their daily reality and investigate how their 'fictional TV episode' might inform a change in their daily lives. Due to the nature of acute illness I have found that patients want to relate the metaphor to the immediate circumstances of their lives otherwise its relevance is lost to them.

The group closed with relaxation and breathing exercises that they might make use of when they were on leave. It was practised so that it would be available to them if there was a time of stress.

Scene two: intensive dramatherapy with acute in-patients

'Intensive' in this context means dramatherapy sessions on a daily basis with each session lasting at least an hour and sometimes two hours. The work is a form of crisis intervention and is an intensive form of individual therapy. The reason for this daily input is due to the nature of acute admission wards that have a very quick turnover of patients. A patient may be admitted to the ward with a severe psychological disturbance – psychotic, depressive, neurotic or suicidal – and the first period of their admission will be concerned with diagnosis and medical treatments. Once the patient has become stabilised medically only then are the appropriate therapeutic interventions activated. During this period the intention is for the patient to be quickly rehabilitated into the community. This therapeutic phase may only exist for three weeks to a month which, for Occupational Therapy activities and Ward groups, is adequate time for practical or supportive forms of counselling. For therapeutic work to take place sometimes a more 'intensive' process of work is required and this 'intensive' form will only be offered to very carefully selected patients. There are many issues here to be considered which this chapter cannot cover and I hope to write more extensively on this in the future. What then follows is a synopsis of how this form of intervention operates.

A patient is referred by a consultant for assessment. I will then visit this patient on the ward over a five-day period. Often the patient is still acutely ill and to begin with each hour I spend with them is an attempt to make contact, to begin to form a relationship with them. My dramatherapy activity follows Gabrielle Roth's (1989: 24) suggestion that the job of a therapist is simply to be 'present'. In so doing, you will respond with your 'beingness' in an appropriate way. Therefore, during assessment I don't structure dramatherapeutic activities unless the patient inspires such an activity in the 'moment'. One patient I assessed later reported to her consultant that she had never felt so completely given attention as she had experienced during the assessment, and that it was this factor that enabled her to rise from her bed, after six months, and become motivated to engage in therapy. Following the assessment, I make a report to the Ward Round and if it is agreed by all staff – the consultant, the social worker and the nursing staff – then the intensive therapy will begin.

The sessions take place off the ward either in my office or in a room I use outside the ward. The time of sessions will be dependent upon my ongoing timetable but I try to keep the sessions at a consistent time. The only break is for weekends or permission I give as the primary therapist for the patient to take any leave from the hospital. The contract is for three weeks – fifteen sessions. After this there will be a review and only if exceptional circumstances demand will there be any continuation. The contents of these sessions will pick up themes that have arisen in the assessment sessions and I will introduce dramatherapy structures with very simple projective exercises which shift the patient's circumstances into a dramatic dimension. The metaphor of drama creates both a distance and a container that enables the patient to engage with 'right brain' material and thereby, through what Murray Cox has called 'poiesis' (Cox and Theilgaard 1987), enables new ideas to be brought into consciousness. However, I don't just stay with the 'metaphor' but weave between the dramatic reality and the patient's everyday reality. I have learnt this from my patients, who do this quite spontaneously. For them, the distress of their acute episodes creates an urgency to relate the drama to the immediate drama of their lives.

One patient I assessed, who had been on the ward for one year and spent most of this time in her bed with acute depression, had been seen by most clinicians and was then referred for dramatherapy. I insisted that she got up from her bed to see me in one of the interview rooms on the ward. For the first three sessions, this patient launched into her story and I was seriously wondering whether dramatherapy would be possible. In the third session she slipped into her monologue an incident in adolescence when she had been stopped from reading *Wuthering Heights* and told to read a religious creed instead. (This patient had been closely involved with the Church.) I was struck by the way this event had been mentioned and, before the next session, followed this up by reading a detailed synopsis of the book, only to find amazing parallels between my patient's life and the story. When I reflected this to my patient she too was caught by the similarities, and the story became the focus of the ensuing sessions.

By first exploring the fictional characters using projective techniques and then using the 'character seat' from which Cathy, Heathcliffe, Linton and Catherine could speak, this patient began to explore key issues of sexual abuse, her sexuality and her faith, as well as her relationship to the Church. Quite soon this patient was able to return home and continue her therapeutic work as an outpatient on a weekly schedule. The intensive dramatherapy sessions had offered a doorway for her to investigate and take stock, because this patient was motivated, then inspired, first by the 'attention' she had felt she had been given in assessment, then, through the charm of re-engaging with an adolescent fiction, it enabled her to safely bring into consciousness parts of herself she had repressed. In so doing she was able to begin the process of transforming the negative patterns in her life.

ACT THREE

Scene one: dramatherapy with out-patient groups

When working in closed dramatherapy groups, at a level that traditional psychotherapy calls 'exploratory', I employ a form of therapeutic theatre which will either involve a rationale employing a para-theatrical model of dramatherapy (see Mitchell 1992a) or a model of dramatherapy which has its roots in ritual theatre; it is this ritual theatre rationale that I will focus on here. It is a form which involves the group in creating their own personal theatre plays (individual healing rituals) and then expanding these individual dramas into a group piece of ritual theatre. The format of a session will interweave four interlocking elements: (1) building an ensemble (by teaching theatre skills), (2) work on personal theatre 'plays', (3) transformation rituals and (4) the composition of a collective piece of ritual theatre.

Building an ensemble

I begin each session with the traditional 'check-in' ceremony, then move into the warm-up sequence. Here I teach the theatre skills, body and voice, sensory exercises, character work, improvisation and work with texts, not with the aim of teaching the clients to act, but to create a common vocabulary of expressive skills which will give them the resources to build their own personal theatre plays.

As the group work with developing theatre skills they are also developing basic interpersonal skills but within the frame of a theatre metaphor. It was Anna Halprin, of the San Francisco Dancers' Workshop, who stated that 'Whatever emotional, physical, or mental barriers that we carry around with us in our personal lives will be the same barriers that inhibit full creative expression' (quoted in Jean and Deak 1976). Therefore, by working on drama skills, the clients are also having an opportunity to overcome inhibitions to self-expression in life.

The further purpose of this work in the initial phase of the dramatherapy group is to build an 'ensemble' or, in therapeutic language, group cohesion. My rosary in dramatherapy is 'safety'. I do not believe clients will take therapeutic risks which will be productive in the long term if they don't feel safe. Therefore, part of my agenda at this stage is to use the development of theatre skills as a way of introducing the group to each other and building an alliance of therapeutic value between myself and the group. Here I would recommend the writings of George Kelly, who suggests that no client is asked to disclose in a group until they feel 'supported by at least one other member of the group other than the therapist' (Kelly 1955: 1160). Also, during this stage of groupwork the dramatherapist will need to observe the 'group dynamic' and set dramatic exercises which will help to encourage the release of tension between group members as they move through the traditional sequences of group life.

Work on personal theatre 'plays'

There are many ways to facilitate the work on personal theatre plays. Each dramatherapist will adopt the methods they feel comfortable with depending on their particular talents. I will often use a guided fantasy called 'The Theatre of Dreams'. The group members are asked to imagine that they are going to the theatre where they will see a scene in a play which reflects an issue in their lives. Then the 'dream' changes to the rehearsal room, where the actors are rehearsing their characters and receiving help from the director. The final aspect of the 'dream' is for them to embody one of the characters and explore the characters in a movement improvisation to music. The guided fantasy closes with the clients sharing their 'dreams'.

Another approach I use spotlights one particular client and the rest of the group participate in helping him or her develop his or her play. The client in the 'spotlight' is asked to imagine they are a *playwright*, to develop the story of their 'play', to imagine they are creating a scene in a drama, TV serial, soap opera, film or dance-drama which, using fictional characters, will depict the dramatic conflict they wish to explore.

The next phase involves the client now taking the role of *director*, and using the group as their 'actors', guiding them in the enactment of their 'play'. In so doing, the client views their process from the projective stance. At this stage the dramatherapist supports by encouraging them to experiment with their *actors*, not simply to accept the first attempts, but to experiment in such a way that the *dramatic conflict* the client is exploring is clarified and the 'play' meets the client's inner vision. The next phase is for the client to enter their 'play', taking over the character which will enable them to discover a new potentiality within themselves. The dramatherapist becomes substitute *director* reflecting to the 'client/character' how they directed their 'actor' in portraying the part. During the creation of the personal theatre play, the client is encouraged to experiment through working 'in character' with new possibilities.

In each session during the formative part of the group all the clients will have the space to develop their own play. At first the plays will most probably operate at what Murray Cox refers to as 'the first level of disclosure' (Cox 1978: 59) as they both learn and test out the methodology. Only after their initiation to the structure will they then feel safe to use the process as a ritual where they can explore deeper, riskier, personal issues.

Transformation rituals

In a dramatherapy group it is part of the therapist's task to provide structures where clients can safely ventilate any feelings, positive or negative, which they wish to express, to encourage the expression of all feelings and to contain for the client, where necessary, intense emotions. The structures the dramatherapist provides I call 'rituals of transformation' because they are designed to shift consciousness from one state to a different state of consciousness.

The rituals of transformation can be approached in two contrasting modes. The first is to work within the context of the dramatic metaphor. Here the dramatherapist works as a Theatre Director with the client in character; using drama exercises or theatre techniques to enable experiments with the character to take place. The second mode will be to devise ritual structures to enable the client to address archaic feelings which are the cause of their emotional blocks and need to be addressed directly. Sometimes this is an absolute necessity if the client is to make an authentic change. If this is the case, the client must make the transition from the fiction of his or her character's needs in the 'play' to their personal needs in 'life'.

The heart of a 'ritual' is for the 'initiate' to enter a *liminal* space, where the givens of daily life are let go and new possibilities can surface. In therapeutic process, a client needs a structure where historic feelings that may have been repressed can once more be brought into consciousness. The dramatherapist needs to have at their disposal a repertoire of experiential structures which can be evolved into safe ritual processes which will allow clients to explore and ventilate their inner psychic life.

The composition of a collective piece of ritual theatre

The aim of the 'ritual theatre' is for the group to encapsulate in dramatic terms the life of the group. It will be both their individual journey with selected images from their personal theatre plays, depicting the dramatic conflict, its resolution and the practical steps they will take in life, to make 'the change', and group images or 'experiences' the group wish to share as they close the group. In the very last session of the group the 'ritual theatre' will be enacted and witnessed by the group's participants as a way of celebrating and closing the group.

In what way a group decide to structure the 'ritual theatre' is a matter for them. I find that groups find it useful to have a structure they can use as a springboard to their own ideas. Therefore I commence the process with a structure called 'The Fool's Dance' developed by Paul Rebillot (for full details of this process see his book *The Call to Adventure*). In brief, 'The Fool's Dance' involves each client creating a series of individual sculpts; each sculpt depicts a certain feeling or stage in the group. For example, you might ask a group in an initial stage to sculpt 'their goal'; at another time, to sculpt 'a negative character'; after a ritual process, 'the resolution', or 'a here-and-now' feeling. Each sculpt is a picture, like a Tai Chi position, a poetic image, containing the essence of a story within their body position. 'The Fool's Dance', like Tai Chi, is a dance. The clients build a series of sculpts and move from one to another, each sculpt depicting a moment on their therapeutic journey.

When the group turns its attention to devising the images for their 'ritual theatre', they will have 'The Fool's Dance' structure. Using this as their point of departure they can weave other images and create group experiences such as 'drumming circles', spontaneous dance, contact improvisation, textual readings, as they wish, to form the composition of images which will be the group's therapeutic journey depicted as 'ritual theatre'.

Scene two: therapeutic theatre with out-patients

I have recently begun a new form of 'supportive' dramatherapy with out-patients in response to the many people who have now been either resettled into the community or are within the acute sector who need ongoing therapeutic support. These clients need a form of therapeutic intervention which is not problem-centred, in respect of working through personal issues, as I have previously described within the 'exploratory' ritual theatre form, but a process of work which is sensitive to their disabilities while at the same time not placing them in a medical-model sick-role. The approach I now employ is a development of Sue Jennings's 'creative/expressive' model of dramatherapy (Jennings 1986, 1987, 1990), where an emphasis is given to the dramatic process rather than interpretation or therapeutic tasks towards change. My work now evolves this drama perspective to a theatre one, which involves clients creating and performing a theatre piece.

This therapeutic theatre model begins with a theatre workshop. A production is then prepared and performances are given. The final phase of this process is for the group to meet and evaluate the task of theatre-making, performance and how they can take the experience into their daily lives. The objective of this process is to treat people who have mental health problems in a non-pathological way, to use the process of creating a piece of theatre and all this entails as the therapeutic process itself. The 'group' becomes a 'theatre company' of actors, writers, technical crew and not a sick or mentally ill dramatherapy group who must be guided towards exploring and sharing their psychopathology.

Theatre workshop

The aim of this phase is to develop theatre skills and build the 'theatre company' who will eventually rehearse and perform the play to an audience. Therefore, the dramatherapist will teach basic acting skills, sensory work, improvisation, how to build a character and image work. This phase will also involve working with body and voice, writing and working with a script.

The 'company' may decide to create their own play about topics that relate to their illness or issues of a social or political concern. In recent years The Grassmarket Theatre Project in Edinburgh has shown what can be both theatrically and therapeutically achieved with their 'home-made' productions of *Bad*, *Glad* and *Mad*. On the other hand the 'company' may choose to work on an established play, create their own collage of a Shakespeare play or another established master. The work of the dramatherapist, whatever the company's choice, is to use their theatre skills to facilitate the theatre process and to allow the healing to arise from the task of making theatre. This may involve guiding the 'company' in choice of plays, or imparting and encouraging play-writing skills. It is not the job of the dramatherapist to be a didactic theatre director, in what Peter Brook describes in his seminal book *The Empty Space* (1968) as 'deadly'. The dramatherapist is not there to theatrically realise their own vision and to use the 'company' to fulfil their own artistic ambitions, but to be a convenor, a resource person, to facilitate in the best traditions of dramatherapy practice.

Rehearsals

Once the play has been written or chosen, the next phase is to cast and rehearse. The dramatherapist may take the part of director or be an assistant to another member of the 'company' who wishes to take this role. The role of director, like that of the role of therapist, can be a powerful and abusing position. What is important is that the dramatherapist is aware that he or she is a dramatherapist and not engaging in his or her own aesthetic aspirations. Like all good theatre directors he or she will not tell the actors what to do but use his or her personal resources as a specialist in theatre techniques to enable the actors to achieve their aims with their parts. (For a full discussion of this role of the dramatherapist and the theatre director see Mitchell 1990, and for ways the dramatherapist might productively develop the rehearsal process, see Mitchell 1992a.)

Performance

As with any theatre project, the rehearsals eventually lead to the moment of performance. The dramatherapist must take care here to shield their clients from the exacting pressures which can be ever-present. This can be minimised by graduating the process of sharing rehearsal work with the general public. As in the established theatre, the 'company' might begin with *open rehearsals* for friends and colleagues before moving towards a series of *previews*. The performances might be aimed towards elderly or disadvantaged residents in homes or hospital wards, not where the threat of failure or harsh criticism might sabotage an otherwise important therapeutic experience. What level of exposure the dramatherapist feels the 'company' can absorb will be dependent, not only on artistic ability, but what 'ego strengths' the different members of the troupe have, to be able to internally assimilate the varying degrees of performance anxiety.

I was first drawn to this dramatherapeutic approach by my colleague, Madeline Andersen-Warren, who had started her own 'Therapeutic Theatre' in Huddersfield. She told me that her clients gained a great deal of self-respect through being able to perform. They had told her how important it had been to their rehabilitation, to be able to 'give something back through performing' (Andersen-Warren 1992). This comment gave me pause to reconsider the dictum 'Dramatherapy is about process not product', particularly in light of the 'supportive' work I have previously described with in-patients and day-patients; where producing a script or radio play has given purpose and pleasure to the dramatherapy group. I now see no reason why both *process* and *product* in 'supportive' dramatherapy should not coexist, particularly if the therapist takes care not to overemphasise the product. When the task of a group is to create a piece of theatre, the *product* is important to the *process* and can be therapeutically as important.

Post-production meeting

The final stage is for the 'company' to meet after the final performance and to reflect upon the project. How much the dramatherapist will focus the evaluation of the production to therapeutic themes will be dependent upon the initial contract with the

54   The handbook of dramatherapy

group. If the contract had involved giving the 'company' space in each meeting to ventilate life issues then the final meetings should reflect the grounding of the group task to everyday life. If the contract, on the other hand, was to create theatre and not structure therapeutic process beyond the experience of making and performing theatre, then the final meetings should be a form of closure and the 'company' will find the appropriate form of closure. This might be to celebrate achievements, plan future enterprises or evaluate and appraise the work so far.

Therapeutic objectives

Where are the therapeutic procedures in this model? It is my belief that individuals can discover important relief from their psychiatric symptoms when they are valued and part of a group that accepts them. We only have to turn to literature such as Yalom (1985, 1989, 1990) to discover some of the important factors in healing: acceptance, the instillation of hope, cohesiveness, altruism, universality, guidance, identification and self-understanding. One of the primary needs in 'supportive therapy' as stated by Bloch (1982: 19) is 'to promote the patient's best possible emotional and social functioning by restoring and reinforcing personal resources; to boost their self-esteem'. It is my belief that the making of theatre can be a process in which the kind of support that both Yalom and Bloch speak of can be present. In many ways, the building of a theatre 'company' can take on many tribal possibilities, of a community joined together in a common task – a task which may be a challenge but within reach of those who are taking part. The need for safety and acceptance I believe are paramount in any therapeutic process and it is my view that a group of clients who are motivated to meet and produce a play will, with the appropriate dramatherapeutic facilitation, experience these needs and thereby have a therapeutic experience.

Scene three: individual dramatherapy with out-patients

I see a number of out-patients each week for individual therapy, all of whom are on long-term contracts. A consultant will first refer someone for assessment and I will meet with this client for five sessions. During the assessment I will slowly introduce dramatherapy structures as I take a history, discover why they are seeking therapy, what resistances to therapy might arise for them and whether I believe a constructive 'therapeutic alliance' is possible. If I do decide that dramatherapy is an option, I will first meet with the client's consultant and, if we are in agreement, in the fifth assessment session a contract for therapy will be offered. This is usually for at least six months to a year with a review at the end of that period – unless the therapy is very task focused. If the client accepts the offer, therapy will commence immediately on a weekly basis, each session lasting sixty minutes.

The 'theatre of self-expression' model in individual therapy offers more of a theoretical framework than prescriptive structures. I have found that the process is a form of creative collaboration which has much in common with the theatre director helping an actor inhabit a role. The work of the 'theatre director' is almost a metaphor for the role of a clinical dramatherapist. They both have the same aim: the director to help the actor play his or her part on stage and the dramatherapist to help a human being to play his or her part in everyday life. Both the director and the dramatherapist know that if they try and tell someone what to do, they'll get nowhere. Each one tries to create a safe environment where experiments with the self can take place, where skills can be both learnt and let go. They will both have what Peter Brook (1968) calls a 'formless hunch' about the voyage of self-discovery they embark upon. And they will both have to ride out the black moments of the creative process, when simply staying with the chaos is the only way forward.

I find in individual therapy that clients have their own rhythm, the pace they wish to go, and allowing them 'time' to work at their pace is a pre-requisite for progress. I also find that I use a whole arsenal of theatre and experiential exercises to enable clients to follow the path they wish to take. My internal map for individual therapy includes the same procedures I have outlined for group work, shifting everyday concerns into a dramatic scene or helping clients to devise a 'rite of passage' that they will perform either indoors or outdoors at a specially selected location. On other occasions I will employ 'para-theatrical' exercises with body and voice, where, through combining projective art work with vocalisation, a client can ventilate or explore a particular emotion or relationship. What is employed, how a session starts and finishes changes with the time span a particular client has been in therapy and what the dynamic of the here-and-now relationship between us is. Yet in most cases, after the client has settled down, I begin with an 'awareness continuum' exercise that will focus him or her into the 'present' feelings and sensations in the body. From here, using breath and sound, they become engaged with the issue which will be the subject of the session's drama.

EPILOGUE

The *theatre of self-expression: therapeutic theatre model of dramatherapy* that has emerged from my clinical practice integrates the honesty required in terms of both therapeutic endeavour and artistic quest. I find it an 'artistic enquiry', not for aesthetics, but for the resolution to the problems the client presents. I believe the dramatherapist gives his/her client the resources, the dramatic tools, to make his/her journey of self-discovery. What do they seek? For each the specific answer will be different, yet, for me, Joseph Campbell comes the closest when he states:

People say that what we're all seeking is a meaning for life. I don't think that's what we're really seeking. I think that what we're seeking is an experience of being alive, so that our life experiences on the purely physical plane will have resonances within our own innermost being and reality, so that we actually feel the rapture of being alive.

(Campbell 1990: 5)

Paul Rebillot, a therapist and teacher of Gestalt and Experiential therapies from Esalen in America, puts it another way:

> I see the work that I'm doing as different from modes of therapy that attempt to fix people up so they can function better. Although that may come as a result of the work people do in my groups. . . my work is to help people open up the vistas of their being so that life becomes more livable – more of an experience and less of a problem. Out of that opening and realization will flow the ability to cope and function more satisfactorily, for the person will have tapped their own creative resources.
>
> (Rebillot and Kay 1979)

This is my aim as a dramatherapist applying the *theatre of self-expression: therapeutic theatre model* of dramatherapy in adult psychiatry. I believe the participation in differing forms of 'theatre structures' (Halprin 1986) offers clients the chance, as Grotowski stated, in a talk in Cardiff in 1982, 'to liberate energies', not simply a focus on resolving their immediate problems. Through the process of dramatic expression, clients can touch their own creative inspiration that will enable them to face themselves and make the necessary changes in their lives. As a 'therapist' I feel my task is to help them on this therapeutic journey, to be a companion, a witness, a guide; to help with my resources, my humanity, presence and the theatre and therapy structures I might have to offer, as they search for their resources that will lead towards a more healthy life.

NOTES

1   Roose-Evans (1989) is the only published account of Anna Halprin's work, although individual commentaries can be found in *The Drama Review* 1960–79.
2   Therefore I am indebted to my teachers and clinical supervisors, particularly Anne Kilkoyne, Marcia Karp, Sue Jennings and Don Feasey, and also the students who have either participated in the Pathfinder projects or have worked with me at the Institute of Dramatherapy in London and abroad, who through their keen and erudite participation have drawn from me what I know and have not known. I also owe much to my colleagues at Lancaster who have accepted my contribution as a dramatherapist and taught me much from their own orientations, in particular Maria Cornell, Dr Elizabeth Taylor, Dr Eileen Healey, Pete Kenny, Judy Mellor, Sarah Blackler and Pen Hutchinson; and all those in the Occupational Therapy Department who have contributed to my understanding of work with long-term patients. Last, but by no means least, I am indebted to all my clients who unknowingly have influenced what I now see as an important and 'artistic way' to healing.

REFERENCES

Andersen-Warren, M. (1992) 'Therapeutic Theatre Project', private correspondence.
Arieti, S. (1976) *Creativity: the Magic Synthesis*, New York, Basic Books.
Bloch, S. (1982) *What is Psychotherapy?*, Oxford, Oxford University Press.
Brook, P. (1968) *The Empty Space*, London, Penguin.
Brook, P. (1988) *The Shifting Point*, London, Methuen.

Campbell, J. (1973) *Myths to Live By*, New York, Bantam.
Campbell, J. (1990) *The Power of Myth*, New York, Doubleday.
Cox, M. (1978) *Structuring the Therapeutic Process*, Oxford, Pergamon Press.
Cox, M. (ed.) (1992) *Shakespeare Comes to Broadmoor*, London, Jessica Kingsley.
Cox, M. and Theilgaard, A. (1987) *Mutative Metaphors in Psychotherapy*, London, Tavistock.
Fransella, F. and Dalton, P. (1990) *Personal Construct Counselling in Action*, London, Sage.
Gersie, A. (1991) *Storymaking in Bereavement: Dragons Fight in the Meadow*, London, Jessica Kingsley.
Gersie, A. (1992) *Earthtales: Storytelling in Times of Change*, London, Green Print.
Gersie, A. and King, N. (1991) *Storymaking in Education and Therapy*, London, Jessica Kingsley.
Halprin, A. (1973) in *The Drama Review* (September).
Halprin, A. (1976) 'Theatre and therapy workshop', *The Drama Review* (March).
Jean, N. and Deak, F. (1976) 'Anna Halprin's theatre and therapy workshop', *The Drama Review* (March).
Jennings, S. (1986) *Creative Drama in Groupwork*, Winslow Press.
Jennings, S. (ed.) (1987) *Dramatherapy Theory and Practice 1*, London, Routledge.
Jennings, S. (1990) *Dramatherapy with Families, Groups and Individuals*, London and New York, Jessica Kingsley.
Kelly, G. (1955) *The Psychology of Personal Constructs*, New York, Norton.
Langley, D. and Langley, G. (1983) *Dramatherapy and Psychiatry*, London, Croom Helm.
Maslow, A. (1970) *Motivation and Personality*, New York, Harper & Row.
Maslow, A. (1971) *The Farther Reaches of Human Nature*, London, Pelican.
Mitchell, S. (1990) 'The theatre of Peter Brook as a model for dramatherapy', *Dramatherapy*, 13(1).
Mitchell, S. (1992a) 'Therapeutic theatre: a para-theatrical model of dramatherapy', in S. Jennings (ed.) *Dramatherapy Theory and Practice 2*, London, Routledge.
Mitchell, S. (1992b) 'The similarities and differences between the theatre director and the dramatherapist', Keynote speech at the Shakespeare Symposium.
Ouspensky, P.D. (1977) *In Search of the Miraculous*, London, Routledge & Kegan Paul.
Rebillot, P. (1993) *The Call to Adventure: Bringing the Hero's Journey to Daily Life*, New York, HarperCollins.
Rebillot, P. and Kay, M. (1979) 'A trilogy of transformation', *Pilgrimage*, 7(1).
Roose-Evans, J. (1989) *Experimental Theatre from Stanislavski to Peter Brook*, London, Routledge.
Roth, G. (1989) *Maps to Ecstasy*, San Rafael, CA, New World Publishing.
Watts, A. (1973a) *Psychotherapy East and West*, Harmondsworth, Pelican.
Watts, A. (1973b) *The Book on the Taboo against Knowing Who You Are*, London, Abacus.
Watts, A. (1976a) *Nature, Man and Woman*, London, Abacus.
Watts, A. (1976b) *The Wisdom of Insecurity*, London, Rider & Co.
Wilson, C. (1986) *G.I. Gurdjieff: the War Against Sleep*, Wellingborough, Aquarian Press.
Yalom, I. (1985) *The Theory and Practice of Group Psychotherapy*, New York, Basic Books.
Yalom, I. (1989) *Love's Executioner*, London, Bloomsbury.
Yalom, I. (1990) *Existential Psychotherapy*, New York, Basic Books.

Chapter 4

An integrated model of dramatherapy and its application with adults with learning disabilities

Anna Chesner

INTRODUCTION

Dramatherapy in Britain has its early origins in work with this client group and this has been clearly documented elsewhere (see Jennings 1973; Brudenell 1987; Chapters 1 and 10 this volume). I shall not be attempting an historical survey here. My intention is rather to outline a broad working methodology based on my current work in this field. I shall be using the metaphor of aviation as a kind of map to illustrate the developmental phases of this work. These phases may take place within one session; it may take many sessions to move from one phase to another; and it may be impossible or inappropriate to move through all phases with one group. Each phase is characterised by a certain level of imaginative involvement, creativity and spontaneity. By placing the group somewhere on this map the dramatherapist may view both how far they have come together and also what kind of challenge may be appropriate next.[1]

SETTING THE SCENE

The institution as community

This chapter is based on my experiences developing a dramatherapy facility within a large residential unit for adults with learning disabilities. Many of the clients I work with have lived here and in similar establishments for years and even decades. A number have moved into 'the community' during the last few years to live in 'group homes', and this trend will continue over the next few years as the unit contracts and eventually closes in its current form.

I mention this at the outset for two reasons. First, the environment of radical change, affecting both staff and residents, is an important part of the context of the work. Second, I wish to acknowledge that the place of dramatherapy with this client group will change alongside their living circumstances. I hope that the observations and suggestions that follow may also be of value to those working within 'the community'.

I put the words 'the community' in inverted commas since those who have not moved out of the unit also live in a community. Since ancient times theatre has been a product of its community, reflecting its conflicts and dreams. Similarly dramatherapy must be seen in the context of the specific and wider communities out of which it grows, and which it reflects. The particular community constituted by the unit (formerly 'hospital') in which I have been working has a history, a variety of traditions, attitudes and norms. These form the backdrop, the broad contextual environment to the specific setting of the dramatherapy studio and the work that happens there.

The relationship between the environment of the dramatherapy studio and the unit as a whole

The dramatherapy studio needs to be both part of and separate from the institution as a whole. There must be links in terms of organisational factors, such as timetabling, and to some extent in terms of clinical input. A client, for example, who is learning to use Makaton sign language with their speech therapist has an excellent opportunity to practise this skill within the context of dramatherapy. At the same time, there must be a sufficient sense of separation to allow for the establishment of different traditions, attitudes and norms. This is crucial to the therapeutic process. The dramatherapeutic experience invites the taking of risks. Clients are invited to journey together into the unknown. It is a matter of respect for the element of risk involved in this process that the boundaries of the therapeutic space need to be established and honoured.

In practical terms this means that the studio needs to be private, so that therapy sessions are not disturbed by extraneous noise, nor intruded upon by people who are not part of the session. Time boundaries are similarly important. Sessions which take place on a weekly basis at a certain time and for a certain duration should occur reliably and punctually. These very simple space and time boundaries help to create a psychologically secure space for the therapeutic process. Within the context of the large institution such basics have by no means been easy to achieve, and considerable time and energy have been dedicated to achieving a compromise of workable conditions in terms of these boundaries. The difficulty may be a reflection of a general problem of liaison and boundary-keeping within large institutions. This aspect of the work can be more challenging for the therapist than what goes on in the sessions themselves. Its importance, however, is analogous to the gardener's preparation of the soil, before the planting of seeds and plants.

Using the dramatherapy studio only for the purpose of dramatherapy sessions generates a sense of tradition for staff and clients alike, and gives clients the security of knowing what kind of activities are possible there. This is an important factor in encouraging spontaneity, creativity and experimentation. There needs to be an understanding that different ground rules may exist in this space than in the home or ward spaces, and than in areas of the unit dedicated to 'training' or 'education'. Clients are sensitive to the difference of atmosphere and working ethos, even though they may not be able to consciously or verbally formulate the differences. In this sense, the physical workspace, its atmosphere and ethos, is of paramount importance in working with this client group. This has been particularly noticeable when clients with profound and multiple disabilities have attended the studio for the first time after a series of ward-based 'contact' sessions. They have been noticeably more expressive, more energised and more alert. I suspect this is due to a number of factors: they have been 'chosen' to come, which means they have been seen as an individual rather than one of the whole group; they come to a space away from the familiar background sounds of the ward/home such as the television or radio, and the sounds of the staff and residents; they find themselves in an environment offering them the space and support to explore without interference.

Setting up a dramatherapy studio

Having looked at the importance of the atmosphere and working ethos embodied in the dramatherapy studio let us look at how a space can be prepared for this use. The key point here is that the layout and contents of the space support the purpose for which it is to be used. There are times when a maximum of empty space is called for, and other times when the space is filled with all manner of objects to stimulate or express the drama. The space must be flexible enough to allow for these transformations.

I have found it useful to have a lot of materials to hand for easy access when required. At the same time this is a client group that is easily distracted from a focal point of attention. Too many exciting possibilities in the space can lead to fragmentation in the group and frustration in the therapist! A balance is required whereby materials can be brought into the action spontaneously, while the space is sufficiently clear to support appropriate concentration.

The therapeutic environment is created by what is absent as much as what is present. One of the choices we made when setting up the studio was to minimise the use of chairs and tables. Whilst these are available when needed, we use bean-bag chairs as a distinctive feature of the space. This decision arose out of the observation that most work and living spaces within the unit are furnished with chairs and tables for the normal day-to-day routine of living. Assumptions like 'That's my chair, that's my table, where I sit every day' seem to encourage a habitual passivity in the residents and corresponding expectations in some staff.

The bean-bag chairs are used in a more flexible way, with the intention of challenging the habit. The experience of sitting on one is more comforting than sitting on a chair, and allows for a wider variety of self-expression in terms of how we choose to sit. The chair, by contrast, tends to impose a way of sitting, and the posture tends to be more formal. Sitting in a circle of upright chairs can be too confrontative and anxiety-provoking, while the use of bean-bag chairs generates a more open and relaxed attitude. Along with a variety of playshapes they have also proved invaluable in terms of scene setting.

The specific style and contents of a dramatherapy studio will vary according to resources, context of the space and individual style of the therapist. Since space is such a vital resource in this therapy, it is a useful discipline for the dramatherapist to question their use of the space in the light of the work that takes place there.

AN INTEGRATED MODEL

I call the model of dramatherapy I use with this client group an 'integrated' model. The philosophy behind it is inclusive, based on the concept of 'drama' as 'the thing done'. In short my attitude is: 'Anything that is action can be used in dramatherapy.'

In practice this means that sessions may include the use of visual art, music-making, dance and movement work, contact exercises, game-playing, story-making, role-play and performance. The choice of activity may be made in advance by the therapist, or spontaneously by the group or therapist.

The emphasis of any activity within the context of dramatherapy is on exploration and communication through action and interaction. The attention of the therapist is on the various levels of interaction:

interaction with the space and objects in it;
interaction with the therapist or therapeutic team;
interaction with the peer group.

The inner world of the participant is expressed implicitly or explicitly at each level of interaction.

Over time the degree of spontaneity, imagination and creativity develops and this allows a fuller expression of the inner world/s of participants. The dramatherapy session becomes a space where anything may become possible through imaginative exploration. Using the analogy of aviation, this corresponds to flying high, an exhilarating experience, but one which requires preparation and is not without risk.

The ritual and risk paradigm developed by Jennings (1990; see also Chapter 6 this volume) has particular relevance with this client group. She draws on the traditions of *rites de passage* to highlight the need for containment within a session. In my own experience it has been essential to begin and end each session with familiar activities and a sense of ritual. In the middle section of the session a greater degree of risk-taking is required of participants. Trust grows as the group comes to recognise the familiar structure of a session. The wider the range of activities that may be included within the dramatherapy session, the more important it is for participants to know that their exploration into the unknown will be contained by a warm-up and closure. When we travel by aeroplane we need to know where we are taking off from and that we will land safely at our destination. The dramatherapy session begins and ends with quite predictable elements, analogous to the predictable processes the traveller goes through at the airport. In the middle phase of the session the client needs sufficient trust of the therapist and group as pilot and fellow travellers.

The integrated model and dramatherapy with individuals

In one-to-one dramatherapy there is clearly no interaction with the peer group. Emphasis is on exploration of the space and its contents, in the presence of and in relation to the therapist. I tend to use group dramatherapy whenever possible, for reasons I give below. Individual dramatherapy sessions are used where the developmental and emotional needs of the client make group work irrelevant (Brudenell 1987).[2]

In these sessions the client is provided with a safe space for exploration of self in relation to the environment, for example by handling a variety of objects which have been set out in advance. These objects may include balls of various colours, sizes and textures; coloured foam play shapes; instruments such as tambour or bells; hand puppets and dolls. The client exercises choice as to which objects to explore. Initial interest may be in a particular ball; then in a variety of balls; from here into other objects of a similar size but a different shape, and which move differently; or to the tambour, which is round, spinnable and gives sound. The client may be absorbed in sensory play with objects, or may be responsive to simple games of give and take with the therapist, either through objects or touch. It is sometimes possible to move into projective play, when the client relates to the doll or puppet as a character rather than simply as an object of a certain colour, shape, texture and plasticity. At this point the imagination and creativity can develop. The therapist's role in this process is to facilitate each stage of exploration; to maintain the safety of the space; and to prepare the space with a sensitivity to the ongoing development of the client, and their need for a combination of the familiar and the new.

Wherever possible group dramatherapy is used, in groups of three to eight clients with a therapeutic team of two to three. This group size allows each group member to be visible, whilst giving them the challenge of working in a group. Group therapy is particularly relevant in the context of the large institution. All live in a group setting, and adapt to this with varying degrees of skill or difficulty.

A common reaction is that there is a minimum of communication within the peer group. The need for communication and friendship is focused on the staff. This pattern of communication is often reinforced over many years through carer–patient, parent–child type interactions, which limit the role repertoire and personal development of the client. This disempowers the client and leads to an undervaluing of the peer group. Institutional life experienced from the role of the 'patient', for whom many decisions are made by staff, leads to low self-esteem. 'They', the peer group, are seen as the same as 'I', limited and worthless, so there is little incentive to build relationships.

Group dramatherapy helps to break this cycle. The group itself is seen as a valued therapeutic agent, to which each participant contributes. Self and peer group begin to be regarded as possible sources of recognition, support, under-standing and meaningful interaction. This involves a radical shift of world view, which is particularly relevant as residents prepare to move into smaller group homes in the community. As they move from the all-embracing and controlling 'parental' figure of the large institution, 'sibling' or peer group support can make a fundamental difference to their experience of the move.

MOVING INTO ACTION: CHECKING IN

From the moment the group arrives for its session the action of greeting is very much part of the therapy. It creates an opportunity for group members to orient themselves to the space and to the particular group of people who come together for dramatherapy. In everyday life we tend to take many processes for granted. Within the dramatherapy session simple structures may be needed to enable participants to engage in these processes (see Cattanach 1992).

When the group has arrived each session begins formally in a circle. Holding hands to close the circle focuses the attention by physicalising the group as container. Each individual contributes to the completeness and sense of con-nectedness. The therapist suggests spending some time looking around the circle to see who is present. This creates the opportunity for eye contact and spon-taneous interaction in groups where this is not already happening. Even the process of saying 'Hello' can be structured in a number of ways. We have developed several hello songs, which include a handshake being passed around the circle, and each person's name being sung. These songs, repeated as part of the opening ritual of the session, gradually become familiar. With familiarity comes confidence and an increased level of participation. As the 'script' becomes known the form is transcended and the song becomes a device for warming up to the group and spontaneous expression.

A very popular 'opener' with some groups is the ubiquitous ball/name game. The idea is to make eye contact, say someone's name, and throw them the ball. The way in which a group masters and develops this game over a period of months can be a fascinating reflection of the changing relationships within the group. The ball becomes a concrete symbol of the communication between group members. At first the lines of communication tend to be to and from members of the therapeutic team, reflecting the pattern of communication described above. In some cases the ball may stop passively in one person's lap. Another person may push it away, but not to anyone, avoiding eye contact and the use of voice. It can be most satisfying when someone first chooses to engage in the game and throw the ball with intention of making contact. Eventually the game is transcended and becomes a device for spontaneous interaction, with the ball taking varied paths between group members. The group may develop expressive and humorous ways of throwing it, often accompanied by greater confidence in initiating verbal interactions. As with many structures used in the dramatherapy session, the aim is for the form itself to recede in importance and for life to come into the foreground. The skill of the dramatherapist lies in finding the appropriate structures to achieve this aim.

Concretisation

Use of concrete elements, accessible to the senses, facilitates the dramatherapeutic process when working with this client group. Objects are easier to work with than abstract ideas, and ideas can be made more accessible by 'concretising' them with the help of objects or props.

In the game described above the ball is a simple therapeutic and dramatic prop. It concretises the flow of communication and attention between group members, and this supports the development of group awareness.

It is a key principle of the work with this client group to use tangible, visible elements whenever possible. We live in a society where much of our communication depends on the abstract. The word, spoken or written, opens doors into conceptual and imagined worlds, often relating to past events and possible futures. As I talk with a friend the words form an invisible bridge between one mind and another. We can have a sense of real contact with each other without moving from our seats, and in the case of the telephone or letter, without even needing to see each other.

I noticed early on in the work with this client group that words alone were often not enough. Attention in the group would wander the longer I talked about something or tried to describe a structure I had in mind. It was as if I was speaking a foreign language and expecting the group to learn it. By contrast if I introduced an object that clients could relate to with the senses and which engaged the body in movement, I felt I had their attention and interest. I was speaking their language, and we had a starting point for exploration and improvisation. So I now try to involve the body and senses even in the introductory or explanatory part of a structure, and use the spoken word more to complement the action than to dominate it. There are elements of clown, magician, ham actor in my presentation as therapist.

The appropriate balance of the concrete with the verbal varies from group to group and sessions are planned with a sensitivity to this issue. Even so there are many moments when spontaneous changes are made by clients and therapeutic team alike in response to the session having become too abstract. At such moments necessity to communicate is the mother of spontaneity and invention.

The use of props

Initially the exploration of the prop is a sensory exploration of the thing itself. A large, round, multi-coloured parachute is a popular purpose-bought therapeutic aid. Initially it provides an opportunity for the group to come together in a large circle connected by the physical presence of the parachute. It can be difficult for some groups to make a circle. If each person holds the edge of the parachute there is a tangible and colourful circle. The group can make it move by raising and lowering their arms. This creates several new sensations. There is the kinaesthetic sensation of the arms moving in space, and particularly stretching upwards. Such a large piece of cloth moving through space creates a breeze that caresses the face in what is usually experienced as a pleasurable way. Visually, the movement of the parachute can be exciting, and it may be possible to see other group members across and underneath the parachute. A game may develop from this, calling 'Hello' to another group member, and changing places by crossing underneath the parachute while it is at its high point. This is a positive experience of co-operation, shared play. There is an element of risk in moving underneath the parachute and managing to come out the other side. It is exhilarating to survive the danger, and the activity can help build confidence in the group.

The prop can facilitate the development of the imagination in the group. By speeding up the movements of the parachute the group may create a 'storm', which builds to a peak of wildness and then subsides. When the group members accept the 'as if' of this idea, they take the first small step towards the infinite possibilities of dramatic imagination. Ultimately anything is possible within the drama. All that is needed is an agreement to pretend, to suspend disbelief, and play within the 'as if'.

It is worth paying attention to the transition from that work which is based in the here-and-now, in the concrete reality of sensory exploration, to activities which have their basis in the imagination. This transition can be facilitated through various structures, using a ball or other prop over a period of time. We have found a foam rugby ball useful in this process. Initially it is a ball, and is thrown from person to person in a name game; then passed around the circle in each direction, still as a ball. When this activity is mastered I have introduced the idea that it is now a 'hot potato', and to be passed on quickly to the next person, to the accompaniment of physical and vocal expressions of heat. These suggestions are modelled, so the group can see and hear what I mean. Another suggestion might be that it is a 'sticky bun'. In this case the hands are as if stuck to it, and a great deal of force is needed to pull it from one pair of hands to the next.

In both these examples the ball is no longer a ball. As it takes on a new reality the group is invited to take on new roles in relation to it, roles dependent on accepting the 'as if' of the ball as something else. Once this possibility is experienced, each group member may be invited to use the ball as something new, and the group may guess what it is. This is an exciting further development. The group itself is coming up with the creative ideas, and the therapist's ideas can take a back seat. Group members are communicating original ideas directly with each other.

TAKING OFF

I have described the process of 'checking in', which gives the group the chance to warm up to each other and to the way of working by engaging in simple activities of greeting and game playing. By 'taking off' I refer to the process whereby the group begins to explore the world of the imagination. This involves a new kind of risk-taking as the here-and-now of the group begins to expand into other locations and other time frames. During this phase the therapist facilitates the group in understanding that anything is possible within the drama, subject to the agreement of the group.

The origin of the material

Increasingly, over time, the material comes from group members themselves, as I shall explore later. Initially it comes from the therapist, who may sense a theme or issue that is present for the group and suggest a structure appropriate for its exploration.

One such theme, which seems to be particularly relevant to the group just beginning to explore the possibilities of imaginative role-play, is the theme of the dangerous journey. There are many versions of this of which I shall describe two.

The first one was inspired by associations with water as both the element of trust and also as a source of danger. The scene is set as a river, the banks defined by chalk lines on the studio floor, or playshapes and mats. A series of plastic hoops are laid next to each other in such a way that they cross the river, creating a bridge of stepping stones. Indeed each group member may step on the previous stone, lay their own stone a little further into the river, and retreat to the safety of the bank. When the last stone is laid the task for the group is to encourage each other to cross the water without getting their feet wet, and to welcome them to the other side when the heroic task has been completed. If the structure is repeated and the group is feeling more confident second time round a water pistol may be used to enhance the danger. This needs to be used with sensitivity, and it is important that the therapeutic team is as likely to be 'got' as the rest of the group.

Another dangerous journey improvisation involves climbing a mountain, and abseiling down. The mountain is built by the group at one end of the studio, using bean-bag chairs, playshapes or whatever else is to hand. An 'experienced mountaineer' climbs the mountain, sends the rope down the studio, whilst anchoring it at one end. The studio floor becomes the mountain side, and each person is encouraged to 'climb' the mountain, by pulling themselves along the rope. Everyone has a moment of being the focus of the group's attention as they take on the challenge of the climb. At the same time the role of climber has been modelled, so there is not too much pressure for each individual to come up with an original idea. Once at the top there is an opportunity for calling down the mountainside, using the voice as if outside and travelling a long distance. When each group member has arrived at the top the group may choose to rest, and reflect on their achievement, or perhaps to celebrate by yodelling or singing an echo song together. There are a number of ways of coming down the mountainside back to base. The rope may be used again, to abseil, or people may choose to run down the mountain with the sense of abandon that comes with going downhill fast. For the truly adventurous there is the possibility of going down by 'sledge'. This is a reinforced car tyre, laid flat, mounted on castors, and with a platform built into the hollow part. The group member sits on this, holding one end of the rope, whilst the other end is pulled from the other end of the studio. The sensation is like riding on a sledge, and is often accompanied by whoops of excitement.

In both examples of the dangerous journey improvisation the basic structure of the session is planned in advance. As the structure unfolds there are spontaneous and very individual responses both to the activity and to each other in doing it. The risk factor is balanced by the opportunity for encouragement, support and achievement. As a matter of principle no-one is forced into anything they do not want to do. Climbing a mountain is a fine analogy of meeting the challenge of something new, which reflects the challenge of moving as a group into more imaginative work. One client standing at the foot of the mountain, said 'I can't do it.' One of the therapeutic team climbed up with him, while other group members called to him in encouragement from the top of the mountain. Once he arrived he said 'It's easy.' At the end of the session he reflected on the whole process and said with clear pride 'I've never done that before.' Not only had he not climbed an actual mountain before, it may also have been his first experience of imaginative role-play. Indeed, it may also have been a long time since he was encouraged to try anything new. It is too easy within an institution to assume that residents cannot do something rather than that they can, with support. No wonder his first statement was 'I can't do it.' Many adults with learning disabilities have internalised this statement over the years, and need encouragement to risk finding out for themselves what their limitations are.

FLYING HIGH

A group gets to 'fly high' at that point in a session and at that point in its ongoing development when it moves into maximum creativity, spontaneity and risk-taking. This corresponds with the ability to enter and explore an imaginary world together, a world created by the group itself, reflecting the fantasies and concerns of the participants.

The 'flight of fancy' takes place during the middle phase of any session, within the containment of a warm-up and closure as mentioned above. The therapeutic team has a facilitative role in providing ways in to the process of improvisation and story-making. A number of devices may be used.

Props

A number of objects are placed on a table, or passed around the group for exploration. These may be a mixture of everyday and more unusual objects, collected over a period of time, e.g. a wicker basket with a lid, a pair of binoculars, a chiffon scarf, an empty bottle, a map, a pipe, a cane and a necklace. As each object is handled, a variety of possible uses is discovered. Each person is invited to choose the object they wish to use in the story, and one person volunteers to start. They enter the area of the studio used for action, and by what they say or do a location or context is defined, and the rest of the group follows. The story develops according to what each person brings to it, as a unique expression of this group of people at this particular time. The therapist often takes the role of narrator, to provide a commentary on the action. This enables the therapist to have one foot inside the imaginary world and one foot outside it, as a safety measure for the group. Other members of the therapeutic team usually participate in the story from within a role, stimulating reaction and interaction in the group.

Pictures

We have collected a wide variety of pictures from magazines and mounted them on card. A selection of these is passed around the group for comment. From these each person is invited to choose a picture of a location and a situation, which interests them. The majority choice is followed as the group choice, perhaps incorporating elements from minority choices. We begin with the physical activity of building the location, by using playshapes and any other objects around in the studio. The clients choose their character using ideas from the pictures, and may improvise costume and props. Music and lighting may be used to set the atmosphere if appropriate to the setting, and the improvisation begins.

Discussion

Themes may arise in discussion at the start of the group. One client may talk about an issue on their mind as soon as they enter: a staff member is leaving, a friend got sick, there was a visit to family, or plans for a holiday. These may be presented to the group as suggestions for a scene. Alternatively, the group may be asked what kind of story they would like to create, and whatever each person says may be incorporated into the story, even if it is a one word suggestion.

The value of improvisation

Improvisation provides a rough framework or starting point for action, and space for spontaneous input. Unconscious and unexpressed feelings or issues find expression within this framework, and this has therapeutic value. There is a tendency to consider people with learning disabilities in terms of their learning difficulties only. In fact the conditions of their life often give rise to powerful feelings. If these are expressed unskilfully or inappropriately the client may be labelled as having 'challenging behaviours' and be put on a behavioural programme with the aim of making the behaviour more acceptable, without necessarily addressing the underlying issues. The dramatherapeutic approach may include aspects of social skills training compatible with the behavioural approach, but it also goes beyond this towards giving space and form for the expression of the underlying material.

Let us consider some of the life experiences and conditions that may contribute to the feelings and issues of adults with learning disabilities living in a large institutional setting. These include physical realities, past experiences and current lifestyle.

Physical realities

It is not uncommon for there to be difficulties or discomfort in mobility. In most groups we have a combination of ambulant and non-ambulant participants. Sensory impairment may add further difficulty for some. However well people cope with these difficulties it is understandable that they have strong feelings, either about the conditions themselves or about the kind of relationships that result at a secondary level, for example, dependency on others for feeding or personal hygiene.

Past experiences

Early experiences are formative. Many may have sensed themselves from an early age to be a source of anxiety or disappointment in the family, and in some way different. At some point the family has decided that it cannot cope full time with a child or adult with learning disabilities, or that others would be able to care more appropriately. These experiences contribute to the client's sense of self, and to feelings of loss, guilt and anger.

Current lifestyle

Limitations in terms of privacy and choice in everyday matters characterise institutional life. Many clients share their room with one or more others. All share their home, not necessarily with people they would choose to live with. Privacy is limited, which may have repercussions in terms of sexual expression. There are many freedoms which most people can take for granted that are not accessible to many members of this client group. Lack of reading skills and the inability to travel independently result in limited access to cultural experience and new ideas. Television and radio may be on, but not necessarily by choice. Verbal skills are often limited and there may be physical difficulty in articulating even if the vocabulary is there. Add to this the current plans to close the unit, which will mean the loss of home and loss of the familiar. These are painful factors, and are the source of frustration, anger, feelings of fear, loss, confusion.

As an improvisation unfolds these experiences may inform the emotional and thematic content of the story; sometimes overtly, and at other times covertly. The theme of control and power, for example, finds its way by hook or by crook into many stories and settings. Out of a large selection of available hats the policeman's helmet, often with truncheon, is one of the most popular pieces of costume.

Some clients have a healthy hunger to be the one with the authority and power for once, and enjoy exercising it over their peer group and the therapeutic team alike. Others put on the helmet but have difficulty in finding the inner authority to fill out the role. They remain passive and essentially within their familiar role.

A less threatening structure for beginning to explore status and authority is a simple improvisation set in a royal castle or palace. Each person in turn is invited to sit on the throne, wearing crown and cloak. From the role of king or queen they may request whatever they want from the courtiers. Even the more timid usually find it possible to make some request, perhaps non-verbally, and so have the experience of being boss for a moment. They may feel reassured by the structure of the improvisation which ensures that the role is temporary and will pass on to someone else.

A recurrent theme for some clients is that of enforced control. An imaginary situation develops in which they assume the role of one who has gone out of control, or is anti-social in some way – perhaps by playing the monkey, kidnapping someone, shoplifting, hijacking a plane, killing. Eventually they are brought under control, and are imprisoned or tried by the group who decide their fate within the story. There is excitement and energy in taking on the role of the villain, but also an element of fear. It is often the group member playing this role who ensures that they get caught. Is this an expression of the internalised message that chaotic behaviour, or expression of negativity, is bad and must be punished? Or an enactment of the need both to express the unacceptable and be contained? Or an exploration of the moral dilemma of self-expression within the context of the social world? The possible interpretations are manifold and it is usually unhelpful to reduce the meaning of a session to one interpretation. What is clear is that these themes are meaningful to the clients and groups concerned, and probably at a multiplicity of levels. The therapist's role is to be open to what is being expressed and to tolerate the unknown.

Another recurrent theme is loss. In one session the group chose to explore the real-life story of how they had to move out of their familiar day-centre into another building, whilst alterations were to be carried out. This event had happened that same week and the group was keen to talk about it. One client kept repeating one simple sentence about the event. The volume of this sentence seemed to increase with each repetition in an attempt, I suspect, to communicate not only the fact of the event, but the feelings, for which this client had inadequate verbal mastery. The action of the session involved building two locations in the space, the old day-centre, and the place they had to move to. Apart from the roles of the two members of staff associated with these locations the group played themselves in the situation. At one level the enactment was a repetition of what had happened. They were told they were moving, moved the contents of the day-centre to the other site and stayed there. The telling of the simple story has therapeutic value itself. It is a way of marking the significance of what happened as a group and of communicating with others, in this case the dramatherapist and music therapist who were conducting the group. The therapeutic value was enhanced by stopping the action at various points to explore the opinions and feelings of the various group members. It was possible to give expression to the feelings of dissatisfaction, anger and ultimately sadness. This was done verbally, physically and through musical improvisation. As the feelings were given space the group made the connection with other experiences of loss, in particular the death of parents and friends.

In the above session the temporary loss of a familiar workspace was more accessible to work with than the more distressing experience of loss through death. One of the advantages of dramatherapy is that the emotional content of an issue can be worked with indirectly. This tends to be less threatening than focusing directly on the deeper psychic wounds. Here the 'story' was an actual experience of the group. It could equally well have been a fictional story created by the group in one of the ways described above, or an interpretation of a known story. The story of Cinderella, for example, begins with the illness and death of the mother, and the grief of the daughter. Here the emotional content of the story is clearly focused around painful issues of loss. The safety factor comes in the fact that the story is fictional and therefore at one remove from the rawness of personal experience.

Improvisation within the dramatherapy session is a group process. The overt task of the group is to create the story. This may involve setting the scene, casting the characters and developing a story-line. Interactions occurring within the framework of these activities give expression to the dynamics of the group and the quality of particular relationships in it. Group members reveal how they see themselves and each other. There are lines of attraction or conflict, and relationships based on competition, co-operation, dominance, mutual dependence and many other variables. The choice of who gets to play which role and who does the choosing is as significant as the content of the improvisation. The here-and-now relationships within the group provide opportunities and incentives to practise new real-life roles in a spontaneous situation. The less assertive person may stand up to a dominant group member, who may in turn be un-characteristically supportive of another person's ideas. These changes often take place when the focus is on the dramatic activities of the session. Change arises in the context of a shared interest in an act of joint creation, rather than by facing the need for change head on.

COMING IN TO LAND

This phase of the work refers to the important process of leaving behind the shared 'flight of fancy' and returning to earth. This involves a process of distancing from the 'as if' world. The studio returns to being a studio, group members return to their own role, and the characters and events of the improvisation become shared memories.

Having journeyed in the middle phase of the session into another time, another place and other identities it is important that the group has the opportunity for reorientation into the present time and space before group members take leave of each other.

This process may need to be broken down into several steps. Taking off any pieces of costume is a concrete way of creating some distance between self and the imaginary role. There may be some reluctance to do this and clients may choose to keep some symbolic representation of the role with them as the group moves into the activity of reflecting together on the session.

Dealing with the baggage

After the journey into the unknown group members are given the opportunity to bring something positive back with them, and to leave behind elements of the experience that they do not wish to intrude on their day-to-day reality.

Reflection and discussion are part of this process, and help to create some distance between the dramatic world and the here-and-now. Each person may be invited to describe or show one moment from the session which they remember or enjoyed. This activity may be facilitated by passing round a talking stick or microphone to hold physically whilst holding the group's attention. I am often surprised by the particular moments that are recollected into the present. Some sessions or moments from sessions are remembered many months on, the experience having become internalised and carried around as a source of pleasure or strength. Sound tapes and photographs of moments within sessions are very popular with a number of clients in this respect.

Finally, goodbyes are said, often in a ritualised way through a song, or group shout. There is a clear ending to the session that involves the whole group, and is based on familiar activities. The journey from the known into the unknown concludes in the known before the group members take leave of each other and get on with their individual lives.

At this point the therapeutic team takes time to reflect on the content and process of the session, and sort through its own baggage with a critical eye. Each session is a learning experience provided we give time to looking at what worked and what did not. The nature of dramatherapy is such that it is impossible to notice everything that is happening at the time. The therapist's attention has to be both with the group as a whole and with individuals within it. Looking back over the session gives the opportunity to compare the dynamics of the group and individual contributions over time. Change happens so gradually that it is easy to overlook it. A creative idea comes from a client who used to be more of a follower; another client begins to communicate more verbally; someone who used to put themselves on the outside chooses to join in the action; clients begin to talk directly to each other rather than through staff. It is important for the therapeutic team to acknowledge these changes. The kind of structures planned for the next session need to take into account both recent changes and the therapeutic journey of the group so far. The aim is to continue to provide a tolerable degree of challenge.

CONCLUSION

The practice of dramatherapy with adults with learning disabilities poses specific challenges to client and therapist alike. The internalised culture of the large institution, where many of this client group live or have lived, may operate as an inhibitor to creativity, spontaneity, self-expression and change – implicit goals of dramatherapy. Client expectations of self and peer group tend to be low, and there may be a corresponding danger that the dramatherapist's expectations of the method and the clients will also drop.

By creating a culture within a culture, dramatherapy is in a good position to challenge these habitual identities and to plant the seeds of change. There may be moments of remarkable breakthrough within a dramatherapy session, but usually the process of change is gradual. It is for this reason that a map of ongoing drama-therapy process is of value, for which I use the metaphor of aviation.

Most groups begin with a here-and-now focus to the work. This phase may continue for a few weeks, months or for the entire duration of a lengthy group process. The work focuses on participants coming together, being together and taking leave of each other. Feet are firmly on the ground and the therapy rests largely in the growing awareness of self and group, and the trust which this engenders. This important process is more about earthing than flying.

A group may need help in taking off into work based in the imagination. It is useful to take this a step at a time rather than leaping into full-blown character-isation, improvisation and performance. It may take time for some participants to learn or re-learn to play. To play together in a shared imaginary reality is a further challenge, for which the trust built in the here-and-now work is a prerequisite.

When a group becomes proficient in flying together, in terms of imaginative dramatherapy work, then worlds of possibility unfold. The limitations of the here-and-now and of the conventionally possible are transcended. Drama-therapeutic journeys in time and location are at the same time journeys into the inner worlds of the participants, in which metaphor and imagery play a part and where personal or group concerns may be explored. As in the case of a real life journey, participants in the dramatherapeutic flight of fancy bring back memories to the here-and-now, and gain value in reflecting on the shared adventure.

NOTES

1 For a more detailed exploration of this model, its development into performance and its application in co-therapeutic alliances with speech therapy and music therapy see Chesner (forthcoming).
2 See Sinason (1992) for psychoanalytically oriented work with this client group.

REFERENCES

Barker, C. (1977) *Theatre Games*, London, Methuen.
Brudenell, P. (1987) 'Dramatherapy with people with a mental handicap', in S. Jennings (ed.) *Dramatherapy Theory and Practice for Teachers and Clinicians*, London, Routledge.

Cattanach, A. (1992) *Drama for People with Special Needs*, London, A. & C. Black.
Chesner, A. (forthcoming) *Dramatherapy and Learning Disabilities*, London, Jessica Kingsley.
Jennings, S. (1973) *Remedial Drama*, London, Pitman.
Jennings, S. (1990) *Dramatherapy with Families, Groups and Individuals*, London and New York, Jessica Kingsley.
Sinason, V. (1992) *Mental Handicap and the Human Condition*, London, Free Association Press.

Chapter 5

A role model of dramatherapy and its application with individuals and groups

Brenda Meldrum

A ROLE MODEL OF DRAMATHERAPY

A *role model of dramatherapy* assumes that the individual's personality is made up of a number of different roles, which he or she plays in different contexts and with various groups of individuals. These roles are biological, occupational and social. Being in one role may give rise to a different set of behaviours and, perhaps, attitudes from playing another role.

The dramatherapist informed by the role model perceives him or herself as a player of a number of roles of which the role of therapist is but one. The dramatherapist sees the client as a person who may be stuck in a restricted number of roles, perhaps even in one role. The task of the dramatherapist may be to encourage clients to find behaviours more appropriate to their role and also to help them increase the number of roles available to them.

The sessions will actively engage the client or clients and perhaps also the dramatherapist in physical involvement with role-play, drama games, story-telling and a number of other drama-based techniques.

The role model of dramatherapy is a drama model informed by the sociological and social psychological model of Erving Goffman. The model of development of the person lies in the social interaction and transactions of the individual with others in the environment.

Therefore, the development of the self is also seen as social and based on the philosophy of symbolic interactionism expressed by George Herbert Mead. Persons construct their personalities through the number and variety of roles they perform with those in the social contexts within which they live, work and play. Although most dramatherapists use role and characterisation in sessions with their client groups, it is the American School of dramatherapists, led by Robert Landy, who base their theories on role theory as such and on Erving Goffman's dramaturgical model in particular.

In the first section of this chapter, I shall look at what is meant by 'role' as used in role theory. I shall then consider in some detail the work of Erving Goffman and critically examine his theoretical position in the light of the work of Bruce Wilshire (1982).

In the next section, I shall look at the symbolic interactionism of George Herbert Mead and his social theories of the development of self. In addressing the question 'How do individuals acquire their different roles?' I shall look at the constructivist position of the personality theorist Sarah Hampson.

The final section will be devoted to an examination of the role models and the practice of the American dramatherapist Robert Landy.

ROLE AND THE WORK OF ERVING GOFFMAN

What is meant by role?

Crucial to an understanding of role in sociology, psychology and dramatherapy are the questions: 'Are the roles I play "myself"?' and 'Is what I do what I am?' Let us look first at some definitions of what role is and what it is not.

Role is a social term. It is not possible to think of being in a role except with reference to other people. So role is the behaviour that the person engages in when taking on a position in relation to others. These others too have expectations of how the person should behave in that role. Take the role of therapist, for example. Part of the training will concern not only the nuts and bolts of the profession, but will also indicate behaviours considered appropriate to the role of therapist, for example, touch. The British Association for Dramatherapists' *Code of Practice* (1991: 3) suggests that

> It is in the nature of dramatherapeutic interventions that patients may touch each other and the therapist and that the therapist may touch them. It is important that this is made clear to clients and patients before treatment commences.

Clients, too, will expect to meet a person with professional skills who will listen to their stories. The therapist will indicate normative behaviours for them both, such as punctuality, an agreed time limit for the sessions and, where appropriate, a fee. While the therapist expects clients to express their emotions and disclose their life problems, the client does not expect the session to be taken up with the therapist's life history and emotional catharsis. There is a role relationship based on normative behaviour and expectancies. The basic psychological function of role is to provide the therapist and the client with a fairly specific model for interaction.

Persons in this occupational role of therapist have their membership defined by the procedure of professional registration and the norms of that professional role apply to them. It is a mistake here to confuse 'role' with 'status'. The role of therapist has status only if others confer status on the therapist role. For example, dramatherapists in Britain, by definition, have successfully completed a post-graduate qualification at an institute recognised by the professional body, the BADth, but may be working in a National Health hospital where their professional skills are not highly valued or regarded as on a par with other professionals. Consequently, their status may be low within that system. On the other hand, their relationship with their clients reflects the normative expect-ancies within their respective roles.

Roles are different from 'stereotypes'. Stereotypes commonly refer to groups of people and ideas, beliefs and cultural images held by one group about members of another group. Stereotypes lead us to minimise differences between people who are members of the same group and exaggerate those differences between them and our group. So stereotypes link norms with groups or classes of people and thus define groups and discriminate between them, while roles associate normative behaviours with differences among individuals within the group.

The essential characteristic of a 'biological role' is that it defines membership of a category of kinship such as mother, father, daughter, son and so on. A woman is a daughter and may also be a mother and hence a parent. However, her own mother may have died and she may have been adopted, so the person she calls 'mother' is not in a biological role relationship with her, but is in the role of parent, as defined by her society.

A 'gender' or 'sex' role, on the other hand, is not necessarily a biological role. A gender role may be a stereotype. A gender or sex role refers to the behaviours and characteristics that are typical of men and of women, but sex role stereotypes refer to society's beliefs about appropriate activities for men and women based on cultural assumptions of biological, physical and psychological differences.

One person, then, may play many roles. She is a daughter and she may be a sister and she may be a mother; these are her biological roles. She may be a wife and that is a social role. She may also be a dramatherapist in a Trust Hospital and that is her occupational role, and she may have other roles such as friend, dog owner, gardener, amateur actor and so on and so on. Each of these roles may require of her different behaviours and different expectations of her actions from the diversity of people, individuals and groups, with whom she interacts. The question is: 'Where is her "self"?'

The theories of Erving Goffman

Goffman, the renowned sociologist, is often quoted in the dramatherapy literature because his is a dramaturgical approach to human behaviour.

Goffman's theory states that people perform in a role for other people and the behaviour they may adopt in this role may be only part of their social behavioural repertoire. They only show slices of themselves. For example, the GP may show the client/patient only her professional self as she enquires into the patient's presenting symptoms. She may well be kind and tolerant in face of the patient's anxiety but she, as doctor, is behaving in ways that she considers appropriate to her role. Her patient is also showing only slices of himself. He may be a powerful person in his occupational role, but here in front of the doctor his behaviour is appropriate to his role of patient. Each has expectations of the other.

The basic assumption of role analysis, Goffman (1972) says, is that each person will have several selves; the problem is if and how they are connected.

The woman performing the role of the doctor sees to it that the impression she makes is compatible with the role appropriate behaviours of detached concern, scientific and rigorous examination and attention to detail in a friendly manner. These personal qualities are attached to the role, but they also affect the individual's self-image. This is also the basis of the image the patient will have of her which she, the doctor, observes. This self-image attached to her position as the GP may please her and she may well become attached to her role and its position. The role of GP is a well-defined social role and the 'front' the doctor adopts is well established.

The client, however, may not like to see himself in the role of 'patient'. In this case, Goffman predicts that he will show 'role distance'. He will behave in some way that suggests that he has a resistance against the role. He may demonstrate that he doesn't really belong in the role; maybe he tries to isolate himself as much as possible by appearing stiff and preoccupied or he may project a childish self. He may find it unusual to be in a lower status to a professional woman and his behaviour will demonstrate his unease in the role by self-mockery. This reaction Goffman labels 'role distance'. Goffman says that there is no saying which is the real person and the patient's capacity for role distance heightens this uncertainty.

People seldom go through their appointed tasks like wooden soldiers; by role distance individuals express their own style, which helps to give the impression that they are nice, well-rounded people. So, behind the role that the individual is adopting, there will be hints of something else: 'something will glitter and smoulder or otherwise make itself apparent beyond the covering that is officially worn' (Goffman 1974: 73). This may seem to be the real self, the personality peeping through, but for Goffman it is no more real, no less illusory than the outward role itself. Providing a sense of what sort of person might be behind the role is part of the game. And the individual becomes a blur.

It is important in the light of its influence on the role model of dramatherapy, so much of which is based on his theories, to take a very close look at Goffman's analysis of role. I shall do this with the help of Bruce Wilshire's (1982) analysis in *Role Playing and Identity: The Limits of Theatre as Metaphor*.

As I have said above, Goffman's is a dramaturgical model. He asks the question 'Is doing being?' Goffman's argument runs like this: if doing is being, then the person will attempt to make their behaviour consistent with their role; they will feel compelled to 'control and police the expressions that occur. Performance will, therefore, be able to express identity' (1972: 88). But, Goffman points out:

> roles may not only be *played* but also *played at*, as when children, stage actors and other kinds of cutups mimic a role for the avowed purpose of make-believe. . . . A professional actor differs from a child in the degree of perseverance and perfection the professional must manifest in the role he simulates.
>
> (1972: 88, original italics)

So, 'doing' for the child and for the professional actor is not being. And doing is not being for the individual in a 'real life' situation who is 'playing at' their role using 'role distance' and showing the audience of other people glimpses behind the mask of the role. But, as we have seen above, for Goffman these glimpses are not the 'real self' but are simply another role peeping through.

Bruce Wilshire's critique of Goffman concerns just thus blurring of self and role, role and self and he too uses the actor as an example of the individual in 'real life'. Wilshire's thesis is that Goffman's analysis of theatre distorts theatre and distorts real life when he applies his theatrical metaphor to it.

Wilshire argues that the actor's performance is not simply a mimetic act of let's pretend or make-believe. 'Impersonation', says Wilshire, 'is a form of mockery; enactment is a form of love' (1982: 7). Enactment is multi-layered. The actor brings himself to the playing of Hamlet. Of course, the actor's self is subsumed by his interpretation of the role, but he cannot play Hamlet just by make-believing he is someone he knows who behaves like a Hamlet-type of person. His self is part of his playing of the character. As an audience member, I am well aware that Alan Rickman the actor is playing Hamlet. I don't think that Alan Rickman *is* Hamlet, but nor do I think that Hamlet is Alan Rickman. Alan Rickman is aware not only of the character and himself as Hamlet, but he is aware of the audience being aware that he is playing Hamlet and so on and so on.

> Above all, the actor is aware at moments that he is expressing via the character some of his own deepest feelings and insights as person and artist, and that this, given the hush of the audience, also expresses others' feelings and insights.
>
> (Wilshire 1982: 275)

The audience member and the actor know that this is not some sort of deceit or mere play-acting. Through his metaphor, Goffman construes role-like activity, both on-stage and off-stage, as a kind of deceit.

The inference is that we are always playing a role and even when the mask of one role slips it only gives glimpses of yet another role. It follows then, as Wilshire says, that either the real self is unknowable or the naked face we see is a non-social mask.

> I believe that this is not only an alienating and demoralising idea of the self, but that it is false. . . . If there is nothing to be found in the way of self – then human life itself can only be taken to be a deficient mode of reality. A person is composed *merely* of appearances.
>
> (1982: 278, original italics)

As I report below, Robert Landy (1990) asserted that he had 'assassinated the self', but Goffman did so before him! So life for Goffman is a multi-layered performance of different roles and the self behind the various social roles is simply another performance; what Landy (1992a) calls the ability to impersonate.

Wilshire argues that Goffman's error is that what the self '*really* is involves integrally how it *appears* to be to others'. The self is the body which synthesises experiences beyond the current context and transcends the roles we play and this self therefore must be apparent to others that it is so doing. What Goffman leaves out of his role analysis is that part of myself which is audience to myself playing the different roles.

> He ignores the self-conscious structure of the self, the I–me polarity, one's accumulating and changing sense of one's passing life in all its episodes, the time-spanning consciousness of self that are integral to the self itself.
>
> (Wilshire 1982: 279)

This type of reductionism that sees all roles as more or less phony leads to the view that the consciousness of role is simply another role, albeit a meta-role that evaluates the other roles we play. To some dramatherapists this view is nihilism.

THE SELF AND SYMBOLIC INTERACTIONISM

The self behind the blur

Perhaps because of its eclecticism, there is a distressing lack of theorising in the dramatherapy literature of a model of development underlying practice. However, there is very little point in a theory which looks only at adult behaviour and does not ask how such and such a behaviour arose. Was it learnt, or is it natural to the person as a result of their inheritance?

As this chapter is concerned with role models of dramatherapy, I shall not be considering the psychodynamic theories of Freud and his followers, nor the object-relations theories of Melanie Klein. The question we are asking is: 'What is the relationship between the self and the social role?'

The theories of self and personality I shall be considering will be those of G.H. Mead, the American philosopher and sociologist, and Sarah Hampson, whose constructivist theories of personality are not incompatible with Mead's. I shall also look into the developmental literature to see how roles and role appropriate behaviour develop in the child and attempt to make a synthesis of the developmental findings with the Meadean and constructivist views.

The symbolic interactionism of George Herbert Mead

G.H. Mead, philosopher, sociologist and social psychologist, gave a number of lectures about the social nature of the mind and the self which were collected and published in 1934 and which have had a profound influence in the debate on the development of self. Central to Mead's philosophy is the understanding of the term 'symbolic'. We see around us objects in our environment which have for us a social significance: they are symbols carrying meanings. 'Interactionism' means that we are able to communicate with each other through symbols because they have shared meanings. Through the interaction of self with the other, the self develops the ability to take on the perspective of the other. The other then feeds back to the self information about the self; thus the self becomes an object to itself. So the essential quality of self is that it is reflexive; we experience ourselves in the same way as we experience other objects and people.

Mead's theory of symbolic interactionism stresses the social context of gestures, not simply as expressions of emotion in the Darwinian sense, but as early stages of the act of one organism responded to by another as indications of the later stages of the social act. Mead specifically thinks of gesture in social terms and from such gestures traces the development of genuine language communication. The mind and the self, in this theory, are social, and language, in the form of the vocal gesture, provides the mechanism for their emergence. For Mead, language is an objective phenomenon of interaction within a social group arising from the gesture. In Mead's view, the world of common or social experience is symbolically formulated.

The behavioural basis of Mead's social psychology lies in the notion that a gesture is a part-action which others complete; therefore the meaning of an action is to be found in the response which it elicits from others. Mead addressed the problem of how the human mind and self arise in the process of action in biosocial terms. Within the ongoing social process of interacting, through the internalisation of the conversation of gestures, mind and self arise. Mead explains it in this way.

The development of the intelligence of humans lies in the long period of infancy. The child's cry of fear leads to a tendency to flight in the parent – a similar physiological reaction – which in turn leads to the parent's encouraging tone and her movement towards the protection of the child. Therefore, the cry of fear of the child is a vocal gesture producing the corresponding gesture of protection from the mother. The cry of the frightened child is heard by himself as well as by his mother in the same physiological way. The child internalises the cry, and the effect of the result of the cry (the mother's response) and then he himself utters the soothing sound the parent makes to calm him and thus the child takes on the parent's role. The long period of dependence in childhood gives infants a remarkable opportunity to play, taking the roles of different people from their social and family group in the play itself. Children thus stimulate themselves to make the sounds they stimulate their parents to make to them.

In so far as the social situation within which the child reacts is determined by his social environment, that environment will determine what sounds he makes and therefore what responses he stimulates both in himself and others.
(Mead 1934: 365)

Hence, out of play, out of addressing themselves and responding appropriately, children's 'self-consciousness' arises.

The child during the period of infancy creates a forum within which he assumes various roles and the child's self is gradually integrated out of these socially different attitudes, always retaining the capacity of addressing itself and responding to that address with a reaction that belongs in a certain sense to another. He comes into the adult period with the mechanism of a mind.

(Mead 1934: 366)

One can readily see that variations of the environment, in particular degrees of sensitivity in the mother or primary caregiver, can lead to very different 'selves'. Indeed Stern (1985: 249) says:

> There is a process that occurs between parents and infants which allows the infant to perceive *how* he is perceived. In this process parents non-verbally 'reflect back' to the infant his own experiences.

One can also relate Mead's paradigm to Shaffer's (1989) descriptive theory of maternal sensitivity and to Bowlby's (1988) attachment theory: the way in which the infant's needs – physical, emotional and social – are attended to by the significant others in her environment, is crucial to her development. Indeed, Dr Mario Marrone (1991), who follows Bowlby's attachment theory, states categorically that adult psychopathology can always be traced to a childhood trauma which was not sensitively managed.

Mead's theory of symbolic interactionism thus sees the development of mind, self and self-awareness as a dynamic process through which infants internalise the responses of adults and take the role of adults which they externalise through play.

Through the symbolic communication of language in interaction we come to see ourselves as the 'me' that 'I' am aware of. This 'me' Mead calls 'the generalised other' and is composed of other people's attitudes to me and is developed through socialisation. If it were possible to imagine a child growing up alone on a desert island, according to Mead's theory this individual would have no concept of self. We know who we are through the way other people interact with us and reflect back to us the consequences of our behaviour towards them.

So the self is composed of the 'me' or the generalised other and the 'I' who reflects on the 'me'. The 'I' impels the 'me' towards action, but the 'I' cannot be pinned down because of its continuous reflexive observation of the 'me'.

The growth of the self is socially and culturally related: it is the essence of socialisation because to have a notion of self is to be able to think about oneself from the perspective of the other person. As Judy Dunn (1988: 79) says:

> Initially it is the child's view of how a particular other sees him or her that is significant in the developing sense of self, but with time it is the child's view of the 'generalised other' of the wider cultural group that becomes important.

As Dunn reports, during the second and third year of life children are very sensitive to the approval, support and disapproval of others and this sensitivity is central to developing self-awareness. The self that develops, says Dunn, is a product both of the culture and of ontogenetic and cognitive change.

We are vividly reminded of Goffman's role analysis when we consider Sarah Hampson's (1988) constructivist position on the development of personality. Personality is:

a social artifact. We attach meaning and significance to behaviour by using it to infer underlying personality characteristics. . . . We are using concepts that are derived in part from our indirect perception of reality . . . and in part from social knowledge.

(Hampson 1988: 9)

Hampson's constructivist view of personality involves the combination of three equally important components: the actor, the observer and the self-observer.

The actor's behaviour is interpreted in a certain way by the observer, who then responds accordingly. The actor's subsequent behaviour is influenced by the observer's response. The actor's ability to be a self-observer will allow the actor to form an impression of the impression forming in the observer's mind and the actor may wish to adjust his or her behaviour in order to manipulate this impression.

(1988: 197)

Thus, the process of personality construction is a process of interaction – of communication. The actor brings her core self and all the genetic factors which may influence her to the interaction; the observer adds social significance and inferred meaning to the actor's behaviour, which in turn affects his behaviour; this is communicated to the actor and she, as self-observer, can see herself interacting with him. We see ourselves as we think other people see us.

We can directly link Hampson's concept of self-observer with Wilshire's critique of Goffman who crucially omits 'myself as audience of myself in my roles'. However, we can hear both Goffman and Landy in Hampson's comment: 'Constructed personality is an elaborate interplay of social roles' (1986: 56). But unlike Goffman and Landy, Hampson does see a 'core self' who is the self-observer in her tripartite theory, with the observer and the actor. Hampson's actor is Mead's 'me' who is impelled to action by Mead's 'I' – Hampson's self-observer. The observer, then, is Mead's 'other'. And so we have made a synthesis between the Meadean theory of self and Hampson's constructivist theory of personality.

We develop the ability to play roles through being born into a particular family in a society within a culture. The biological role we have of either being a daughter or a son is not by definition learnt, but the behaviours deemed appropriate to what it means to be a daughter in our particular society are learnt. She may be taught: 'Little girls don't do that!' or she may learn through observation: only her brothers are taken to the football match by their father. But it is certain that the number and complexity of the roles we play are socially constructed and are not inherited.

If we return to our question 'What is the relationship between the self and the social role?', we see that for G.H. Mead and Sarah Hampson self, personality and social role are inextricably mixed. Indeed, with Mead, both self and mind are social and with Hampson, the personality is socially constructed. Mead, Hampson and Wilshire, unlike Goffman and Landy, however, see a tripartite

notion of self: the actor, the generalised other and the self-observer in a trans-
actional dynamic.

ROBERT LANDY'S ROLE MODEL OF DRAMATHERAPY

The dramatic basis of role theory

While Robert Landy (1991) thinks it is important for dramatherapists to move
towards what he calls a 'healthy eclecticism', he also thinks it is imperative for
them to 'address the one thing that makes drama therapy unique among psychotherapeutic disciplines – that is, its roots in drama' (1991: 29).

At the heart of any dramatic experience is what Landy calls 'the principle of
impersonation', which is the ability of the person to take on a role. The paradox of
the dramatic experience is that when I am in a dramatic role I am 'me' and 'not-me'
at one and the same time. An explanation of the dramatic paradox is the concept of
role which is the essential medium of the actor. Role theory, then, is for Landy at the
root of the dramatherapy model and it is role that is the significant feature that
distinguishes drama therapy from other forms of psychotherapy.

Wilshire (1982: 7), as we have observed above, would not agree that that
actor's task is impersonation, for he contrasts 'impersonation' (as mimicry) with
'enactment'. He would argue that it is not the actor's task simply to take on a role
and play it. To understand Wilshire's critique more clearly, we may draw a
distinction between 'entertainment' (a West End musical) and 'theatre'
(*Tamburlaine the Great* at the RSC). The problem with overtly making this
distinction is to lay oneself open to the accusation of elitism. I shall make it
anyway. As an entertainer I play a role; in a farce, I play a role. Compare playing
Mistress Quickly in Shakespeare's *Merry Wives of Windsor* with playing Lady
Macbeth. Mistress Quickly is a one-dimensional character while Lady Macbeth
is a complex part and the actress has to build into her characterisation – her
enactment – layers of feeling and experience, both from what is contained in the
text itself and from her own knowledge and experience. Landy would say that the
role of Lady Macbeth incorporates many sub-roles and the actor/character
switches from one to another as the play develops.

Landy's model is similar to Erving Goffman's role theory. For example,
Landy (1992: 104) talks of role seduction. He says that throughout the centuries
actors have been 'seductive' to audience members who fuse actor as person with
actor in role. Furthermore, he says, some actors through enacting a role, a
character, a part, have become the part. This is reminiscent of what Goffman
(1972: 79) calls 'role attachment' when:

> The self-image available for anyone entering a particular position is one of
> which 'me' may become affectively and cognitively enamoured, desiring and
> expecting to see himself in terms of the enactment of the role and the self-
> identification emerging from this enactment.

This is really a strange way for Landy to regard actors. In the theatre very, very few audience members confuse the actor as person with the actor as role because the stage performance itself produces aesthetic distance. Landy is saying that for some actors 'doing is being'. The British tabloid press, however, deliberately confuse the soap opera actors with their roles in the drama because it sells more newspapers and links in with the fantasies of the reader. The private lives of individual actors have often become common property, as though they were indeed characters in a play, but not in the theatre itself where Landy bases his role theory.

I believe that Landy, like Goffman, lifts from the theatre a role model which he applies to 'real-life' role-playing. Goffman compares the presentation of self with the presentation of a character or role by an actor: as the actor in the theatre plays a role, so we in our lives act like actors. This, in my view, is to confuse the actor, who stands in for us the audience in a character or role in the play, with the character and personality of the actor herself.

Role theory and the self

In his book *Drama Therapy* (1986), Landy describes his theory of self in rather different terms from his most recent work. The two basic building blocks of Robert Landy's model were self and role. But to understand the relationship between self and role, one must consider a third building block – the other. In the model these three are interdependent concepts; the self – one's essential uniqueness – relates to the other (who is a representative of the social world), through the role. Thus role is the mediator between the self and the other, and the self and the social world. Landy made a complex analysis of the synthesis of self and role, self and other, identification and projection, which in the normal course of human development strive towards balance. However, there are times when the balance is disrupted, which can be more or less severe and at these times, intervention may be necessary. One may be caught in the trap of a single role when we need to re-establish our ability to mediate between self and world by taking on and playing out appropriate roles and it is then that the dramatherapist needs to understand the crucial concept of distancing.

'Distancing' is a key concept in Landy's dramatherapy theory. The over-distanced person keeps rigid boundaries between self and other, projecting onto others their own feelings and thoughts, thus seeing the other as a reflection of themselves. The under-distanced person identifies him or herself too readily with the emotions and behaviour of others, losing boundaries between the self and other. The distancing paradigm is a balance between the two extremes, where the person is able to find a comfortable balance between him or herself and other, person and persona, one role and another role and where the boundaries are flexible and amenable to change as the self or the interaction with the other changes. This point, midway between the two extremes of over-distance and under-distance, Landy calls aesthetic distance.

For the dramatherapist, the therapeutic goals are to move towards balance, towards aesthetic distance and to strengthen one's ability to use role as a mediator between the self and the social world.

This attempt to formulate a model of dramatherapy set out in his book *Drama Therapy* (1986) was expanded by Robert Landy in his address to the British Association for Dramatherapists in September 1990, when he explained that his point of reference in therapy is role and roles. But, he asked, how do roles work in therapy? Why are they the most significant bridge between the external and the internal? Landy explained that he wished to find a theoretical structure or construct to form a bridge between theatre and psychotherapy. Further, he wanted to make the structure more scientific – to find a theory applicable to dramatherapy and he chose role theory.

The concept of role in social psychology, Landy said, has been taken away from its dramatic roots, yet the word 'role' derives from the theatre. In the earliest forms of theatre the text of a play was written on a scroll. Prompters would open this scroll, which was called the role, and give the actor his line. Therefore 'role' was originally a dramatic term. Nowadays, playing a role is seen as doing something other than being one's true self. And he, Landy, has 'assassinated the concept of self'.

Thus, between the publication of *Drama Therapy* in 1986 and 1990, Landy's position regarding the self as one of the three major building blocks in his model of the person changed. The self is now fused with the role.

'Self' as a concept, said Landy, has no real place in the theory of role. For him, the concept of 'self' is too mystical. The personality is like an onion; each layer of the onion is another role and when you have taken away the last layer, there is nothing. A central understanding of the core is one's ability to generate roles. Perhaps that core is the ultimate role – the role of the impersonator.

> At the centre of the person is the ability, the potential to take on other persona. This ability to impersonate, very different from imitation, which is essentially an external act, is a creative act in that a new part is generated, a new mask is fashioned, a new persona enters into the person's dramatic repertory.
>
> (Landy 1992a: 422)

We remember that Wilshire calls impersonation 'a form of mockery' and enactment 'a form of love'. This could be construed as a major criticism of Landy's theory, but I suspect that he and Wilshire do not share the same definitions of the word 'impersonation'. And yet, my reading of Wilshire's philosophy is that he would indeed criticise Landy's position in the same way as he does Goffman's, that this assassination of the self is reductive and alienating. Where is the self-observer, the 'I' who watches 'me' impersonating another and forming another mask or role? I fear Landy has assassinated him or her and, in doing so, has rejected both Mead and Hampson.

Landy's position is that the dramatic role model, which I shall discuss in detail below, puts 'role' in the prime position held for so long by 'self'; that the 'era of the primacy of the Self as core object is dead and that we are now living within the era of the Role' (1992a: 421).

His theory states that role contains all the properties that define us as human: somatic, cognitive, affective, social/cultural, spiritual and aesthetic.

A dramatic role model theory of dramatherapy

Landy proposes a dramatic role model to be applied to dramatherapy that examines role type, role quality, its function and its style. He has been working on a taxonomy or a typology of roles in an attempt to produce a system of theatrical archetypes. This taxonomy of roles, Landy argues (1991, 1992a), can be used as a 'blueprint for the possibilities of being'. He defines role as 'the container of all thoughts and feelings we have about ourselves and others in our social and imaginary world'.

Aristotle preceded Landy in finding a taxonomy of roles. Aristotle used drama as a mirror through which to observe nature. He was an interpreter of the Greek drama and the characters he saw on the stage gave him insights into the roles he saw people around him playing. Like today's psychologists and educators, Aristotle recognised the primacy of motivation in human behaviour. Through watching the drama he realised that thinking through and choosing courses of action are an indispensable indication of character (Castellani 1990). He also recognised that characters in the drama fall into certain groups or types, who display similar emotions and behaviours because of their age, their social status or personality traits. Aristotle's ethical expositions recognise typologies of humanity from drama; moral types from the comedies and ethnic classes and individual roles from the tragedies. 'Type classes' are categories such as 'the young', 'the old', 'slaves'; 'type names' or roles are labels such as 'pimps', 'usurers', 'shameful profit-makers'. As in Robert Landy's taxonomy of roles, Aristotle linked certain behaviours with certain types of character; for example 'the bashful old man' or 'the nervous wreck', 'the obsequious flatterer' and so on. Castellani writes that 'Drama and theatre worked on [Aristotle] to give him data on human motivation and behaviour, to give him exemplars and even names for things' (1990: 32). Thus, like Robert Landy centuries later, Aristotle links behaviour with human roles and types derived from the theatre.

Landy says that a role is only part of the person. Roles have meaning only in their intrapsychic and interpersonal counterparts. Landy's role as father relates to his age role as adult and his cognitive role as a person with knowledge and his interpersonal role as father to his daughter and so on. 'There exist roles for most all forms of human activity. The role is like a cell or atom. It is a primary building block' (1992b: 422).

Presumably, the individual develops roles through interaction and socialisation. If the number of roles presented is limited, then the child is unable to generate roles within herself and may become 'stuck' in a few, possibly psychopathological roles. From his clinical work and experience Landy has encountered people who are very ill, psychically, emotionally and mentally; their illnesses, he surmises, were a function of how broad or how narrow were their role systems. As a therapist, he sees his primary role as one who provides the fuel that will generate more roles for the client. He does this by helping the client generate further roles and by using his relationship with the client as a methodology to inspire the development of further roles.

The role method helps the therapist to find answers to questions such as:

1 What are the roles the client is playing in this session and in his or her life?
2 What are the qualities of these roles?
3 What is the function of these roles for the client?
4 How, in what style, does the client play these roles?
5 How do these roles intersect with other of his or her roles, both intrapsychic and interpersonal?

The goal or aim of therapy is to help clients live with their various roles so that they are not overpowered by one role and so that they can accept the ambivalence of others. The therapist helps the client move through the taxonomy of roles with facility, for this taxonomy, as we have seen, is intended by Landy to be a 'blueprint for the possibilities of being' (1992b: 431).

A taxonomy of roles: a system of theatrical archetypes

In trying to find a way to make a system of roles, Landy took an understanding of role back to the theatre. In his research on theatrical forms, he picked out the primary role types and asked himself the question: does the system of theatrical roles mirror other systems? He tried to create this system based on theatre that would hold the specific roles in categories. The taxonomy of roles consists of nine parts:

1 *The Domains*   These domains form the largest category and contain all aspects of our humanity: the somatic, the cognitive, the affective, the social, the spiritual, the aesthetic.
2 *The Classification within the Domains*   This is where the domain is sub-divided into the kinds of roles within the major category. Sub-categories within the Somatic Domain, for example, are age, appearance, sexual orientation and health.
3 *The Role Type*   This part is akin to Jung's archetypes or universal forms. This role type, which Landy describes as universal, will be a role type found in the theatrical literature of all ages. So in the Somatic Domain, the archetypes under the classification 'age' will be the Child, the Adolescent, the Adult, the Elder; under the category 'sexual orientation' the role types will be the Eunuch, the Homosexual, the Transvestite. 'Appearance' and 'health' will be similarly divided into role types.
4 *The Sub-type*   This is a further subdivision of role type each of which implies a different aspect of the role type. For example, in the Cognitive Domain, the

role type 'The Simpleton' has sub-types of 'The Fop', 'The Pedant' and 'The Ideologue'.

5 *The Quality* This domain describes the characteristics associated with the role type. So the qualities of the Child include playfulness, fun-loving, ego-centric and so on.

6 *The Alternative Quality* This domain describes the opposites of the charac-terics associated with the quality. So the 'fun-loving' child may also have a 'temper' and be subject to tantrums.

7 *Examples* This domain gives examples of the role types and their qualities from the panorama of world literature. So an archetypal representation of the Child – naive, playful, guileless – would be Hedwig in Ibsen's *The Wild Duck*. These examples testify to the universality of the Role Theory System.

8 *The Function* This is a description of the way in which the role serves the individual; for example Hedwig asserts the playful spirit of innocence.

9 *The Style* This is the form in which the role is enacted. Theatrical style may be representational, or reality-based, but a presentational style is more abstract and universal, 'the mask rather than the face'. 'Each style implies a specified degree of affect and cognition. The former implies a greater degree of emotions, the latter a greater degree of cognition.'

(Landy 1992b: 422)

Landy (1992c) uses the taxonomy to illustrate how he worked with one particular client and in a further paper (1992d) he elaborates on the use of the taxonomy with a dramatherapy group.

In conjunction with the taxonomy, Landy's role method of treatment involves eight steps:

1 invoking the role;
2 naming the role;
3 playing out/working through the role;
4 exploring alternative qualities and sub-roles;
5 reflecting upon the role-play: discovering role qualities, functions and styles inherent in the role;
6 relating the fictional role to everyday life;
7 integrating roles to create a functional role system;
8 social modelling: discovering ways that the client's behaviour in role affects others in their social environments.

The invocation of the role appears to be the most important part of the process, not simply because it is the first step, but because the theory is based on the notion that invoking the role is a projective technique, enabling the client unconsciously to focus on a single aspect of the personality. The client moves in the therapy space, focusing on a part of the body which becomes the basis for a physical-isation of the role. When the role is named (step 2) the client can further concretise the physical character. The therapist helps the client play out or work through the role in various enactments or improvisations (step 3). Then the client works, perhaps by making a puppet or a mask, on a variation or sub-type of the particular role type. 'Exploring alternatives is important because one begins to recognise options and work with them. In many ways, this allows the clients to work through their ambivalences toward their roles' (1992d: 9).

Landy admits that step 4, although important because it embodies for the client contradictions and ambivalences, does not fit well with the role model of dramatherapy. Certainly, one imagines that it requires a considerable degree of sophistication on the part of the client.

After the enactment and role-play, the closure of the session consists of reflection and an attempt to find meanings for the characters in the roles played within the story. This important step (5) allows the client to make the link for the character between feeling and thought. The fictional role is then examined in the light of the client's real life role or roles (step 6). The therapist helps the client return to reality. 'To understand how my fictional roles serve me in my everyday life, then I must be able to see both fictional role and its reality-based counterpart clearly' (1992d: 10).

The goal of the dramatherapy role method is to assist the client in constructing a viable role system which allows for contradictions and ambivalences. In step 7 the client recognises how the various roles are integrated one with another. Finally, in step 8 the client is able to change their behaviour in real life roles.

Landy uses the seven steps towards this eighth stage, where the knowledge and new role system the client has achieved through therapy are integrated into real-life social systems. While recognising that it is a model of treatment, Landy does not see it as a stage model. That is to say, a client does not have to complete one step before tackling another; the dramatherapy role model is intended as a set of guidelines rather than a rigid, linear system.

Landy hopes this model and the taxonomy may be applied in practice, in diagnostic assessment, in treatment and evaluation and as a research instrument. He expects the dramatherapist to be versatile enough to shift from role to role, while maintaining an actorly reserve and a balance between being over-distanced and under-distanced from the client. (The dramatherapist, then, is like the actor in rep who 'plays as cast'!) I can myself testify to the value of steps 1, 2, 3, 5 and 6 in therapeutic work with clients and in the theatre as rehearsal techniques. Invoking a role or character through physicalisation, naming the character, playing the character in improvisations and reflecting upon the work is an excellent way in getting in touch with aspects of the self which we bring to characters in texts. I have found step 4, exploring alternative qualities and sub-roles, very difficult to put across, however, possibly because I do not understand it too well myself. I get round it by asking clients and actors to find a character who is the opposite to the first role we have worked on. I have not worked on steps 7 and 8 because we seem to cover so much in our discussions and reflections after the work, and there is rarely time enough. I have found, however, that this is a powerful method of working and it has been necessary to de-role carefully.

Landy's taxonomy of theatrical roles (1992b) is an amazing piece of scholarship; it is not, however, easy to understand how he puts the whole system into dramatherapy practice. Landy sees his model as based in the theatre and brought back into the psyche.

We can see that Landy's theory is based on a synthesis of mind and body. The mind, the self, is a construct formed in layers of role upon role developed from childhood experiences, not from intrapsychic forces and instincts. By performing in the body the various roles in dramatherapy, the clients and the therapist increase the number of roles and role types for the clients, allowing them to free themselves from the tyranny of psychopathological roles by generating others.

CONCLUSION

In this chapter we have looked at the concept of role: roles imply norms and values, status and stereotypes, and the individual's self-image may be affected by the roles she or he takes. If the role enhances the self-image, it may be embraced if it does not, she or he may show role distance.

In the final section, while recognising the quality and immense scholarship of his taxonomy we await clarification of the ways Landy's system might be used in dramatherapy practice.

There is one caveat that in conclusion I think it is important to make. This denial of a core self is crucial to Landy's role model and it must be addressed. For it is hard to see how role theory dramatherapists can persuade their clients that there is no core self, while their colleagues, coming from alternative models of dramatherapy, see as their major therapeutic task that of helping their clients find the self in the chaos of their internal lives within an ever more alienating social environment.

REFERENCES

Bowlby, J. (1988) *A Secure Base: Clinical Applications of Attachment Theory*, London, Routledge.
British Association for Dramatherapists (1991) Membership List and Code of Practice, London, BADth.
Castellani, V. (1990) 'Drama and Aristotle', in James Redmond (ed.) *Themes in Drama 12: Drama and Philosophy*, Cambridge, Cambridge University Press.
Dunn, J. (1988) *The Beginnings of Social Understanding*, Oxford, Basil Blackwell.
Goffman, E. (1972) *Encounters*, Harmondsworth, Penguin Books.
Goffman, E. (1974) *Frame Analysis*, Cambridge, MA, Harvard University Press.
Hampson, S. (1986) 'Sex roles and personality', in David Hargreaves and Ann M. Colley (eds) *The Psychology of Sex Roles*, London, Harper & Row.
Hampson, S. (1988) *The Construction of Personality: an Introduction*, London, Routledge.
Landy, R. (1986) *Drama Therapy: Concepts and Practices*, Springfield, IL, Charles C. Thomas.
Landy, R. (1990) 'A role model of dramatherapy', Keynote speech to the Conference of the British Association for Dramatherapists, Newcastle.

Landy, R. (1991) 'The dramatic basis of role theory', *The Arts in Psychotherapy*, 19, 29–41.

Landy, R. (1992a) 'One-on-one: the role of the dramatherapist working with individuals', in Sue Jennings (ed.) *Dramatherapy Theory and Practice 2*, London, Routledge.

Landy, R. (1992b) 'A taxonomy of roles: a blueprint for the possibilities of being', *The Arts in Psychotherapy*, 18(5), 419–31.

Landy, R. (1992c) 'The case of Hansel and Gretel', *The Arts in Psychotherapy*, 19, 231–41.

Landy, R. (1992d) 'The dramatherapy role method', *Dramatherapy*, 14(1), 7–15.

Marrone, M. (1991) Address to the Institute of Dramatherapy, London.

Mead, G.H. (1934) *Mind, Self and Society*, edited by Charles W. Morris, Chicago, University of Chicago Press.

Shaffer, R. (1989) 'Early social development', in A. Slater and G. Bremner (eds) *Infant Development*, London, Lawrence Erlbaum.

Stern, D. (1985) *The First Relationship: Infant and Mother*, London, Fontana.

Wilshire, B. (1982) *Role Playing and Identity: the Limits of Theater as Metaphor*, Bloomington, IN, Indiana University Press.

Chapter 6

The theatre of healing
Metaphor and metaphysics in the healing process
Sue Jennings

INTRODUCTION

The twentieth century is noted for its swing away from ritual and its emphasis on technology; in particular, there is often confusion about birth, death and age-stages which, I suggest, contributes to identity and role chaos.

This chapter looks at the importance of ritual drama, and its relevance to the practice of dramatherapy. It considers how ritual and ceremony structure our passage through life and how many clients who come into therapy have been cut off from the appropriate ritual form to complete necessary rites of passage.

Shamanism is considered in relation to the evolution of healing rituals in dramatic form, as is the importance of symbol and metaphor. The dangers of assumptions regarding shamanism are discussed as well as the attitude that dramatherapy is necessarily 'a good thing'.

The work of theatre artists as well as anthropologists and clinicians contributes to our understanding of a model of dramatherapy practice that is based on ritual. The ritual model of a 'theatre of healing' ultimately needs to make a metaphysical as well as a physical statement about illness and health. This model does not place ritual 'out there', as having a rarefied existence of its own, separate from human beings and their corporeality; rather it emphasises the interplay between the several aspects of the human personality and, in particular, the interaction of the physical and metaphysical through the imaginative dramatic act.

AWAY FROM RITUAL

Traditional ritual which accompanies major life stages is performed less often in contemporary society; there is less attention paid to rituals of birth and death, naming, coming of age, marriage and so on. In fact the rites of passage described by Van Gennep (1960) which mark our passage through life, for the most part receive little attention. Many of the traditional ritual roles, such as village midwife, matchmaker and healer, have been taken over by high-tech medicine and professional counsellors, for example. Modern medicine is 'acted upon' patients by doctors, rather than being 'interactive' between doctor and patient.

Historically, communities had their own ways of ritualising death and mourning, with elaborate ceremony, costume, artifacts and an overt statement of ritual relationships. Nowadays, most funerals tend to be brief, perfunctory rites, where we find that medication is frequently given to damp down grief, and we now have bereavement counsellors.

The decline in ritual seems to have followed the decline in religious belief and practice, and a continuing dualism between mind and body, thought and feeling. While there are various attempts to revive rituals or invent new ones, it appears that society marginalises such attempts, placing them outside of central belief and practice; they are equated with non-science and are therefore non-proven. For example, attempts to have childbirth take place at home or in places that are considered more 'natural' are undermined, and fear is inculcated that 'something could go wrong'. Most births take place in hospitals where there are new purifying rituals, but in particular there is the availability of high-tech apparatus. Childbirth is seen as a disease rather than a 'natural' life event, and the new rituals seem to be based on individual decisions rather than collective values. Treatment is given by individuals to individuals and the symbols and support of the social group are less in evidence.

As yet another father faints in the delivery room at witnessing the pain of his child being delivered from his best beloved wife, it makes me wonder about the importance of male childbirth rituals. In some societies men participate in the 'couvade' (rituals where men go through the confinement or dietary requirements for childbirth, which are usually the prerogative of women; from the French word 'to hatch'), or enjoy a transitional pub ritual on the eve of fatherhood or the 'baptism' of the new child by 'wetting its head', and thereby gain both attention and reassurance for themselves. We do need to ask whether, behind the brave face of the new world, it really is working as satisfactorily as it could. Do we need to reconsider the importance of ritual and symbolism in order to make sense of the universe and our place in it?

As I write this chapter, not only religion but also the arts are in a rapid decline, accelerated by economic starvation and political manoeuvre. Nevertheless, it is not only in this century that drama and ritual have declined; a look at the history of theatre or philosophy will show, for example, how Plato vilified the actor, denigrated the image and prized the idea. Every age seems to bring an ebb and flow, against or for, the artistic and the rational.

While there are various influences working against ritual and drama – with the emphasis on pathologising society, high-tech solutions and artistic redundancy – there are also strong currents working for the artistic and metaphysical. It is surely a positive sign that there are five postgraduate training programmes in dramatherapy which provide a recognised qualification. Although we are facing severe cut-backs in relation to the arts generally and to educational drama, yet there appears to be an increase in therapeutic theatre and the creation of drama-therapy posts. Many actors are now training in dramatherapy as a second career, and are also eager to extend the remit of their work in relation to performances in hospitals and prisons. It is a travesty that drama is not in the National Curriculum and perhaps increased lobbying may change this. However, for any healing art to be able to report growth in the current recession surely gives room for some optimism, even though it may be tinged with scepticism, that the anxieties and de-skilling caused by such a recession may be calling into being the need for more therapy!

Perhaps the most encouraging sign for us at the present time is that there is an attempt at dialogue: high-tech hospitals are employing dramatherapists and art therapists, intuition is being acknowledged in the scientific mind, poetics have their place within psychological medicine:

> Clinical experience leads us to the conclusion that conventional and supportive psychotherapy can be facilitated by the use of image and metaphor. We suggest that deep affective material in the patient's inner world can be contained, changed, or consolidated by the appropriate use of 'poiesis' in which new resources are called into being. And these resources fulfil the criteria of 'poiesis' because, as far as the patient is concerned, something has been called into existence, in the shape of new capacities and enhanced resilience, which was not there before.
>
> (Cox and Theilgaard 1987: 18)

Whether we work with individuals or groups of clients, or teach in difficult situations or wait for an artistic muse or struggle with a failed experiment or search for the sub-text of a scene, it is reassuring to remember the regenerating effect of the dramatic imagination and theatre art on human processes:

> Where historical life itself fails to make cultural sense in terms that formerly held good, narrative and cultural drama may have the task of 'poiesis', that is, of remaking cultural sense, even when they seem to be dismantling ancient edifices of meaning, that can no longer redress our modern 'dramas of living' . . .
>
> (Turner 1982: 87)

CAN WE DEFINE RITUAL?

Ritual, like drama, seems too complex to define with any clarity, and anthropologists pay more attention to what ritual does, than to what it is. However, I attempt a simple statement, if only to separate ritual from other forms of activity such as habit or stereotypical behaviour, and to place it firmly within the arena of active symbolic and therefore artistic expression. This definition is not original but is a compilation of various thoughts and statements that I have gathered over the past twenty years, from many influences and sources.

Dramatic ritual is a set of performed actions involving metaphor and symbol which not only communicates to us about change, status and values but also affects us. Ritual sets us thinking; it may remind us or reassure us or stimulate us. Our responses to ritual are likely to be at several levels: physical and corporeal, affective, cognitive, imaginative and metaphysical.

> Ritual is not done solely to be interpreted: it is also done (and from the point of view of the performers this may be more important) to resolve, alter or demonstrate a situation.
>
> (Lewis 1980: 35)

This multiple level response or engagement leads us to question whether ritual itself became too powerful to continue – religious or dramatic or sporting rituals have often provided a threat to the existing order – whether the division of ritual properties and the separation of the concrete from the symbolic and the corporeal from the cognitive, i.e. establishing the duality, enabled the effective control and detumescence of dramatic ritual expression.

Drama was thrown out of the churches, masks were banned from religion; the church, hospital and theatre are three separate institutions, rather than a single entity which integrates our several levels of experience. Freud and Marx have argued that religiosity and ritual are wish-fulfilling illusions and opiates; and the unconscious, the laboratory and science have gained supremacy; however, as Rycroft (1985: 288) points out:

> Even though Freud prided himself on being a scientist, his insight into the importance of Oedipal guilt led him to formulate an anthropological theory about the murder of the Primal Father which he himself described as a 'just-so' story, and to invoke a Greek myth, as an expository device for getting across what children feel about their parents.

I shall explore the dramatic context of the Oedipal story in a future publication (Jennings, forthcoming b); here it is important to note how the story or myth is called upon when scientific words, or perhaps everyday words, are not enough. I am inspired to continue this endeavour by the reflections of James Hillman (1983) when he quotes from an interview with Freud who says:

> Everybody thinks that I stand by the scientific character of my work and that my principal scope lies in curing mental maladies. This is a terrible error that has prevailed for years and that I have been unable to set right. I am a scientist by necessity, and not by vocation. I am really by nature an artist . . .

Hillman goes on to say that

> Psychoanalysis is a work of imaginative tellings in the realm of 'poiesis' which means simply 'making', and which I take to mean making by imagination into words.
>
> (Hillman 1983: 4)

I would like to take this a step further and suggest that, following Hillman's thesis, dramatherapy is in the realm of 'mimesis' and 'poiesis', which means making by imagination into actions and words. In dramatherapy it is the dramatic action which is created from the imagination, the action that is embodied and vocalised, projected into images and dramatised (i.e. the dramatherapy

Dramatherapy Developmental Paradigm		Normal Development
Embodiment - Projection - Role (EPR)		
EPR	(basic — all ages)	0–5 years
Embodiment:	movement system	body play
	gesture	sensory play
Projection:	sculpting	projective play
	drawing and painting	
Role:	drama games	dramatic play
	enactment : role-play	
	improvisation	

Figure 6.1 Dramatherapy developmental paradigm. For a full analysis of EPR and charts, see Jennings 1993a.

developmental paradigm: Embodiment–Projection–Role (EPR); Figures 6.1 and 6.2 show the basic and extended dramatherapy developmental paradigms; see also Jennings 1987, 1990, 1992a).

SHAMANISM AND RITUAL DRAMA

The term 'shaman', although now in more popular use, is used with unease by British anthropologists who tend to use terms like 'spirit possession' and 'spirit mediumship', whereas shaman and shamanism are used more extensively in America in studies of cultural anthropology (Lewis 1986). Many anthropologists

Dramatherapy Developmental Paradigm

EPR (condensed and expanded)*

	Miniature	**Life Size**
Embodiment:	finger play	physicalisation
	body parts/singing games	dance
Projection:	micro and mini sculpts	body and chair sculpts
	'small worlds'	painting
Role:	puppet and doll play	role-play
	stories	dramatisation
		improvisation

*   The qualities of condensation and expansion are part of symbolic and ritual processes; they also are part of the drama and dramatherapeutic process.

Figure 6.2 Dramatherapy developmental paradigm, condensed and expanded.

have sought to make a distinction between the shaman who undertakes a mystical journey to the heavens or the netherworld, and one who is possessed by a spirit, usually a spirit-guide in the course of the healing process. There is extensive literature on the nature of trance and whether shamanism in itself implies a trance state. Anthropological literature has tried to distinguish various shamanic 'cults' with sometimes arbitrary categories, which seem imbued with the perceptions of the observer. Lewis (1986) points out that there is far more epidemiological study of magic, witchcraft and sorcery than there is of possession rituals and shamanism, and he suggests that there is a concentration of interest on the social roles of shamans at the expense and even neglect of sociological analysis:

This striking difference in analytic emphasis results partly, no doubt, from the dramatic aspects of spirit-possession that so readily seize the attention of the investigator and deflect interest away from any detailed examination of the categories or persons most prone to be selected as mediums by spirits.

(Lewis 1986: 25–6)

I have attempted elsewhere (Jennings 1992b) to articulate ideas on a shamanic model of dramatherapy, which emphasises two realities: everyday reality and dramatic reality, and the dramatherapist's role in assisting the passage or 'transit' from one to the other and back again. I suggest that some degree of trance is always present: whether a slight degree of absorption or engagement, or an altered state of consciousness or some point in between these two extremes of experience.

However, it is interesting to note that whereas there is anthropological debate regarding 'spirit possession' and 'mystic journeys' there is also theatrical debate concerning the nature of character and role: whether one allows a role to inhabit the self, or whether one goes into role? Does a role come into me or do I go into a role? What happens if the 'role' is an inappropriate one for me? Is it possible to go into role and not get out again? Historically, of course, this used to be the criticism from clinicians, who thought it highly dangerous for psychotic people to do drama. Grainger (1990: 92) has adequately demonstrated that the experience of dramatherapy can actually bring about more ordered thinking with people who have thought disorder, and that by doing drama we will not necessarily make people more 'mad' than they already are. However, we have still obscured what I call the elements of rigour and discernment which should underpin dramatherapy practice and theory.

Thus much of the literature is taken up, as I have said, with discussion of the psychological status of trance states and the extent to which shamanistic healing rites possess genuine therapeutic value.

(Lewis 1986: 26)

There is an assumption that dramatherapy and going into character or role is necessarily a 'good thing' and that such experiences are, by definition, therapeutic. I suggest that dramatherapy and shamanism can both fit a set of pre-determined assumptions which do not necessarily bear examination. For example, why should we consider that certain sorts of drama are necessarily therapeutic and that certain sorts of roles are good for us?

Landy (1993) has already made a substantive contribution to our understanding of the nature of role through his analysis of 500 plays and their characters in order to develop a role taxonomy (see also Chapter 5 this volume). Gersie (1991) has illustrated the necessary care she takes when choosing a myth or story for therapeutic application:

In many of these stories there is, however, more at stake than immortality. In some tales we discern the disquieting sense that life and death are irreconcilable. Life is so very much 'something', a source which runs through us:

changing our cells, empowering our heartbeat, stimulating our breath. Death is so very much 'nothing', a nothing of a very specific kind. Whereas life equals presence, death equals absence, irrevocable absence. Thus we might be tempted to conclude that life or presence, and death or absence are mutually exclusive processes, processes which do not belong together. This apparent opposition when combined with the sequentiality of life and death, nourishes our wish to create an explanation whereby life and death are linked together.

(Gersie 1991: 55)

Lahad (1992) reinforces the autonomy of the client by discovering the strengths rather than focusing on the 'weaknesses' or problems through his application of the Fairy Story Method (see Chapter 10 this volume). My own work has taken me extensively into the use of developmental dramatic stages that parallel normal human development. The three stages of EPR have proved a safe and useful paradigm and basis for dramatherapeutic intervention. They enable participants to develop a range of artistic skills in movement and voice, to develop the imagination, and to have choices about the scenes, scenarios and stories that they may wish to explore. Within this process I see myself as a guide/director who can wait at the dramatic threshold, or in the wings of the therapeutic stage, until people wish to go further.

There is a safeguard in that people develop greater autonomy through acquiring artistic skills: they report feeling more confident, behave more assertively, are more articulate, have greater unity of body and mind, of liking themselves more. Therefore, these skills enable people to expand their worlds and to have choices about how they will explore them.

It is crucial that the dramatherapist should always question his or her particular choice of material at any given time. It may well be that our intuitive decision was appropriate, but have we allowed for the fact that it might not be, and that we are way off-beam and perhaps need to re-locate our responses to participants' needs?

With this caveat, I want now to propose that this paradigm of Embodiment–Projection–Role (EPR) is also applicable in 'larger-than-life drama' (see Figures 6.3 and 6.4), in the areas that I term the ritual theatre of healing. Here I take some of the major concepts from Antonin Artaud and illustrate how an integration of some of his ideas provides us with the basis of a theatre of healing, which can be structured with EPR. As far as possible, I no longer wish to use the term 'shamanic' in this context, since I feel that it adds to the confusion rather than helps the clarity. I do admit to my own aversion to the use of 'partial systems'; the magpie-ing of themes and artifacts from other cultures and superimposing them onto our own. I do not see myself as a modern shaman, although I can see that there are similarities between dramatherapy and shamanic traditions. I see myself as a theatre artist with clinical training, who applies a 'theatre of healing model' with people with needs.

Dramatherapy Developmental Paradigm

applied to

RITUAL THEATRE OF HEALING

(Metaphysical Dramatherapy)

EPR (expanded in movement and voice, objects and space)

	Larger than Life
Embodiment:	physicalisation
	extended movement
Projection:	effigies
	epic sculpts
	large masks
Role:	ritual
	myths
	metaphysical drama

The narrative or the chorus may be used as dramatic devices, as well as group movement and masks.

NB: These are all processes which are not just linear but also spiral.

Figure 6.3 Dramatherapy developmental paradigm applied to the ritual theatre of healing.

THE CONTRIBUTION OF ANTONIN ARTAUD

Antonin Artaud has made a profound impact on our understanding and practice of theatre art. For many years he became a cult figure and a kind of totem for the 'avant-garde', especially because of the extended time he spent in an asylum. Some have regarded him as a seer, others, such as Peter Brook, consider him a guide. Artaud wanted Western theatre to rediscover its own archetypes through digging deep into its own tradition to construct 'a primal dramatic language'. He emphasised the importance of rediscovery and was not in favour of imposing

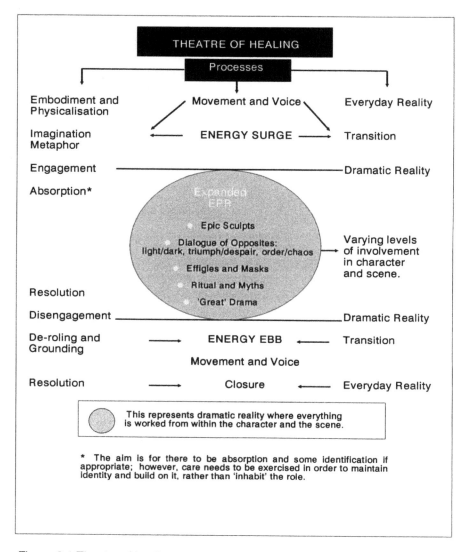

Figure 6.4 Theatre of healing processes.

rituals from other societies onto western theatre. Nevertheless, he was influenced by Balinese theatre and also his travels to Mexico, and sought to translate the images and processes into new theatre forms. He is remembered in particular for his development of the ideas of a 'Theatre of Cruelty', a 'Theatre of the Absurd' (or Grotesque), and 'The Theatre and its Double', as well as his own thoughts on catharsis. Since all these ideas are linked and illustrate Artaud's attempts at dramatic synthesis, I will briefly summarise these main areas as part of our understanding of a metaphysical dramatherapy.

Theatre of Cruelty

> Instead of harking back to texts regarded as sacred and definitive, we must first break theatre's subjugation to the text and rediscover the idea of a kind of unique language somewhere in between gesture and thought.
>
> (Artaud 1970: 68)

Artaud journeyed to Mexico in 1935 in search of Mexican ritual theatre, which he also thought could be inside himself. The Theatre of Cruelty grew from his ideas on 'solar drama' which is characterised by action, revolt, self-assertion and upward energy. It takes several forms, but ultimately necessitates a gesture of defiance or cruelty. Artaud was clear that this 'cruelty' was metaphysical and neither psychological nor social: it represented a metaphysical defiance against the gods. The Mexican sacrificial and peyote rituals, with their symbols of blood, sun, plumed serpent, eagle and fire, served to illustrate his proposed new forms of theatre. For these he wanted new sounds and gestures, larger-than-life effigies or the simulation of a disaster on the stage. He emphasised that the 'cruelty' was not sadism, but harsh gestures and definitive movement that will provoke a sense of danger.

Artaud also thought it was possible to achieve catharsis through 'Theatre of Cruelty', especially through the use of major disasters such as the Plague. He emphasised the importance of taking people by surprise and, unlike Aristotle, he acknowledged the equal importance of comedy as well as tragedy. As Aristotle said in the *Poetics*: 'the comic mask is ugly and distorted but it does not imply pain'.

Theatre of the Absurd (or Grotesque)

Whereas the 'solar drama', the messianic act and the surging energy was epitomised for Artaud by the Mexican rituals, the 'lunar drama' which developed into the Absurd or Grotesque Theatre grew from the major influence of oriental theatre. In particular he was impressed by the Balinese dance-drama which he saw in Paris in 1931, and by earlier exposure to Cambodian theatre as well as the ideas of Buchner, Jarry and Apollinaire (Sellin 1968). Lunar drama takes place after the fall of the gods and is characterised by hopelessness, defeat, waiting and the ultimate belief in the triumph of the pessimist.

> Their gestures fall so exactly on that woody, hollow drum rhythm, accenting it, grasping it in flight so assuredly, on such summits it seems this music accents the very void in their hollow limbs.
>
> The women's stratified, lunar eyes.
>
> Those dream-like eyes appearing to engulf us, before which we see ourselves as ghosts.
>
> (Artaud 1970: 48)

The Theatre and its Double

The idea of the double permeates most of Artaud's thinking and writing, through his belief that the theatre is the double of life and life is a double of the theatre. His work makes frequent reference to mirrors and reflections and the unity of binary opposites; indeed, the relationship of solar and lunar drama is itself a struggle to reconcile doubles and oppositions:

> for if the theatre is the double of life, life is the double of true theatre. . . . This title will correspond to all the doubles of theatre which I thought I had found over so many years: metaphysics, the plague, cruelty.
>
> (Artaud 1964: 272–3)

There is a major theme throughout concerning the discovery of a new language through gesture and sound and not by adherence to the words in a text:

> It is in this light of magic use and witchcraft that one must consider the arts of staging, not as a reflection of a written text and of all that projection of physical doubles which are given off by the text, but as the burning projection of everything of objective consequence which can be derived from gesture, word, sound, music and from combinations thereof.
>
> (Artaud 1964: 88)

Whereas he suggested that people should delve into themselves to discover new truths, he also said that we could impose forms from the outside, such as the postures in Balinese theatre.

> I propose a return in the theatre to the elementary magical ideas, picked up by modern psychoanalysis, which consists of bringing about the cure of a patient by making him assume the external attitude corresponding to the state to which one would seek to restore him.
>
> (Artaud 1964: 96)

Artaud is preoccupied with the search for new forms, in particular through sound and gesture, and with the use of space and dimension. He sees the theatre as capable of transformation and even 'transfiguration' as well as a reconciliation. However, his own lunar side is also fatalistic about the impossibility of reconciliation of the opposites or doubles.

Although it is tempting to become fascinated by Artaud the man, and his journey through mental breakdown and asylum, it is important in this context to look at these concepts in relation to a 'theatre of healing'. Here I want to address the following dramatherapy principles which have been inspired by the writings of Artaud, in my practice of ritual dramatherapy, a theatre that is larger than life, a 'theatre of healing': first, the search for new language through sound and movement; second, the use of larger-than-life images and effigies; third, the dialogue of opposites and reconciliation; fourth, triumph and despair, order and chaos; and finally, resolution through integration of the metaphysical.

The search for new language through sound and movement

Theatre artists, as all other artists, continually seek for new 'languages' to express those things that are difficult to express. Most psychotherapy and psychoanalysis relies on existing language and especially the language of words; however, it is possible to discover completely new means of communication through intensive work on the body and the voice. If we are talking about a 'theatre of healing' that is participatory rather than passive, then we need the skills to be able to enter the experience. The development of the body and voice belong to the embodiment stage.

Once we have practised these skills, then it is possible to experiment and to discover new modes of communication. There are many movement 'systems' – whether Balinese dance or pure mime or Laban or Alexander or Yoga. If we adhere to just one system, then this will control the extent to which we can improvise. The movement, shapes and patterns, and the limits of our creativity, will be dictated by the form. So it is worth suggesting that we take on a more flexible approach to our movement education and perhaps combine at least two 'systems' or perhaps have a major and a minor.

Clinical example: a dramatherapy group in a psychiatric day hospital

Following a slow movement 'warm-up', which involves gentle stretching and shaking and attention to breathing, we focused on the parts of the body, as today I have planned to exaggerate body-parts as a preliminary to ritual workshop.

We took zones of the body and relaxed and moved them (knees downwards, and so on), and then we took specific limbs. We were focusing on our elbows, and one elderly lady said: 'Look at my elbow – it can disappear.' She became engrossed in the fact that she could make her elbows disappear and appear again, by turning her arms. This was the first time she had become engaged in the dramatherapy; usually she carried on a monologue just too low to be heard but nevertheless very disruptive!

We went on to explore parts of the body that could disappear and appear again (such as heels and elbows); those that we could not see (such as backs and ears), and those that were difficult to make disappear (such as noses and knees). We found new ways of moving the body and differentiating between the different limbs, on their visibility and the way they moved. People in the group came up with different ideas and it eventually led into pair-work where different body-parts joined up (such as elbow and knee). This led to a whole-group exercise, where different body-parts joined to create different 'worlds': a stormy sea, a steep cliff, the dark wood, the maze and so on. The work was already moving beyond the physical into the realms of the imagination, and had worked through a sequence from individual, to pairs, to whole-group.

In the next session we worked on breathing and sound and voice exercises which led into sounds to accompany the movements: so there were sound-effects for the stormy sea and the dark wood and so on. We then experimented by having two groups – a movement group and a sound group – and changed over. The sound and movement exercises were now based in a dramatic reality.

The group then went on to build events and happenings that occurred in these places, and they decided to link some of them together: so we had a journey across a stormy sea and landing, an entrance to the dark wood and the finding of a maze and its central treasure.

These metaphors are 'epic metaphors' (Jennings 1990), that are signposts in the aesthetic and metaphysical process. They may well illustrate psychological and social truths, but my preference is to allow the generation of these healing processes to continue 'working'.

We can see how this group moved from the embodiment techniques or skills of movement and voice, to the imaginative act whereby they could create through movement and sound. This was a step from the concrete to the symbolic and can take time to develop. However, many people 'choose' to stay in the concrete in tangible shapes and forms that they can identify; others are 'unable' to move out of the concrete, and they should not be pushed. As a client poignantly said: 'It really is very difficult when you want to be in Siberia, when all the time you know you are in the drama room.'

Larger-than-life images and effigies

I was first introduced to the idea of the larger-than-life image by a professional puppeteer, John Phillips, who taught an introductory session to dramatherapy students at St Albans using 'junk' to make collaborative puppets. Students worked in small groups to create an image from old materials: string, boxes, bamboo canes, newspaper. Its creation in itself became a social skills exercise as students collaborated in a single creation. However, the 'image' or puppet had to 'work': either limbs moved or the mouth opened and so on, and it was large enough for at least two people to be inside it. Students improvised dramatically and then brought several images into one 'story'. I had initially been unconvinced of the significance of this way of working; yet, after a single session, it was apparent how strongly the students identified with the images they had created and had then needed enormous creative energy or an 'energy surge' to project through the image into the story. This became the preferred way of working before any mask-work or smaller individual puppetry. I cannot overemphasise how important it was to have the skills of a professional in the creation of these and other puppets. After 'larger-than-life' images, students and clients alike become more adventurous and creative with 'life-size' puppets.

Clinical example

A group of trainees used the story of Androcles and the Lion to develop as a workshop presentation with a very vulnerable group of people with serious mental health problems. The story was developed as a series of 'epic sculpts' of:

the rich family,
the poor family,
the accusation,
the prison,
the escape,
the desert night,
the wounded lion,
the capture by soldiers,
the lion's den and dénouement.

A narrator told the story as trainees created the nine 'larger-than-life' sculpted images: the nine images represent the dominant 'units of action' of the story. It was agreed that the characters in the story could have many different 'motivations' which would influence the 'unit' (for an elaboration of this analysis, see Jennings 1993).

We then set up three groups: the rich family, the poor family and lions and soldiers, and clients were invited to join or observe a group and contribute to the development of ideas.

The rich family developed an image of being spoilt by being overwhelmed by too much, showered by gifts, drowned in generosity.

In *the poor family* concern was shown for the helplessness of the wife whose husband was a compulsive gambler. They developed rituals of cultivation – planting, hoeing and watering.

The lions displayed roaring and clawing and then the gentle interaction of the thorn in the paw.

The soldiers showed marching and drilling (this enabled me to go in 'in-role' and suggest to the sergeant that he tidied up the groups, which he promptly did!).

The trainee group then presented their version of the story which made use of large 'junk masks' for the lion, the soldiers and Androcles. They expanded the nine sculpts into a dramatisation which used movement, gesture, postures and sound, all of which was 'larger than life'. The client group were able to engage with this drama as: (1) narrative story with sculpts; (2) workshop of characters; (3) audience of the image-drama.

It is important to register the structure that was used with a group of quite disturbed people. The 'engagement' happened with the narrative story, which served as a warm-up. The involvement in 'dramatic reality' developed in the workshop of the characters. The return to everyday reality and distancing took place with the trainees re-owning the performance, which the client group observed. The experience was finally 'grounded' by the audience giving the trainees feedback, including ideas for developing the story as a piece of Brechtian theatre and also as political theatre.

I would suggest that this was probably the only way to engage this particular group in the dramatherapeutic process: they were far too vulnerable to work with drama that would further reduce their fragile defences. The following is a rationale for the 'larger-than-life' approach in this particular situation: first, physicalisation of sculpts communicates at a primary level (E), second, the character workshop provides choices and solutions (P and R). (Most of the drama was embodied, and the roles were either projected (P) onto trainees, or developed as (R) but still embodied.) Additionally the masks allowed for dramatic distance and engagement and fragile defences were strengthened by the structure.

It is a reminder that drama can strengthen and enhance, and, at the same time, enable people to go beyond their limits. As Artaud suggests, the larger-than-life effigy can create a new way of communicating. I would suggest that the above story would fall into his category of 'solar drama'. It had the effect of facilitating greater communication in this group, and participation in the drama process by people who had never participated before. However, it was important that the trainee group was skilled in maintaining the containment of the ritual and not letting it slip into the 'life-size' or personal.

The dialogue of opposites and reconciliation

Many of the people with whom we work as therapists find that they are in a polarised position, such as perceiving themselves as 'all bad' or 'all mad' or 'completely helpless' or 'completely confused'. If we are working in hospitals, there may be diagnosis of mental illness or personality disorder or neurosis. However, I find that prisoners often have similar self-images, without the diagnosis, unless you include 'recidivist' or 'villain'.

Opposites need to be brought into dialogue with their polar partner through the dramatic image and metaphor. All major myths and dramas build on polarities such as: good/bad, light/dark, heaven/hell, sun/moon. The polar opposites are often seen as mutually exclusive rather than aspects of the same. So, for example, one of the prisoner groups insisted that they were unable to enjoy life 'being good': they created 'the good side' and 'the bad side' with a barrier down the centre and said that it was impossible to cross over. 'Being good is boring'; 'Being good is depressing'; 'Being good means expectations' are some of the responses in a sculpt we created about the good or light side. The bad or dark side was seen as exciting, glittering (the lights of the dark side!), stimulating, adventurous: 'Being bad is big.'

We created exaggerated stereotyped scenes of the good side and the bad side, and the group found postures and sounds to make larger-than-life statements in each position. Then one pair decided that they wanted to try to be in the middle and listen to the voices of persuasion from each side. The bad/dark side was able to say that it held the secrets of excitement and all things that people want; it had mysteries and adventures. The good/light side had difficulty in saying anything beyond the banal and regressive: 'We will look after you', 'It is warm here', 'We have kept your place', 'We don't want to blame you.'

It was not until they created effigy masks of light and dark and had struggled with the idea of transformation that a move towards artistic authenticity became possible. I use the phrase 'artistic authenticity' and not 'reality' because we are in the 'larger-than-life domain' which belongs to dramatic reality and not everyday reality. Authenticity enables movement and change from the stereotypic assumptions and banal response. As Elizabeth Rees (1992: 152) says: 'If you are going to create a paradise – don't make a boring one!'

It was an important step when, within the masks, they were able to express the 'danger' inherent in the light and the dark, the danger of standing still and the danger of change. They introduced a new binary opposition: the light side is warm and the dark side is cold.

Triumph and despair, order and chaos

I have selected these two pairs of opposites as themes that constantly recur, not only in the work of Artaud, but also in the dramas of client and student groups. Triumph and despair are the dominant symbols of solar and lunar drama and, pushed to their extremes, become the hyperactivity and depression of people with manic depression.

Ceremony and ritual are frequently the means whereby we can celebrate the triumph or acknowledge the despair. As I said at the beginning of this chapter, ritual is performed action with a common set of symbols which affects us. Without the signposts of ritual and ceremony, is it surprising that many people become lost on the way?

At the beginning of Androcles and the Lion, the trainee group created a lunar sculpt of the accusation of Androcles who lay prostrate on the floor. We experimented with various 'j'accuse' gestures – pointed fingers and outstretched arms – and then played with the ideas of different levels. The image had the most power when we had four different levels for the accusers to stand over Androcles. This is an example of 'working from the outside in', where we experimented with gesture and posture externally until it 'felt and looked right'. We were all reasonably certain that this sculpt probably had the most powerful effect on the group; certainly there was a *frisson* of attention when we adopted this sculpt during the narrative story.

The masks that were created by the prisoner group described in the previous section were an interesting mixture of solar and lunar images, and were developed along the theme of good/bad and light/dark. What transpired in the masks was far more connected with triumph/despair and order/chaos (for illustrations of these masks, see Jennings and Minde 1993).

One mask was a hollow triumph, with glitter, drugs, alcohol, sex with pierced condoms and the idea of the 'high time' and 'rolling fun': the mouth on this mask was large and cavernous, with teeth made from dollar bills. The overall impression was one of despair. Another mask, created all in black (apart from one yellow 'ray of hope'), included 'boils of badness' and a 'lying nose' – very much a mask of despair and acknowledged as such by the group who created it. A third mask said that it was lost and confused and contained question marks, and the final mask (already mentioned above as warm/cold) which included danger in all states, was a triumphant statement. The mask had movement and took risks to move from one state to another. Unlike the condoms with holes, the risks were personal risks with the self, and a recurring theme with the mask was that the people who made it said that they all had to learn to trust – themselves, as well as other people.

> Therefore we must create word, gesture and expressive metaphysics, in order to rescue theatre from its human, psychological prostration. But all of this is of no use unless a kind of real metaphysical temptation, invoking certain unusual notions, lies behind such an effort, for the latter by their very nature cannot be restricted or even formally depicted. These ideas on Creation, Growth and Chaos are all of a cosmic order, giving us an initial idea of a field now completely alien to theatre. They can create a thrilling equation between Man, Society, Nature and Objects.
>
> (Artaud 1970: 69)

Resolution through integration of the metaphysical

It is important to state again Artaud's idea of the drama that goes beyond the social or the psychological – the defiance or revolt against the gods or the cosmos, rather than sadistic acts or cruelty against humans. In the progression of masks (see Jennings 1990) which starts with the mask/puppet on a pole and ends with the mask for the whole head, we can see a development through the separation of the effigy to the 'second skin' of the whole-head mask. With the second skin, people are likely to completely identify with the mask, which is why I suggest its use should be limited. However, within the 'larger-than-life drama', I am more interested in the giant masks and oversized effigies, which not only keep the person's identity intact, but also give a form for them to interact with: they may identify with the effigy, but they do not take on the identity.

Clinical example

Trainees chose to work with *King Lear*, using effigies built on wooden broomsticks which ranged from the most complicated mask – hat and jewellery (Lear) – to a simple pair of sunglasses (Gloucester). The division of the kingdom became an experiment using single lines from the play. Characters paired and explored the situation through gesture, sound and then the line. Time was spent exploring the Lear family when the children were young and before the death of 'Mrs Lear'. They created her funeral, a ritual which was very important to the patient group for whom it was performed (see Jennings 1992b and forthcoming a, *Shakespeare's Theatre of Healing*). 'What ceremony else?' Laertes' plea seems to echo the needs of these groups.

The journey in the storm with Lear and the Fool became a journey through all the effigies as they called and cried through the storm sounds. The ending had several versions, depending on whether the play was seen as solar or lunar. The overall consensus was towards the lunar nature of the play and the idea that Lear is stripped of all trappings (just as Poor Tom is stripped of all his clothes), and stands in despair at the loss of everything, even his daughter. Even so, he makes his peace, within his own limitations.

Below is some of the feedback from this session.

'Lear's storm made it possible to meet the storm in my own life.'

'In playing Lear, I had the opportunity to act out some of my own longing, holding that baby; I did not for one second get confused by the fact that I sat with a stick.'

'My hatred is so big. Where does it come from?'

'I know my father, I have to smooth to the last minute.'

The above piece shows how the multi-level experience can bring about the integration of the physical and the metaphysical – feeling and thought – through the ritual drama. It is becoming more common now to look for the communication, the connection, rather than the polarity or the splits, as I have suggested earlier, through the mimesis and poiesis.

The use of ritual drama in a Theatre of Healing is not merely functional, such as 'coming to terms' or 'acting out' or 'resolving the problems', it is also that it 'feels right' – that the particular dramatic form is the best way to do it and it is recognised as being just that.

As Parkin points out in his essay 'Reason, emotion and the embodiment of power':

Emotions thus make for aesthetic as well as functional appropriateness. . . . Many such pleasing images involve the use of people's bodies. Thus, magicians often heighten the drama of their performance through stylistic movements and gestures. Bodily drama and emotion here draw on each other and at the same time result in acts, decisions, and suggestions that are regarded as reasonable as well as pleasing.

(Parkin 1985: 142)

A RITUAL THEATRE OF HEALING

In this chapter I have considered some of the ways in which ritual is a necessary part of the healing process, and that it needs to be applied with forethought and consideration. I have suggested that 'shamanic' approaches are not necessarily helpful when considering ritual, and that rigour needs to be applied when planning this type of intervention.

I have taken the major theories of Artaud: the theatres of Cruelty and the Absurd, solar and lunar drama and the Double, and developed them in relation to a metaphysical model of dramatherapy. I have suggested several stages in this, in particular the EPR developmental progression which can be applied in any dramatherapeutic setting. This allows for the acquisition of skills that are appropriate to expand people's experience and enable the engagement necessary to work within dramatic reality.

In particular, I have emphasised the use of larger-than-life masks and effigies as a way into the metaphysical, while still building up the strengths and identity of the individual. In the main, we are working from the 'outside in' in this form of dramatherapy: the skills of movement and voice are established externally and then make an impact on the internal world. The movement and sounds create metaphors and images which are able to reach our internal world (see Cox and Theilgaard 1987). They by-pass our defence systems which are necessary for fragile identities.

I have not addressed in this chapter the biological impact of all dramatherapy and metaphysical Theatre of Healing in particular. This will be the subject of future work; however, it is exciting to realise that 'Performing artists are forever playing around – not only with codes, frames, and metaframes of communication – but with their own internal brain states' (Schechner 1990: 40). I want to take further the interconnecting impact of the physical and metaphysical, which must include a biological basis within the aesthetic experience.

It is important to acknowledge the integration possible through this dramatherapeutic form and to place 'artistic authenticity' or 'aesthetic congruence' as an essential part of the healing process. A Theatre of Healing must be aesthetic as well as functional; and indeed, I imagine that the healing property is that they have both been brought together into a relationship.

REFERENCES

Artaud, A. (1964) *Oeuvres Complètes IV–V*, Paris, Gallimard.
Artaud, A. (1970) *The Theatre and its Double*, London, John Calder.
Cox, M. and Theilgaard, A. (1987) *Mutative Metaphors in Psychotherapy*, London, Tavistock.
Gersie, A. (1991) *Storymaking in Bereavement: Dragons Fight in the Meadow*, London, Jessica Kingsley.
Grainger, R. (1990) *Drama and Healing: the Roots of Dramatherapy*, London, Jessica Kingsley.
Hillman, J. (1983) *Healing Fiction*, New York, Station Hill.
Jennings, S. (ed.) (1987) *Dramatherapy Theory and Practice 1*, London, Routledge.
Jennings, S. (1990) *Dramatherapy with Families, Groups and Individuals*, London and New York, Jessica Kingsley. (Also translated into Danish.)
Jennings, S. (ed.) (1992a) *Dramatherapy Theory and Practice 2*, London, Routledge.
Jennings, S. (1992b) 'The nature and scope of dramatherapy: theatre of healing', in M. Cox (ed.) *Shakespeare Comes to Broadmoor*, London, Jessica Kingsley.
Jennings, S. (1993a) *Playtherapy with Children: a Practitioner's Guide*, Oxford, Blackwell Scientific.
Jennings, S. (1993b) 'Shakespeare's theatre of healing', *Dramatherapy*.
Jennings, S. (1994) *Introduction to Dramatherapy*, London, Jessica Kingsley.
Jennings, S. (forthcoming a) *Shakespeare's Theatre of Healing*, London, Jessica Kingsley.

Jennings, S. (forthcoming b) *The Greek Theatre of Healing*, London, Jessica Kingsley.

Jennings, S. and Minde, A. (1993) *Dramatherapy and Art Therapy*, London, Jessica Kingsley.

Lahad, M. (1992) 'Storymaking: an assessment method for coping with stress. Six-piece storymaking and the BASIC Ph', in S. Jennings (ed.) *Dramatherapy Theory and Practice 2*, London, Routledge.

Landy, R. (1992) 'A taxonomy of roles: a blueprint for the possibilities of being', *The Arts in Psychotherapy*, 18(5) 419–33.

Landy, R. (1993) *Heroes and Fools, Victims and Survivors: a Study of Role in Theatre, Everyday Life and Therapy*, New York, Guilford Press.

Lewis, G. (1980) *Day of Shining Red*, Cambridge, Cambridge University Press.

Lewis, I.M. (1986) *Religion in Context: Cults and Charisma*, Cambridge, Cambridge University Press.

Parkin, D. (1985) 'Reason, emotion and the embodiment of power', in J. Overing (ed.) *Reason and Morality*, ASA Monograph 24, London, Tavistock.

Rees, E. (1992) *Christian Symbols, Ancient Roots*, London, Jessica Kingsley.

Rycroft, C. (1985) *Psycho-analysis and Beyond*, London, Hogarth.

Schechner, R. (1990) 'Magnitudes of performance', in R. Schechner and W. Appel (eds) *By Means of Performance*, Cambridge, Cambridge University Press.

Sellin, E. (1986) *The Dramatic Concepts of Antonin Artaud*, Chicago, IL, University of Chicago Press.

Turner, V. (1982) *From Ritual to Theatre*, New York, Performing Arts Journal Publishing.

Van Gennep, A. (1960) *The Rites of Passage*, London, Routledge & Kegan Paul.

Chapter 7

Dramatherapy and psychodrama
Similarities and differences

Anna Chesner

INTRODUCTION

'What is the difference between dramatherapy and psychodrama?' This question is often asked by newcomers to either method, and the two are often muddled. Before focusing on their differences it is important to acknowledge that there is common ground. Indeed, this is why there is often confusion as to their differences.

I shall begin by focusing on the similarities between dramatherapy and psychodrama, in terms of the broad principles of their foundation in drama. I shall then highlight the differences by taking a closer look at each method in practice, using sample sessions to illustrate the patterns and principles of each method.

In the interest of clarifying major similarities and differences I shall not be able to do justice to the full range of personal styles and therapeutic orientations that create such diversity within each method. I shall inevitably generalise, and there are probably exceptions to each generalisation.

My own background is in drama. I trained initially as a dramatherapist. At the time of this training I had my first experience of psychodrama, and am now, more than a decade later, in the process of completing my training as a psychodramatist and group analytic psychotherapist. Group analytic psychotherapy clearly differs from dramatherapy and psychodrama by being a verbal method conducted within a physically static group environment. Participants sit in a circle on chairs and talk. However, the experience and philosophy of this method can shed light on the processes of the other two, and I shall refer to it below when highlighting the differences between dramatherapy and psychodrama.

SIMILARITIES

Drama

The most immediate similarity between dramatherapy and psychodrama is the central place of drama in both methods. The current definition of dramatherapy, adopted by the British Association for Dramatherapists, is as follows:

Dramatherapy is the intentional use of drama and theatre processes and related techniques in order to achieve the therapeutic goals of symptom relief, emotional and physical integration, and personal growth.

(Barham 1992; see also Appendix 1)

J.L. Moreno, the originator of psychodrama, describes this method as: 'The science which explores the "truth" by dramatic methods. It deals with interpersonal relations and private worlds' (Moreno 1953, quoted in Holmes 1992: 6). A participant in either a dramatherapy or psychodrama session can expect elements of the dramatic idiom to be present in the experience.

Drama is a creative art form, and both therapeutic methods draw on the use of artistic form to give shape and stimulus to the therapeutic process. Therapist and client use their internal creative resources and shared cultural sources in the therapy. The implicit message is that we are, in our healthy state, creative beings, and that creative action is central to the process of becoming whole.

Drama involves doing. The dramatic world is one of action, where participants enact and are active. These therapies involve the use of action methods, ways of engaging participants in action. This is in contrast to the verbal, non-action psychotherapies that have their origin in the work of Freud.

Drama and the body

When we express ourselves through action we engage at a physical level. The presence of physical movement and possible physical contact within the therapy session has a powerful impact. There is a profound connection between body, senses, emotional and mental states. By engaging at a physical level the client has easier access to their emotional and inner world.

This same connection between the physical and the psychic informs the training and work of the actor, who learns physical and vocal flexibility in order to inhabit a dramatic role more effectively. Without this training their range of expression remains limited to the habitual, and they may end up 'playing themselves' in each role. For the client in therapy physical engagement means both a fuller expression of the habitual self, and also the chance to adopt new and alternative roles in action.

There is also a connection between the body and the unconscious. The psychoanalyst Joyce McDougall explores this link in the significantly titled *Theaters of the Body* (1989). Physical symptoms reveal themselves to be communications of inner pain, the historical origins of which are discovered in the course of the analysis. Similarly, in psychodrama a physical symptom explored psychodramatically through physical action may be the doorway to a series of significant memories that make sense of current difficulties. In both dramatherapy and psychodrama the physicality of the experience brings the emotions and the unconscious onto the therapeutic stage.

The use of space in theatre and therapy

The therapeutic space corresponds in some ways to the theatrical stage.[1] It is a space where illusion and play are acceptable, and where they can be given three-dimensional expression in action. When we go to the theatre we accept that the action on stage has a different kind of reality than the action that takes place on the street or in the foyer of the theatre. Coleridge described this process as the 'willing suspension of disbelief'. Performers and audience alike agree to play. The word play is used to denote both a theatrical production and the recreational activities typical of childhood. As the lights dim at the start of a show the audience accepts the invitation to suspend disbelief in a similar way to children on hearing the words 'Once upon a time . . .' or 'Let's pretend . . .'. In the context of therapy clients are invited to bring the worlds of memory, fantasy and myth onto the therapeutic stage. Whether working through dramatherapy or psychodrama, clients are invited to try things out in action in the safety of the therapeutic, dramatic space, where the context of illusion and play give permission for more freedom of exploration and expression.

The particular quality of reality held by the theatrical stage and the psychodramatic or dramatherapeutic space can be described in terms derived from anthropology and *rites de passage* as 'liminal', existing between one state and another. A related concept from the writings of D.W. Winnicott (1974) is the 'potential or transitional space' in which play takes place. The particular quality of this space is that it is intermediate, between the inner and outer reality of the child. The importance to the young child of the 'transitional object', often a teddy bear or piece of blanket, is that it is allowed to exist at a reality level somewhere between 'me' and 'not me', forming a bridge between subjectivity and objectivity. It exists in the external world in a concrete way, but is creatively endowed by the child with significance from its inner world. This quality is tremendously powerful and developmentally transformative. The therapeutic space in dramatherapy and psychodrama is also 'transitional', operating as a bridge between inner and outer worlds. The dramatic idiom relates closely to the experience of play, and the agreement to play can be as facilitative of exploration and change in the adult as it is in the child.

Drama and dream

The drama of the inner world is familiar to us through our experience of dream. Freud called dreams the 'royal road to the unconscious'. It is interesting that the unconscious chooses to speak to us not through words alone, but through an essentially dramatic mode of communication. In dream we find dramatic elements such as story, location, plot, scene changes, spatial relationships, characters and dialogue.

The meaning is expressed through each of these elements and through the atmosphere they create as a whole. Even in daydream, which is more accessible to the conscious mind, the psyche makes use of dramatic dialogue and imagery to explore the dynamics of conflict. The process is natural and psychically familiar to us.

The dramatherapist and psychodramatist use the same elements to facilitate expression of conscious and unconscious material. Stories which have their origin in the imagination, fantasy or memory can be externalised and shared through the drama. The manner in which the therapist enables this to happen differs between the two methods. There is common ground insofar as drama is the means of communication through which inner concerns are expressed.

Drama and role

The dramatic concept of role has an important place in dramatherapy and psychodrama. Moreno defined role as:

> the actual and tangible forms which the self takes. We thus define the role as the functioning form the individual assumes in the specific moment he reacts to a specific situation in which other persons or objects are involved.
>
> (Moreno 1961, quoted in Fox 1987: 62)

The concept comes from the dramatic tradition, and Moreno applies it to life in action, from the moment of birth onwards. He categorises roles into three groups: psychosomatic roles, social roles and psychodramatic roles. Psychosomatic roles relate to the way in which the individual functions at a physical level, e.g. 'light sleeper', 'fussy eater', 'shabby dresser'. Social roles describe the individual in relationship to others, e.g. 'reluctant mother', 'competitive sibling', 'confident teacher'. Psychodramatic roles exist more as internal images of self in relation to others, which then colour our actual interactions, e.g. 'doomed victim', 'good girl', 'precariously balanced tight-rope walker'. In Moreno's theory, roles may change from moment to moment according to context and the particular specialities or habits of the individual. Some roles tend to be overdeveloped at the expense of others which are underdeveloped. There is a tendency for some roles to become fixed, and while these may serve us well in some contexts, in others they may be dysfunctional and problematic.

This status quo is challenged through dramatherapy and psychodrama. A variety of unfamiliar roles may be played out and played with in the therapeutic space. As the role repertoire develops, the individual has the option to exercise greater freedom of choice in each moment. Spontaneity in relation to role is a key concept here, at the heart of Moreno's work on role and existential philosophy. The word comes from the Latin *sponte*, 'of free will'. The idea of spontaneous action does not refer to being out of control or lacking appropriate boundaries. It is more a question of being sufficiently free of past and future to act freely in the present moment. It is the force which 'propels the individual towards an adequate response to a new situation or a new response to an old situation' (Moreno 1953, quoted in Fox 1987: 42). Psychodrama addresses itself specifically to the development of spontaneity in this sense, and it is a core concept in dramatherapy too.

Having considered some basic similarities between the two methods let us now take a look at their differences. To do this we shall look at an example of each therapy in practice.

DIFFERENCES

There are two key differences between dramatherapy and psychodrama: the way in which they operate as group therapies, and the specificity of technique, structure and therapeutic intention within psychodrama compared to the broader range open to the dramatherapist.

Dramatherapy and psychodrama as group therapies

The focus of the psychodrama session is on the psychodramatic journey of one group member, the *protagonist*, and once this person is identified, the roles taken by the other group members are largely a reflection of the protagonist's inner world. In dramatherapy the focus may come to rest on one individual for most of a session, but it is more likely that the focus will move freely around the group.

These differences will emerge more clearly as we look at two sessions in some detail, but first I should like to introduce the concept of the *group matrix* which may help to highlight the difference between these two methods as group therapies. The term was used by S.H. Foulkes in the context of group analytic psychotherapy:

> By *matrix* is meant a psychic network of communication which is the joint property of the group and is not only interpersonal but transpersonal. As the matrix develops into a more embracing network of communication and relationship, the individuals become more clearly defined, find themselves in an ever-moving dynamic interplay.

> (Foulkes 1990: 182)

In group analytic psychotherapy the matrix emerges in the group through free-floating discussion. Whatever is communicated in the group, whether verbally or non-verbally, sets up a resonance in other group members including the group conductor. Themes become apparent and are worked through verbally in the group.

The matrix is where the energy and the concern of the group is at any moment, whether it be an analytic group, a dramatherapy group or a psychodrama group. Individual members relate to and create the matrix through what they bring to the present moment in terms of past conditioning and habitual roles. In the context of dramatherapy the therapist proposes structures to the group, through which the matrix is explored by the whole group. In psychodrama the concerns of the group must be held by the issues of the chosen protagonist, who then works on behalf of the group as a whole.

Structure and technique of psychodrama

A core difference of technique between dramatherapy and psychodrama stems from the historical fact that psychodrama originated in the work of one man, Moreno (with some significant developments made by his wife Zerka Moreno). The practice of 'classical psychodrama' is still in use and is a central reference point for variations such as strategic psychodrama, analytic psychodrama, person-centred psychodrama, etc. Dramatherapy, by contrast, has its sources directly in a variety of dramatic and theatrical traditions, such as shamanic ritual, story-telling, dramatic and creative play, and the work of a variety of theatre practitioners from Stanislavski to Grotowski (for a more comprehensive survey of these sources see Landy 1986).

In practice this means that the psychodramatist (also called the psychodrama director) uses a more precise map in structuring the psychodramatic journey, and this reflects a more precise therapeutic intention. Each session consists of three phases: warm-up, action, sharing/closure. The action phase in particular is highly structured. Let us look at each phase.

Warm-up

The function of this part of the session is:

1 for the group members to warm up to each other in the context of the psychodrama group;
2 for the group members to warm up to their inner world, to get in touch with areas of unresolved conflict, issues and feelings;
3 to identify a central protagonist, who will be the focus of the action phase of the session. The protagonist (a term taken from Greek theatre and meaning 'first actor' or central character) must have the support of the group to explore their psychodrama, as the other group members will be called upon to play roles from the protagonist's inner world.

The methods used for the warm-up can be quite varied, ranging from active games to guided fantasy or verbal reflection. The director's task here is to allow the group matrix to emerge, and to facilitate the group in finding the person whose psychodrama will most resonate with the group as a whole. This is a subtle and intuitive process. A number of group members may put themselves forward to work as protagonist. There are a number of ways of choosing the protagonist: each group member may be invited to stand behind the person who holds the issue they most resonate with; the potential protagonists may choose between themselves through open discussion; the director may make the choice and ask for the group's support.

Action

It is in this phase of the session that psychodrama differs most from drama-therapy, and where the concept of the map is important. The American psycho-dramatists Elaine Eller Goldman and Delcy Schram Morrison have devised an actual map, in the form of a psychodramatic spiral which charts the classical psychodramatic journey. The principal direction followed by the psychodrama is 'from the periphery to the core' and back again to the periphery (Goldman and Morrison 1984: 27).

This journey usually (depending on the therapeutic contract) involves an element of time travel. It starts with the present moment or recent past, and travels back to a formative time in the past in which the present problem has its roots. Finally there is a return to the present and the real challenge of change.

That is the general flow of the action phase. It is often an intense journey, during which the protagonist may experience a variety of powerful emotions, and achieve insight into themselves and significant others from their present or past. Particular techniques are used to explore each phase of the psychodramatic journey. Let us look at the process in more detail using the example of a fictional protagonist, Helen.

Helen's psychodrama

The *warm-up* puts Helen in touch with difficulties she is experiencing at work, where she feels she is being overlooked while her colleagues are promoted around her. She is chosen by the group to be protagonist.

There is an agreement between Helen and the director (the psychodramatist) to explore this situation. Helen would like to find out why it is she gets over-looked. This *contract* provides the focus for the psychodrama. At some moments in the psychodrama there may be a number of different directions that could usefully be explored. At these moments the director bears the contract in mind and chooses options relevant to the agreed focus. It may be necessary for Helen to explore other options in future psychodramas.

The psychodrama begins with a *presenting scene*, a scene from Helen's life through which she shows the group how and where she experiences her problem. She shows the group a recent moment at work, where she learnt that a junior colleague had been invited to apply for promotion over Helen's head. The director helps her to *set the scene* which warms Helen up to the immediacy of the situation. 'Then' and 'there' becomes 'here' and 'now', as Helen's subjective perception of the scene is replayed in the session. Helen recollects the layout and atmosphere of the office, and arranges the dramatic space to represent this. The scene takes place 'as if' it were happening now. Helen projects her memory of the scene into the dramatic space.

Group members are chosen to play the other people in the scene, or *auxiliary egos*. The director instructs the protagonist to *reverse roles* with her boss and her colleagues in the scene. This is often considered the most important technique in psychodrama. As Helen takes on the role of her boss she embodies her perception of him. She has the chance to see herself through his eyes and to identify briefly with his perspective, rather than her habitual one. The director interviews Helen in role as her boss and it emerges that he just hadn't thought of Helen in terms of promotion. He sees her as insignificant, not special, a bit of a mouse, although she does make a good cup of coffee. The young woman whom he expects to promote by contrast stands out from the crowd, and deserves recognition for her hard work. It is important to note that this is Helen's subjective perception of the situation, and if her real boss were present he might disagree. The psychodrama concerns itself with the protagonist's inner world, which colours her experiences in external reality.

Whilst the protagonist is engaged in the process of showing the presenting scene, the director makes a *role analysis*, an assessment of the protagonist's dominant roles in relation to others. The director uses techniques such as interviewing, soliloquy, asides, thought bubbles, to make this analysis. There are five key elements of the role analysis to be highlighted. These are: the context in which the role arises; the feelings experienced in the role; the actual behaviour in the scene; the belief system or identity this behaviour is based on; and the consequences of all this for the protagonist.

In Helen's case this analysis reveals the *context* to be at work, in a situation of potential competition with a peer, and potential recognition from a person in authority. Her *feelings* are of unexpressed hurt and anger, while her actual *behaviour* in this situation is to hide these feelings and try to please. She puts on a cheerful smile, makes everyone in the office a coffee, and withdraws into herself. She does nothing either to push herself forward or question her boss's judgement. Her *belief system* seems to be: 'No-one ever notices me, but it's selfish and bad to make a fuss. I should keep my feelings to myself and be nice to people.' The *consequences* of all this is that Helen feels badly done by and fails to get recognition and promotion.

The role analysis here is based on one scene and the director may choose to check whether this pattern affects other aspects of Helen's life or is specific to the work situation. The director asks Helen if she gets to feel overlooked anywhere else in her life at present, and Helen says yes, occasionally at home with her husband.

A second presenting scene between Helen and her husband Harry is set up and explored using the same techniques. It emerges that at home too she feels taken for granted. Harry always gets priority use of their car, which means that Helen has had to abandon her evening class in pottery. Again she has strong but unexpressed feelings of hurt and anger, but avoids confrontation with Harry, which she believes would be selfish and destructive of their marriage. He does not even know how important the pottery class was to her. It is often the case that a pattern of relationship exists in more than one area of a protagonist's life. The familiar roles that make Helen feel recognisably herself exist at an internal level, as part of her psyche, and she is drawn to situations where these internal roles come into play. Even roles which are unsatisfactory are perpetuated in this way. Psychodrama aims to make a change at an internal level, within the externalised world of the protagonist's psyche.

So far the psychodramatic exploration has been at the periphery of the spiral. The protagonist has explored conflicted areas of her current life with the help of the group and the director. Through the role analysis the director notices that the protagonist's belief system is inappropriate to these current life situations. Helen lacks spontaneity in the sense defined above. Her response to the situations at work and at home is inadequate and unsatisfactory.

The journey turns now towards the centre of the spiral in the search for the time when Helen learned or consolidated the belief system that underlies her current behaviour. The place where this occurs is called the *locus nascendi*, the place where the belief system was born. In terms of the psychodramatic spiral this is located at the centre of the map.

The information from the analysis of the presenting scenes helps the director guide the protagonist to find this *locus*. The salient points are summarised by the director, who asks the protagonist to recall an earlier time in her life where she learned to hide her hurt and anger, to be quietly helpful, perhaps while someone else achieved recognition or got their way. Helen is very warmed up to this whole complex of feelings and given a little time recollects an earlier scene. Helen's internalised experiences of the past influence her present perceptions in an unconscious way. The director's questions help her identify a possible source for a belief system that has become familiar and habitual, and a role which is overdeveloped and inappropriate in a number of present-day contexts. By return-ing psychodramatically to the past Helen has the chance to disentangle the past from the present, and to make some conscious choices over her future.

Helen goes to a time when she was 7. The scene takes place on the psycho-dramatic stage as if in the present, and Helen relates to it as a 7-year-old. She has just come home from school and is carrying a painting. She is proud of it and is looking forward to showing it to her parents. Her mother is preoccupied with looking after Helen's younger sister, Jane, who has always been sickly, and is currently quite ill. As Helen approaches her mother with the painting she indicates to her to be quiet, as Jane has just managed to go to sleep and must not be disturbed. Helen must be a good girl and wait until later. When father comes home his first enquiries are about Jane and yet again Helen has to take a back seat. Through role reversal with mother, father and sister Helen reveals that this moment is typical of many moments in which she learns to put her own needs for recognition and attention aside, in favour of being undemanding and helpful. Jane is the special and important one, while Helen sees herself as the least significant member of the family. While Jane's every whim seems to be answered, Helen's own needs seem selfish and bad, so she hides her feelings, withdraws, and tries to be helpful in the hope that if she is good enough her moment of recognition will come.

The protagonist's problem is not so much that she had to put her own needs to one side for a moment, but that she appears to have been doing so ever since. The director assists Helen in changing her perspective and her behaviour in the scene. Helen is given a *double*, an empathic group member who stands with the protagonist, adopts her posture and gesture, and tries to give voice to the thoughts and feelings that Helen finds difficult to voice. The task of the double is to empathise, not analyse. When the double gets it wrong Helen corrects them, and gradually the underlying feelings are given expression in the scene. What emerges is anger at parents and sister alike, and a child-like fear that if Helen asserts herself and wakes her sister that Jane will die, and it will be her fault. This fear acts like a hand over Helen's mouth, hushing her voice. The director asks if there was anyone in young Helen's life who would understand how she feels and would be able to help. The protagonist remembers that her grandmother always felt like an ally, but she was not around at this time.

The action moves into a different mode, which Moreno called *surplus reality*. In surplus reality anything is possible on the psychodramatic stage, and the protagonist can have a new experience, denied to her at the time. In this case, grandmother is brought into the scene and young Helen confides her feelings of hurt, jealousy, anger and fear with her. The double stays in Helen's role, and Helen reverses role with this supportive grandmother. As grandmother she is very impressed with the painting, and tells Helen how special and talented she is. The director asks Helen to return to her own role and the scene is replayed so that Helen has the chance to take in the new experience from the role of the 7-year-old.

It is important for Helen to confront her parents and sister if she is to avoid being dominated by an inappropriate idea of how she has to be in relation to authority figures and peers, and a replaying of these patterns in her adult life. The work with grandmother builds up her self-esteem so that she is able to face the other family members.

She confronts her parents first, an emotional moment, where she gives voice first to her anger, then to her pain at always being put second. She asks them why they never noticed her need. Using role reversal she is able to answer her own question, and from their role describes the worry of having a sick daughter. Also from the role of her parents she experiences contrition at not appreciating young Helen, and a desire to make amends. They reassure her of their love, and show how proud they are by putting up her painting in pride of place in the living room.

Helen is given the option to spend some time with Jane in this psychodrama. She decides to go and talk to her in her sick room. It takes courage to risk waking her up, but Helen does so and describes to her how she feels about her sister always getting the attention. She is clearly frightened that by doing so she will destroy Jane, but learns from the reverse role position that Jane will not be destroyed, and does not want to hold Helen back.

This is not simply the rewriting of Helen's personal history. The roles of 'preoccupied, uninterested parents' exist at an internal level within Helen's psyche, and are matched by the corresponding reciprocal role of the Helen who hides her feelings and never demands recognition. As her psychodramatic parents hang Helen's painting 'in pride of place', the protagonist is symbolically valuing herself in a new way.

In so doing she is making a significant shift in her belief system, that could have profound consequences in her life. The work with the sister helps to challenge the unconscious belief that her needs for recognition are destructive.

Helen's work in the locus leads her to important insights into her way of being in the world. She learns to activate new roles and begins to internalise a new belief system. In a sense her world changes at an internal level, and the rest of the action focuses on making a bridge back to the real challenges of Helen's present life. The past is gone, and any change can only take place in the present and future. In terms of the psychodramatic spiral there is a return to the periphery and the presenting scenes. The protagonist brings her new insights back to the *status nascendi*, where she is encouraged to put her new roles into practice, through *role training*. It would be hard for Helen to go to work next day and have the task of applying the fruits of her psychodramatic work in real life. The psychodramatic map gives her the chance to practise the new roles within the safety of the transitional space.

This is not always easy. She manages quite well to tackle her husband and set up a re-negotiation about the use of the car. However, when she returns to the work scene, she has difficulty in standing up to her boss. She knows what she wants to say, but has difficulty in contacting the appropriate role in a situation where other people expect her to be her 'old self'. The director makes use of *concretisation* to give concrete form to Helen's difficulty. Two group members take on the role of the inner voices that tell her not to be selfish, but to smile and make a cup of coffee. Their physical task is to push Helen into the background where the kettle is, and keep her from her intended meeting with her manager. Helen needs to find the appropriate physical and vocal energy to overcome the stultifying power of these thoughts, and as she finds it she also finds the words and the energy to make her stand with her boss. She makes it clear to him that she no longer wishes to be passed over, that her own achievements at work have been considerable, and that she would like to be informed next time there is a possibility of promotion.

Sharing/closure

As the psychodrama comes to an end, the action phase of the session is finished. The focus moves from the protagonist to the rest of the group. Group members are invited to share their own feelings and experiences in response to the protagonist's work. From the protagonist's side this gives reassurance that she is not alone in her vulnerability and humanity. The other group members share how they identify with the protagonist in terms of their own life experiences. The focus returns to the group as a whole, and each group member is invited to resonate with the themes of the psychodrama. The group matrix is redefined in the light of the work that has taken place. The director's role at this point is to ensure that the sharing happens in a non-judgemental way. The protagonist is considered to be too raw at this point to be able to tolerate analysis of what she has presented. Having been the central focus of the group's time it is reassuring for Helen to know that her work was also of personal value for the other participants. The response to her psychodrama may well generate a starting point for a future psychodrama in which another group member will be the protagonist.

The psychodramatic journey is highly structured. As the idea of the spiral indicates it is the intention from the outset to explore a present situation, discover the origins of habitual dysfunctional behaviour in the past, recapture spontaneity, gain insight, and practise a more spontaneous role in the present. The method is extremely powerful, and penetrative. A protagonist may deal with more material in a 2-hour psychodrama than they would in several years of verbal psycho-analysis. That is not to say that the therapeutic process takes place in one session. It is ongoing, involving a continuity of experience in which the group member participates as protagonist, auxiliary ego and witness on a number of occasions. Nonetheless, most classical psychodramas involve a completed journey into the depths and back. The structured map and the familiar psychodramatic techniques are essential to contain and guide this therapeutic process.

Structure and technique of dramatherapy

Let us look more closely at dramatherapy. There is some similarity in terms of the overall tripartite structure of a session. While psychodrama involves warm-up, action and sharing, the dramatherapy session can be divided into warm-up, development and closure.

The warm-up

The dramatherapy warm-up aims:

1 to facilitate a sense of connection and trust between group members;
2 to warm group members up to being expressive, physically or vocally;
3 to allow themes or concerns to emerge in the group.

There is noticeably no requirement for an individual protagonist to be found. Dramatherapy differs here from psychodrama, and is very flexible. The group may continue to work as a whole throughout the session, or an individual may hold the group theme and be the focus of the work.

A central concept in the dramatherapy warm-up is that of ritual. The warm-up often involves an element of game playing. Simple games with rules give a structure for spontaneous interaction. The structure itself is formalised, and this provides containment for interaction. There is a balance between ritual and risk (see Jennings 1990), form and spontaneity. The dramatherapist is aware of this balance at each phase of the session, and their task is to find appropriate struc-tures to provide tolerable challenge to group members (Grainger 1990: 78).

Development

The structure of the session flows from relative safety at the start, into greater risk-taking during the development phase, and a return to ritual and safety at the closure. Over time the group is encouraged to take greater risks in terms of the expression and exploration of their inner worlds, and of their shared social world in the here-and-now of the group.

The techniques used in this process can be drawn from any aspect of drama or theatre. These may include working with text, performance, improvisation, story-telling, make-up, mask, puppetry, movement, voice, game, sculpting and many more. The dramatherapist uses their skill and understanding of dramatic processes to create structures appropriate to the needs of the group at any time. As mentioned above, the central phase of the dramatherapy session does not follow the precise map which underlies the psychodrama. There are many options open to the drama-therapist. I shall give an example of the development phase of a fictional session, through which I shall highlight some of the principles at work. The particular dramatic elements used in this session are movement, mask and improvisation.

Stage 1

The group explores moving in the space, initially with the focus on the physical sensations of stretching and breathing. They start at floor level and discover the possibilities of movement while the body maintains contact with the floor. They are then invited to move up to a crawling level, and again to discover what is possible here in terms of the mechanics of moving and the sensations of stretch-ing and breathing. They are asked to come up to full height and explore in a similar way.

Principles   This is a physical warm-up. Its structure is designed to be less threatening than asking a group to 'move freely around the space'. The therapist gives rules, such as staying at ground level. This corresponds with our earliest experiences. We learn to move as babies at this level before we take the risk of crawling and finally walking. The group is even told where to focus their attention, just on the sensations of the body stretching and breathing. The inten-tion here is twofold: first, to encourage an awareness of self at a physical level, in other words, to 'earth' group members in physical awareness. This is the 'embodiment' phase of the work (see Chapter 6 this volume). Second, the intention is to limit what is expected of the group, so as to give them an experience of being adequate to the task.

Stage 2

The participants are asked to carry on moving but to change level when instructed. They are also to start to move according to four adjectives: spiky, light, heavy, flowing. The level and the mode can change at a moment's notice, at the therapist's instruction. A further ingredient is added, the voice. The group is invited to make any sounds which stem from the movements. The therapist encourages them to begin to relate to each other.

Principles   The therapist is beginning to demand an increase in spontaneity and an increase in interaction. The risk level rises, and there is an element of fun as the group meets the challenge. No-one is the centre of attention. Indeed, everyone is engaged on the same task at the same time. There is an element of anonymity which allows group members to move and use their voice under cover of the whole group activity.

Stage 3

The therapist gives the instruction for the group to drop to the ground, close their eyes, and concentrate on their breathing. There is a period of rest, which is welcome after all the physical activity. While this is going on the therapist lays out around the room a selection of animal masks. The group is invited to get up and take a look around, without engaging in conversation. When they have seen all the masks they come together in a circle, close their eyes, and are asked to notice which mask comes to mind. It may have made an impact because it is attractive, repellent or amusing. Whatever the reason they are to go and stand by it. If more than one have chosen the same mask there may need to be some negotiations until each person has a mask, which they bring back to the circle and place in front of them.

Principles   An element of ritual is present in this phase. The masks are laid out while the group have their eyes closed. The intention is that they are relaxed and receptive as they walk around the room and silently encounter the animal faces. It might distract from the impact of the faces if the group were to converse. The directive to avoid conversation has the purpose of maximising the impact of the masks, and encouraging identification or resonance with qualities in the animal faces. The ritualistic atmosphere builds expectation. There may be echoes of shamanistic ceremony. Here the mask is treated with great respect as the container of a particular energy. Wearing the mask allows the wearer to embody its personality and energy. As each group member looks at the masks they see qualities and potentials 'out there', in the external reality of the mask. The reaction to these qualities depends on what qualities and roles are overdeveloped and underdeveloped within the individual.

There is an element of projection from the inner world onto the mask, which usually takes place at an unconscious, instinctual level. The mask holds an aspect of the looker's internal world. This parallels the relationship of auxiliary role to the protagonist in psychodrama to some extent. Wearing the mask is then analogous to the process of role reversal. Both processes allow the participant to experience themselves as Other. Mask work is one of a number of projective techniques the dramatherapist uses to facilitate the externalisation of the inner world, and the activation of inner roles.

Stage 4

In pairs the group members work on finding a movement and sound repertoire that goes with their mask. While one person in each pair puts on the mask and begins to move with it their partner acts as a mirror for them, by showing them what they are doing, and also making suggestions. When one mask has been 'activated' in this way it is put to one side and the process is repeated for the other partner.

Principles   There is a move towards greater risk-taking as each person begins to develop their own interpretation of the mask. They must draw on considerable creative resources, and are supported in this challenge by being with a partner. The whole group is still working, which provides a certain amount of anonymity, but there is also a growing individuality.

Elements of preparation and rehearsal are used in this phase. It is a time to try out ideas, which can be abandoned if they do not work, or elaborated on if they do. For participants whose habitual life roles forbid them to try out new ideas or make mistakes this process itself is therapeutic. The context of dramatic exploration helps develop new roles and subvert old patterns.

Stage 5

Preparation moves into improvisation. An abstract set is constructed out of tables, chairs and anything to hand. It may represent a jungle, a garden or a desert to different animals. The group members are invited to don their mask when ready, and to enter the set. They may stay there as long as they like, and see what happens as other animals come onto the scene.

Principles   This is the phase of maximum freedom and maximum risk for the group. The structure allows for personal choice as to how involved each character becomes. There is an unknown element. For the first time the entire group is free to interact from within their roles. The characteristics that were projected onto the masks are now embodied by the wearer of the mask. The intention is that the mask gives permission to enter another role. At the same time it offers the psychological protection of distance. It is the owl which is predatory, watching and swooping. From behind the mask the group member experiences the characteristics of the owl with the protection of the idea that 'This is not me'.

At this point it would be possible to move into a new stage. The group might consider the characteristics of the various animals, and use these to improvise a further scene, based on human roles with the same characteristics as the animal ones. The setting might be a family get together, or passengers on a cruise ship.

This elaboration of the work would give the opportunity for group members to look at the connection between the masked animal characters and situations closer to real life. This is a matter of choice and judgement for the dramatherapist, who might pursue this idea in a future session. The pace of therapeutic exploration is flexible. In this fictional session the therapist decides to remain with the metaphor of the animals.

Stage 6

Reflection and de-roling. When the improvisation is over participants are invited to remove the masks and bring them with them to a circle. The group reflects on the experience in a free flowing way. The therapist asks them to identify something about the role that was different to them and something that was similar. They may also consider whether the role reminded them in any way of someone they know. They may wish to take some aspects of the role away with them, and leave other aspects behind in the group. Each mask is returned to a box in the centre of the group, and group members are invited to take leave of each other.

Principles   At this point in the session the group distances itself from the dramatic roles, initially by removing the mask, and then by talking 'as themselves' about the experience. This process may yield insights into habitual ways of being, and thoughts about what kind of change might be appropriate. The person who played the owl might reflect on one or two people in their own life that they would enjoy swooping down on in the dark, or they may notice that in real life they tend to be victim rather than predator.

It may also be that group members have little energy for applying the experience to their own life. Within the dramatherapy method this may be quite acceptable. Change may be happening gradually through an accumulation of experience, and it might even be considered psychically damaging and counter-therapeutic to shine too bright a light directly onto the significance of the dramatic work to each individual. There is a dynamic between disguise and revelation, and too much revelation may inhibit the therapeutic work. Dramatherapy may take place under cover of relative darkness, while psychodrama tends to shine a torch of conscious awareness into the dark recesses of the psyche.

CONCLUSION

We have looked at two sample sessions, using psychodrama and dramatherapy. Structure is important in both methods. The psychodramatic map gives a precise pattern to the process for the protagonist. The details depend on the history and current problem of the protagonist. The role of the director involves following the map in a way that is relevant to the protagonist. This may mean deviating from the classical map as described, by starting in the locus for example, or by remaining in the presenting scenes for exploratory work throughout the whole psychodrama. The director's first concern is with the protagonist, and the map provides a standard for the kind of journey that may be taken.

In dramatherapy the therapeutic process is sketched more roughly. In a session where the whole group works without particular attention on an individual there may be many roads travelled within the session. The dramatherapist chooses precise techniques to facilitate the group, as the psychodramatist does in guiding the psychodrama, but the dramatherapist does not expect necessarily to complete such an intense psychic journey within the one session. The structures used in the dramatherapy session make it safe for the participants to make some exploration of their inner world and their shared world. The question of change is tackled obliquely and gradually. Participants have the protection of working through metaphor, role or story at some apparent distance from their own issues. This process is similar to children's play. If the session focuses on the problems of an individual in the group then the dramatherapist may well use some of the psychodramatic techniques developed by Moreno for this work. To conduct a full psychodrama requires a separate training, but the methods of role reversal, doubling and mirroring are often used in the context of dramatherapy.

The role of the therapist

The methods differ in pace and in emotional intensity. Consequently, the roles of dramatherapist and psychodramatist are somewhat different. The psychodramatist is also known as the psychodrama director, and the role of the psychodramatist is indeed more directive at a therapeutic level than the dramatherapist's.

The relationship between psychodrama director and protagonist during a psychodrama involves a strong empathic link on the one hand, and a clear analytic mind on the other. The empathic link is essential if the protagonist is to regress to early vulnerable states for psychodramatic exploration. The director must sense their emotional needs, even when the protagonist has difficulty expressing these. At the same time the director is the map-reader. This involves making therapeutic judgements and influencing the direction the psychodramatic journey takes. If too many paths are followed the protagonist may be over-whelmed with material and the journey may not be successfully completed. So the director takes responsibility for guiding the work away from some paths that could be counterproductive or irrelevant to the agreed goals of the psychodrama.

The psychodramatist has particular responsibility in relating the warm-up and sharing parts of the session to the group matrix. The individual works in a sense for the group as a whole, and the psychodrama warm-up and sharing are essential in locating the work in the emerging and changing matrix.

The role of dramatherapist also requires empathy. The therapist must sense the therapeutic potential of each exercise and structure used, and be attuned to the group as a whole, its current mood, and the ongoing themes and concerns. The dramatic structures proposed by the therapist are an invitation to the group to explore the matrix. In the sample session given above, the mask work could reveal group concerns related to aggression, status, freedom, disguise, belonging and a large number of other possibilities, including the ongoing dynamics between the group members. The freedom of the group to explore the mask work is analogous to the free-floating discussion used in group analytic psychotherapy. The themes emerge in the shared space of the action, through an interplay between the participants. The role of the dramatherapist, like the group analytic conductor, is to be sensitive to what is emerging, and if appropriate to make an intervention to enhance the exploration. These interventions, as in group analytic psychotherapy, may focus on the group as a whole or on an individual.

The general sweep of the work is broader than that of psychodrama. This enables the dramatherapist to be less directive and less prominent in the detailed working through of material. There are relatively directive dramatherapists and relatively non-directive psychodramatists, but in general terms the psycho-dramatic method calls for more directive intervention on the part of the therapist.

Summary

I have explored the similarities between dramatherapy and psychodrama, which stem from their common roots in the dramatic tradition.

I have described two sessions as examples of each method and to highlight their differences. These are:

1 The focal point of the session. It is usual for psychodrama to work through one protagonist, as the holder of group concerns, while dramatherapy often focuses on the whole group.
2 Methods used. Dramatherapy draws on any aspect of the full range of dramatic activity as a therapeutic source. Psychodrama exploits the particular techniques developed by Moreno to direct a precise therapeutic journey.
3 The pace and intensity of the therapeutic process. Dramatherapy addresses issues obliquely and gradually, through the use of metaphor and a variety of projective techniques. Psychodrama confronts issues more directly. It defines itself clearly as a psychotherapy, while dramatherapy is as yet ambivalent about this label.
4 The relationship with the group matrix. The group matrix is explored in a free-floating way in dramatherapy. In psychodrama it is identified within the first few minutes of a session and informs the choice of protagonist.
5 The role of the therapist. The nature and pace of the process tends to lead to a more directive therapeutic presence from the psychodramatist than the drama-therapist, who may be more facilitative.

NOTE

1 For a more detailed exploration of the spatial and temporal boundaries in therapy and theatre, see Antinucci-Mark (1986).

REFERENCES

Antinucci-Mark, G. (1986) 'Some thoughts on the similarities between psychotherapy and theatre scenarios', *British Journal of Psychotherapy*, 3(1).
Barham, M. (1992) unpublished document.
Foulkes, S.H. (1990) *Selected Papers*, London, Karnac.
Fox, J. (1987) *The Essential Moreno*, New York, Springer.
Goldman, E.E. and Morrison, D.S. (1984) *Psychodrama: Experience and Process*, Dubuque, IO, Kendall/Hunt.
Grainger, R. (1990) *Drama and Healing: the Roots of Dramatherapy*, London, Jessica Kingsley.
Holmes, P. (1992) *The Inner World Outside*, London, Routledge.
Jennings, S. (1990) *Dramatherapy with Families, Groups and Individuals*, London and New York, Jessica Kingsley.
Landy, R. (1986) *Drama Therapy: Concepts and Practices*, Springfield, IL, Charles C. Thomas.
McDougall, J. (1989) *Theatres of the Body*, London, Free Association Press.
Winnicott, D.W. (1974) *Playing and Reality*, London, Pelican.

Chapter 8

Dramatic play with children
The interface of dramatherapy and play therapy

Ann Cattanach

FINDING THE SELF AND THE WORLD BEYOND THE SELF

I one my mother.
I two my mother.
I three my mother.
I four my mother.
I five my mother.
I six my mother.
I seven my mother.
I ate my mother.

This rhyme is described as 'malicious' in the book *I Saw Esau* (Opie and Opie 1992). The poem is beautifully illustrated by Maurice Sendak, first showing a child crying on mother's lap then a series of drawings of the child gradually eating mother. This is what I might describe as a play therapy preoccupation: what is part of me and what is not part of me, can I really eat my mother or will she eat me?

From the same book, a skipping rhyme:

Mother, Mother, I am ill!
Send for the doctor! Yes, I will.
Doctor, Doctor, shall I die?
Yes, my child, and so shall I.
When I die pray tell to me,
How many coaches will there be?
One, two, three, four . . .

All   Then we're respectable.

This seems to me a dramatic play preoccupation, life, death, a place in the world and an interest in the way the world outside the self functions.

The play therapist plays with children, the dramatherapist stimulates dramatic play with children and the reason for the play and the drama is to help children make some sense of their known world in the safety of created symbolic worlds.

The difference between play and drama in this context is in the relationship between therapist and child and therapist and group and the media used to find the best symbolic way to make the therapeutic journey.

When play and drama are used as therapy by the dramatherapist and play therapist using an arts therapy model then the play and drama are the medium for healing. Play and drama are placed at the centre of the therapy rather than as a stimulus for talking or interpretation. In this form of therapy we move from everyday reality into symbolic worlds through the medium of play and drama.

In individual work with a child, play and drama can interweave according to the needs of the child and the developmental level she has reached. A very young child may not yet have the skill to undertake role-play and dramatic play but often there is a shift from play to dramatic play in the course of one session with a child.

PLAY THERAPY MODEL

In my book *Play Therapy with Abused Children* (Cattanach 1992a) I described four concepts basic to the examination of the use of play as therapy in the context of the arts therapies. These are: first, the centrality of play as the child's way of making sense of their experience and coming to terms with their world; second, the notion that play is a developmental process when the child in play moves backward and forward along a developmental continuum as a way of exploring the self, past, present and future; third, that play is a symbolic process; fourth, that play happens in a therapeutic space which is a physical space and which is also the space between child and therapist.

The centrality of play

Children *have* to play as a way to think things out. Children play to make sense of their experiences, and children in trouble are able to use play to resolve unsolved problems from the past, to cope with present concerns, and prepare for the future and its tasks. Play is the place where the child can learn and develop an understanding of what is 'me' and 'not me', a place where the child can discover their relationship to the world outside the self. Play is the place to sort out and separate out objects and the environment from the self.

Grainger (1990) writes:

I select an object from the outside world and bestow an identity upon it, so that, despite being mine, it now belongs to itself and this first and foremost is achieved by learning to play.

Play as a developmental process

In Chapter 2 of this book, I have described the developmental model of drama-therapy. In play therapy this paradigm is explored through the three developmental stages of play described by Sue Jennings (1990, see also Chapter 6 this volume) as embodiment play, projective play and role-play.

Embodiment play

In play therapy embodiment play is regressive play when the child starts to explore the world through the senses, in the way the baby explores her own particular world. Many children start play with Playdoh, 'slime' or other tactile materials and use them to touch, sniff and smell. Abused children constantly use these materials as a way in to their fearful memories and play in this way for many hours before they feel safe enough to begin to explore their abuse. Other children have never learnt to explore in this way or have adapted to violence by shutting down their senses so the pain is less. If they are safe from abuse it is their delight to be able to go back to the beginning and start again. Oh the delight of getting messy, prodding sticky substances, blowing bubbles, watching water slip through your fingers! I mourn the passing of 'Ghostbusters' and their tubs of ectoplasm, the most perfect 'slime', not too sticky and not too runny, just perfect for messy play.

Projective play

From sensory play, children begin to discover the world outside themselves through toys and objects which begin to be used in play. This is the beginning of symbolic play when children begin to experiment with symbolic alternatives to reality and make-believe play begins.

Role-play

As children develop skill in creating fictional worlds through projective play then dramatic play develops. Role-play begins with self-representation where a child acts events like sleeping or eating in play, not in the everyday context of those activities. Then from playing at being herself the child pretends to be someone else. This kind of play often begins with the child acting herself but also acting for a doll so creating another person's role. From such beginnings the child becomes involved in make-believe play with other children. Schwartzman (1978) described the make-believe play of children in a day-care centre. She says that in order to be a successful player, one must be able to communicate information that simultaneously (and para-doxically) defines one as a player subject (e.g. adopting the play role of witch, mother, etc.) and as a person in the defining social context (e.g. the day-care centre) and therefore a play object. For example a child, Linda, must be able to communicate to other players and that she is both Linda (i.e. a person who leads, dominates and directs activities as she is known for this in the general classroom setting) and not Linda (i.e. a witch or mother in a play situation). So play becomes dramatic play through the paradox of the duality of roles.

Symbolic play

Symbolic play can be described as the use of self, toys and objects to create an 'as if' fictional world in play. In play therapy the child makes fictional worlds which symbolically represent aspects of their experience which the child can explore to make meaning and resolution of those events. At the beginning of therapy the child often spends much time searching for an appropriate symbol for herself and the experiences which she wants to play. I worked with a girl of 5 who wanted to find a character which expressed the abuse she had experienced and, after much play with a variety of materials, she created a blood red snowman, bleeding on the outside but frozen and immobile on the inside. With this character as hero, she made up stories and rituals which explored the meaning of the snowman. This character which she had invented clearly expressed her own feelings about being abused, but because it was a snowman, an object of play and not her, she was appropriately distanced from herself so the explorations were safe for her.

Symbolic play is also part of a developmental process and children learn more complex levels of meaning through symbols and metaphors as they grow. The process starts through play with objects, then making simple action sequences through more complex sequences until the child can transform objects and create make-believe play. When a child can use play in this way then there is a possibility to transcend and transform experience.

The therapeutic space

This space defines both the physical space where therapist and child meet and the psychic space between the two which develops as the relationship grows. Children play in special spaces chosen for their safety, away from the reality world. I remember having a special room in the attic which was especially safe because the door could be bolted from the inside. I could fly up the stairs closely followed by my angry sister, slam the door shut after a struggle, then force the bolt across the door. Oh, the immense feeling of relief when I knew I was safe and could get back to my private world, door shut and bolted, safety assured. This was my space, set apart for my use, where I could explore a thousand different lives.

Children relish these spaces just on the borderland of their social world. The den, the treehouse, the attic, under the table. Many frightened children in care begin to heal themselves through their play under the table, back to the wall, wary eyes looking out but secure under the table top; too difficult for adults to crawl under the table.

Jane, aged 3, had sat and played under the table for eighteen months before we began therapy and in our safe place continued her under-the-table play. She had already begun to heal herself, she needed her experience validated by someone who would listen.

It is important in therapeutic play to replicate the safety of the play space, with boundaries to the space but with access to a more social environment. The child has the choice to play but also access to the social environment. So what is required is a room with space for imaginative possibilities but a way out which the child can control. A room which is too intimidating becomes less safe for the child. Sometimes a room is too big a space so a mat or a corner can be the place on the 'fringes of structured time' as Gersie (1987) describes.

The psychic space between child and therapist is similar to the potential space between mother and child described by Winnicott (1971). Through the developing relationship the child experiences play as being alone but in the presence of someone. The therapist is reliable, is available and continues to be available when remembered after being forgotten. The therapist is felt to reflect back what happens in the playing.

The child can then allow two kinds of playing. Initially the therapist and child can play together but the therapist fits into the child's activities. Then the therapist can introduce her own playing so the child experiences ideas that are not her own. The therapist and child have then established a relationship.

THE PLAY THERAPY PROCESS

When the child first comes for play therapy it is important to establish with the child why they have come and who referred them. I explain to the child that we are going to play together for an hour and that I will tell them when it's time to stop. I will warn them when we have ten minutes left. If children have a limited concept of time, instead of the 10-minute warning, I tell them that there is time to play with just one more toy then we must stop.

I have explained elsewhere (1992a) the kind of materials appropriate for play and ways to give a boundary to the space, according to the facilities offered in the workplace.

Toys should be selected which encourage embodiment play such as Playdoh, bubbles, sand, water. Projective play will need items like small family figures, animals, monsters, puppets and other objects for story-making as well as drawing and painting materials. In play therapy much of the make-believe play is through projective play with toys and objects, but many children enjoy role-play, or acting their stories themselves or with the therapist, so there should be objects, clothes, etc., to facilitate this form of play and encourage role-play.

First meetings

Gersie describes what the therapist observes during the first contact. She states that the therapist is looking for:

1 the generation of information, which can be related to similar children (age group/sex/background), others in the same predicament and to the child herself in other situations;
2 the exploration of presentation and interaction, relevant to the child's situation and experience;

3   a formulation of a tentative hypothesis regarding the child's difficulties and a first attempt at describing likely developments with or without professional intervention of one kind or another;
4   the initiation of relief. Gersie states that it is of paramount importance that we explore how some immediate relief might be offered to encourage the child to sustain the energy needed to overcome her difficulties and to foster her will to do so!;
5   a tentative formulation of a proposal for possible treatment and follow up.

This information can be obtained by talking with the child and making observations of the play during the session. It is important that the child and therapist make a contract about the nature of the intervention: whether it is limited to a number of sessions or ongoing, what is being explored through play and the boundaries of behaviour acceptable to both child and therapist. For example, no hitting is always a rule for me and I boundary my role as therapist; the nurture the child will receive is from the play. I am not the child's carer, I am her therapist.

DRAMATIC PLAY WITH CHILDREN

The concepts which embody play as therapy are equally appropriate for a model of dramatic play with children when used as a healing process.

Drama for healing

The centrality of drama as the healing process, the safe space for the individual or group to meet, the developmental model of embodiment, projection and enactment, the symbolic processes inherent in drama, are all aspects of drama for healing and are dealt with in more detail in Chapter 6 of this volume.

The dramatherapist working with children uses dramatic play to help them make transformations of their experience which enable them to make a shift in their experience. This is the core of drama as a healing process and is experienced when we move from everyday reality into dramatic reality. Sue Jennings (1992) defines this as the human capacity not only to accept but also to create what is not actually there through fictive drama and this lies at the very core of our understanding of dramatherapy.

Dramatic play is the way children are able to transform experience through the symbolic form of the fictions they create. As the group make dramatic action they create a fictional present by using both the remembered past and the imagined future. In dramatic play children can face life experience through the fictions they create and in this fictional present they can try out possible futures or re-work situations of the past but appropriately distanced from the everyday reality by the fictional nature their play. Courtney (1985) describes this process as a way to face life experiences at a functional and symbolic level. Not only do children 'try out' possible futures and 'act out' problems of the past, but they engage in problem-solving in a deep personal way through the fictional present.

Sarah, aged 9, was experiencing difficulties coping with her mother, who had been an alcoholic for some years and was now working hard to stop drinking and have her children back home with her. Sarah expressed her fear of the present each time we met through creating stories and using dramatic play. Her stories were always about islands and through these fictional islands she could make sense of her present predicament. The fiction kept her safe and distanced but the power of her fictional worlds validated her reality experiences. It was interesting to observe the process of her creation. She always made the contours of the islands in slime, enjoying the embodied experience of the actual material. Then she placed figures and objects on the island and finally made enactments in the form of dramatic play or story-making.

This is a description of one of her islands. This island is about being back home with mum. It is always interesting to observe the way children use what they are taught at school. Hadrian was the history topic of the day.

> This is Hadrian's Island. It has a place for bowling next to a place for storing doughnuts, a gym and a TV room. There is a model of Hadrian in the middle of the Island.
>
> There is a bedroom in one corner of the Island, he's built a wall with seaweed as a place to store swimsuits.
>
> Each morning he goes to the model of himself, inspects himself to see if everything is there.
>
> He wants to be how the model is but he is very fat and is disappointed.
>
> Sometimes he swims to see if he can find anybody but he is lost, can't find anybody, because once when he was little, he wanted this and his words came true.
>
> He is looking outside to find a lamp to find his way back home.
>
> He gets furniture from wrecks washed ashore, and paint, to paint his house up.
>
> Sometimes he is happy, and sometimes he has his bad days.

Drama as development

Courtney (1980) describes dramatic action in developmental stages. He defines four stages:

1 The identification stage (0–10 months)
2 The impersonation stage – the child as actor (10 months–7 years)
  (a) The primal act (10 months)
  (b) Symbolic play (1–2 years)
  (c) Sequential play (2–3 years)
  (d) Exploratory play (3–4 years)
  (e) Expansive play (4–5 years)
  (f) Flexible play (5–7 years)
3 The group drama stage – the child as planner (7–12 years)

4 The role stage – the student as communicator (12–18 years)
   (a) Role 'appearance' (12–15 years)
   (b) Role 'truth' (15–18 years)

In each case the later stage has within it each of the previous stages so that the adolescent as communicator is at the same time an actor and a planner.

It is perhaps at the third stage described by Courtney that the therapist would define the therapeutic intervention as dramatherapy rather than play therapy, as the focus of the work changes from the child as individual actor towards group drama where the child learns to share ideas and actions in the group.

Dramatic play as a group process

When children make a group for dramatic play then all the negotiations and interactions which are part of any group with a task apply to this group.

The children will need to negotiate with each other about the way their drama is to develop, who will play the witch and who will play the king and queen, whose ideas are chosen, whose ideas are rejected, how to deal with that rejection. Many processes interweave: the emotional and internal process of each individual, the creative development of each individual, the group dynamic process in the group and the creative development of the group.

Perhaps the most complex understanding in the group is the acceptance of the reality roles and the fictional roles of individuals in the group.

Children are learning these skills and sometimes find it difficult to hold onto their feelings without instant reactive response. Sometimes in the healing process the pain cannot be contained and the play stops. This also happens in play therapy when a child will be exploring a fictional play and suddenly stops. 'I'm not playing that anymore.' It is important that the therapist accepts this as the rules of play which children use when playing with each other.

I remember James, whose father had attacked his mother in front of him on several occasions. He played 'good' families and 'bad' families again and again until he could define his terms to his own satisfaction. When he played 'bad' families enacting some violent behaviour he would say 'I'm not playing anymore' and choose other stories. Sometimes he would say, 'It's too scary' and this is often an explanation I use if I think a child wants me to enact an inappropriate role. Children understand this explanation as part of the rules of play and accept it as a practical reality.

Dramatic play as dramatherapy

When organising a group using dramatic play with children as a therapeutic intervention it is important to define the aims of the therapy and offer the group a focus and a structure which will achieve the therapeutic goals.

Sue Jennings (1990) identified models of practice in dramatherapy, describing four models: (1) the creative–expressive model, (2) the tasks and skills model, (3) the psychotherapeutic model and (4) the integrated model. There are two models of practice which could be the basis of dramatherapy using dramatic play with children. These are the creative–expressive model and the tasks and skills model.

Creative–expressive model

The focus of this model is on the healthy aspects of people and the stimulus of the work is to help individuals and the group to discover their own creative potential in drama. This model uses the forms of play and dramatic play and emphasises communication in the group both verbal and non-verbal. The dramatic explorations in this model are to experience forms of play through the development model of embodiment play, projected and symbolic play to role-play. In this way children have permission to move back and forward along the developmental continuum making fictions which exist in a sequence of time.

This therapeutic form emphasises nurture of the individual and the group. There is no pressure to resolve issues from the past. The focus is to build on the skills of the group and develop self-esteem and a sense of self through exploring what everybody is good at.

I remember a group of three children of 8 who were experiencing difficult family situations. One of the children was an elective mute. The group decided for a time to make up stories using mime and because there was no pressure for Julie to talk she felt validated as a person in the group. The other children negotiated ways of communicating non-verbally and gradually Julie began to talk a little to the other children.

This group was part of Julie's treatment but it became her safe place where speaking was not the only way of communicating although the other children talked endlessly as they prepared their mimes. Julie could still make connections with the other children and be valued for her skill in a specific form of communication because Julie was skilled at mime and the other children included her in their drama because they valued her skill. This model employs the skills that are available in the group emphasising what each individual can achieve and how that skill can be integrated with the skills of the rest of the group.

In this kind of group some children want to re-enact a younger childhood more pleasant than their reality experience. This is often the case with groups of sexually abused children who do not want to explore their past experience of abuse in the group but who want to make stories and be playful in a way not possible in their abusive homes. When their creativity is valued and not distorted or manipulated by adults they can discover that their bodies are not offerings for adult appeasement but belong to them.

I worked with a group of seven children in their first year of secondary school who were finding it difficult to adjust to the experience of a large school. We met in school once a week for a term. Some of the group responded to the experience of school by aggressive behaviour, others had become depressed and a few were frightened. We established rules of respect for each other in the group and no bullying or physical violence. Each session began with a burst of physical activity for those who needed that release of energy, then a quieter game of observation skill. Children who are uncomfortable in their environment are often watchful and so develop a heightened awareness of what exists in their immediate world. I could never achieve their skill in observation so I could gasp in admiration as they showed their skill and they felt good about that.

The group explored themes about hiding your feelings, what you show on the outside and what you feel on the inside. They made masks to express this and used movement and sculpted stories to express these themes dramatically. There was no talking; they found it easier to develop their ideas through a series of images rather like freeze frames in a film. The roles they took were basic stereotypes. From that theme they explored the meaning of the hero male and female from crude macho men to more subtle forms of goodness. Here the shy fearful members of the group were able to express their fear of the boisterousness of the tough talking members. Slowly, little by little, the group learnt to respect each other's skills in drama and learn ways of talking to each other.

There were some small victories. Jim, who responded to reprimands from the Head by smashing up his office, managed to accept a reprimand for his inappropriate behaviour, control his anxiety and leave the room as he found it. June, who found the playground overwhelming with what seemed to her like a mass of children swirling around, managed to make contact with some of her classmates and felt less overwhelmed.

When individuals in the group were treated with respect and everyone learnt to keep to the ground rules for the safety of the group then self-esteem began to grow.

Tasks and skills model

This kind of drama group involves the concept of dramatic play as a rehearsal for living and the task-based group is a place where members can practise the skills needed for everyday life.

The dramatherapist still approaches the task through the medium of play by dramatising situations using fictional characters to explore ways of solving problems of everyday living. An initial part of treatment for sexually abused children can be a programme to help them learn about body boundaries. Making stories and fictional situations is a powerful way for children to learn. The fictional form of the drama means that some characters can get it wrong and in the safety of the role the child can explore strategies to cope. After all that stupid rabbit isn't me but a silly rabbit who we'll have to help in a better way this time.

I worked with another group of adolescents aged from 12 to 15 years who were compulsive stealers and constantly victimised by their peers or siblings. When the children talked about how they were manipulated by their peers they could offer plausible talk about ways they could avoid further difficulties but in creating and improvising scenes about victimisation they found it difficult to resist the role of victim. We explored strategies through drama and they discovered that it was much harder to stay with the strategy in dramatic play than to talk about how they would manage. The children were all fluent verbally and could bend the truth with words but were confronted by their victimisation in dramatic play. The shock of this revelation motivated the group to learn more strategies to be able to cope with pressure from their peers.

THE INTERFACE BETWEEN PLAY THERAPY AND DRAMATIC PLAY

There is a flow and continuity between the processes of play therapy and dramatic play so that one form frequently merges into the other. This can happen in the course of a single session of therapy or as the child moves through the longer therapeutic process.

The child in play therapy uses forms of play which will help the function of playing so sometimes dramatic play is the most appropriate form to contain the metaphor being explored. Then the child and therapist play together, each taking roles to dramatise the story created.

I worked with an 8-year-old girl called Tania who had difficulties making a relationship with her mother. She decided that she wanted to work with fairy stories and chose to act scenes from Little Red Riding Hood, Hansel and Gretel and The Goose Girl.

She chose scenes which reflected her feelings of being overpowered by her parent and scenes where children didn't heed the advice of their mother. In reality, Tania often got herself into difficulties on her journeys to and from school. She found the advice of mother not to stray in the woods most powerful when creating the story of Red Riding Hood and perhaps internalised the advice when she played the role of mother, warning her daughter of the dangers of loitering. Equally, she enjoyed pushing the witch into the oven in Hansel and Gretel.

Tania always used dramatic play after warm-up activities with play materials so in each session she used embodied play and projected play as a means to focus her dramatic play. Dramatic play had the most meaning for her but she needed the stimulus of other forms of play.

Many children in need of help are not used to any kind of play and sometimes the function of therapy in the initial stages is to help the child begin to play. These children need to experience play through all the levels of development and make-believe play will emerge in due course. I worked with John, aged 5, who had no idea how to play with toys but he spent each session taking out play figures looking at them and putting them away again. He enjoyed this activity and gradually we began to make simple connections between the figures until he could invest the figures with symbolic roles. Then for the first time he was able to express his own despair through the play figures. John was not developmentally ready to use himself as a symbolic object in make-believe play so he used materials which he could control and contain.

Many children who have learnt make-believe play would still be unable to function effectively in a small group because they are not ready to cope with the social interactions and still need time in individual therapy. Susan was such a child. She could cope with dramatic play with me but in a small group of her peers was not able to contain her anxiety.

Sometimes, as with adults, it is possible for a child to go to a group for dramatic play after some time in individual play therapy. The therapist will need to assess the best possible way to help heal the child according to the developmental level of functioning, the kind of relationships which the child can contain, how the child wants to play and what the child wants. After all, sometimes it's a matter of what suits best. As the rhyme says,

Up the ladder and down the wall,
Penny an hour will serve us all,
You buy butter and I'll buy flour,
And we'll have a pudding in half an hour.

REFERENCES

Cattanach, A. (1992a) *Play Therapy with Abused Children*, London, Jessica Kingsley.
Cattanach, A. (1992b) *Drama for People with Special Needs*, London, A. & C. Black.
Courtney, R. (1980) *The Dramatic Curriculum*, New York, Drama Book Specialists.
Courtney, R. (1985) 'The dramatic metaphor and learning', in J. Kase-Polisini (ed.) *Creative Drama in a Developmental Context*, Lanham, University Press of America.
Gersie, A. (1987) 'Dramatherapy and play', in S. Jennings (ed.) *Dramatherapy Theory and Practice 1*, London, Croom Helm.
Grainger, R. (1990) *Drama and Healing: the Roots of Dramatherapy*, London, Jessica Kingsley.
Jennings, S. (1990) *Dramatherapy with Families, Groups and Individuals*, London and New York, Jessica Kingsley.
Jennings, S. (1992) 'The nature and scope of dramatherapy: theatre of healing', in Murray Cox (ed.) *Shakespeare Comes to Broadmoor*, London, Jessica Kingsley.
Opie, I. and Opie, P. (1992) *I Saw Esau*, London, Walker Books.
Schwartzman, H.B. (1978) *Transformations: the Anthropology of Children's Play*, New York, Plenum Press.
Winnicott, D.W. (1971) *Playing and Reality*, London, Tavistock.

Chapter 9

The Dramatherapy Venture Project

Steve Mitchell

As we walked towards Kes Tor rock we entered a world of rushing winds and driving rain. The air moved forcefully around, above and through us, as we battled forward, gasping for breath, reminding me of the struggle for survival down the centuries in this harsh wilderness. One by one, we climbed to the top of the rock and stood battling against the ferocity of the wind with arms outstretched, as we let go of all the things in our lives, which were hindering us. Then, we climbed the rock again together and stood in a line holding hands, defying the worst of the blast hurtling towards us, as we shouted together into the wind with a new-found courage. . .

Like forest Indians, we sank silently to the ground, forming the radii of a circle with our outstretched bodies, with our heads towards the centre. Slowly, I closed my eyes and experienced the unfamiliar closeness to the earth mother. The sun shone on my face creating flickering light patterns. On my back, I could feel the dampness of the grass; the lumpiness of the pine cones; the prickliness of the holly leaves. Insects crawled up my arms and swirled around my face, biting me. The earth felt so secure and I felt at one with the source of life and with the medium to which I will finally return. . .

(From the diary of a group member 1990)

INTRODUCTION

The Dramatherapy Venture Projects have as their particular inspiration, the para-theatrical activities of Grotowski's Laboratory Theatre.[1] Here I will expand on these ideas by focusing in what ways para-theatrical activities can be employed as dramatherapy processes when working both indoors and outside.

I will present here a synthesis of two clinical groups, both of whom used this rationale to structure the work. The groups represented two different psychiatric populations: one was an acute out-patient group, the other a rehabilitation group. Both groups were involved in a time-intensive period, a one-week residential, on the edges of Dartmoor National Park. In essence the two groups participated in the same activities, although the out-patient group occasionally worked using more intensive experiences; these I will indicate where appropriate in the text. They both used the elements to give a conceptual framework to the work and they both met to participate in the week-long project. This does not always have to be the case and I will indicate how a dramatherapist might interweave indoor para-theatrical work with an outdoor event at the close of the chapter. I will begin, however, with a section on preparation.

PREPARATION

Administration

The success of any dramatherapy enterprise reflects the process of preparation prior to the running of the group. This is obviously important when you are intending to take a group of clients out of the hospital and into the wilderness. A group leader who has no understanding of wilderness conditions or no respect for the changeability which can so quickly take place should *not* be tempted in any form to work in the wilderness. If the dramatherapist has no training or experience, then they must have as an assistant, a 'guide', who does. The importance of this cannot be stressed enough because it can actually be a matter of life and death. We have all read newspaper reports about leaders who have got lost because they couldn't read a map or compass, and the justified scathing reports by the authorities who are called out and have to pick up the sometimes tragic pieces.

If you intend to take a group deep into the countryside or into the wilderness you must have given the area you intend to work in a thorough reconnaissance. This is not only to discover work locations for 'group experiences' but to know, at every step of the way, all emergency exits – what is the quickest, safest, route to help at any moment during the event. It is also important to know where the nearest telephone, doctor, casualty department, chemist shop or grocery store is. It is also important to plan for the unpredictable, the unwanted scenario, and have in place back-ups for any group casualties – including injuries to the staff team – making sure that in such a situation the rest of the group is left safely managed. This is as much an essential part of preparation as facilitating the practical work of the group. In all dramatherapy work the need to create a safe environment is necessary and no more so when you take clients away from their natural habitat and everyday routines. Hospital management and your own immediate line-management will also require evidence in writing that all these safety factors have been thoroughly entered into, and evidence of procedures in cases of emergency.

As well as concerns for safety, management will be concerned with how the project will be financed – what it will cost. Therefore, the dramatherapist will need to research all aspects of the project and make out a feasibility study which clearly demonstrates the costs of each aspect of the work. I found it useful to organise my budget sheet under the following headings:

1 hire of the centre;
2 hire of transport;
3 fuel for the journey and activities in Devon;
4 food;
5 equipment required;
6 insurance;
7 contingency.

The clients

Once line-management has given the go-ahead, the next task is to publicise the project and organise the selection of clients. The publicity for the project needs to be out six months prior to the project taking place. The feasibility study has to be organised to meet management needs, whereas any publicity put out has to meet another set of criteria. Often, when working from within an institution such as a Psychiatric Hospital and Community Service, referrals for the project will come from other professional colleagues such as consultants, nurses, occupational therapists, CPNs, psychologists and social workers. They are not going to be concerned about costs but about therapeutic factors. Therefore, the language used to convince managers has to be modified and translated into answering concerns about psychological safety and therapeutic rationale. To back up any publicity sent out to teams and departments or specific individuals, you may decide to write or arrange to meet with them. At the meeting you can give a brief outline of the project, answer any questions and guide staff as to the kind of referrals you are seeking. I preferred arranging meetings with teams so that I could respond to their particular concerns and articulate in their particular language or orientation what the therapeutic aims of the project were aspiring towards. I would then leave with the teams a separate leaflet designed for clients.

Selection of clients

In the leaflet I sent out, clients who were interested in taking part in the project were asked to contact me personally to arrange a time when we could meet informally to discuss it further. At this meeting I would tell the client about the project and answer any initial questions. The meeting would last about thirty minutes. If at the end of this time they still wanted to be short-listed, I told them that they would have to attend a formal assessment interview. Before they came to the formal assessment interview they were asked to get permission from their consultant or GP and make a list of medication they took on a daily basis.
     The structure of the formal assessment interviews was as follows:

1 The clients were invited to my office in the hospital by letter – they were asked to confirm the appointment.

2 A list of 15 questions was prepared to cover different aspects of the project.
   • Who is your consultant or GP?
   • Are there any physical/medical problems we need to know about?
   • Any specific dietary requirements?
   • What medication do you take on a daily basis?
   • If you take a depot injection when is it due?
   • Are you travel sick?
   • What outdoor clothing do you have: waterproofs, gloves, sun-hat, walking-boots – what do we need to get you?
   • How do you control sunburn?
   • Regulations relating to alcohol and smoking – will you agree with the ground rules concerning them?
   • Staying together is part of the project – will this pose any difficulties?
   • Who do we contact in case of emergency?
   • Will the pre-group meeting cause any problems?
   • Do you have any concerns or particular difficulties with any of the elements we will be working with: earth, fire, air or water?
   • Is there anything you want to ask or need to know?
   • Are you still interested in participating in this Special Project?
3 One of the assistants to the project took written minutes of each answer, so we had a record and could take action on any point that arose.
4 The interviews were 25 minutes each. Unless there was an outstanding problem, the clients were told immediately at the close of the interview if they were to be invited to participate.

It might be argued that the formal assessment interviews are intimidating and it is true that certain clients were anxious about them beforehand. But they told us later, at the close of the project, that they respected the process and, though it had been a concern at the time, at a later stage in the project it made them feel safe as it was part of the security we had created. Any people the leaders felt would be unsuitable were invited to a separate meeting with me. Here, as with any dramatherapy group that turns down an applicant, we sensitively found alternative possibilities.

Pre-group meetings

It had been decided that one of the important ways of making the clients feel safe would be to meet before departing. We designed four weekly sessions which introduced the group to each other, some of the drama tools they would be working with on Dartmoor, the Centre they would be staying in, the organisation of menus, kitchen rotas, and the checking of personal and work equipment. The format the meetings took was:

Session one

1 A walk together from my office to the church hall.
2 Candle Ceremony.
3 Percussive improvisation.
4 Introductions.
5 Information re Dartmoor, the Centre, travel, etc.
6 Tea and close.

Session two

1 Candle Ceremony.
2 Partner work – introduce partner.
3 Working out menu, kitchen rotas, etc.
4 Tea and close.

Session three

1 Candle Ceremony.
2 Sensory work.
3 Equipment lists.
4 Tea and close.

Session four

1 Candle Ceremony.
2 Baggage check.
3 Equipment check.
4 Preparations for journey.
5 Tea and close.

DAY ONE

The outward journey to Dartmoor

The final session had involved the group bringing to the workspace all their personal baggage as the session took place the day before departure. Everything was checked and stored overnight in the Dramatherapy Office. The group met the following morning, loaded the mini-bus and departed for Devon. This was a 7-hour journey so we stopped at the motorway services approximately every two hours for 30 minutes each time.

Arrival and organization of the Centre

The Centre is an old village infant school which is now used as an Adventure Centre for schoolchildren or adult parties who base themselves there for expeditions on Dartmoor. It has one large room, a small staff bedroom, a large kitchen, an entrance hall, washroom and two outdoor chalets, which in the summer are warm enough to sleep eight people each. Outside there is a complex of outhouses and male/female toilets. At the back there is a grass area which offers space for three or four tents. The Centre offers basic accommodation and when we arrive it is important to transform it to our needs. Each group will transform the Centre in its own way but this usually entails storing the old furniture from the main room in one of the out-houses, and using the main room as a dormitory with mattresses on the floor by night, and as a drama studio by day. Some members of the group will allot themselves sleeping areas in the chalets, the bedroom or put up tents.

Part of making ourselves 'at home' is to unpack not only personal equipment but the food. The main meal of the day is a pre-cooked hot meal which will be kept frozen until the day required. All other meals, breakfast, lunch, snacks and drinks, are the corporate responsibility of the group. One of the first acts on arrival was to put the evening meal into the oven to heat up while we settled in.

The Candle Ceremony

The first session takes place after the evening meal around the cloth which has been laid out in the centre of the 'drama studio'. The Candle Ceremony is a structure that the group had been introduced to from the first preparatory session back in Lancaster. The Ceremony is employed as a ritual to both open and close sessions. It involves the group sitting around the ceremonial cloth, which has a candle placed in the centre. A member of the group is asked to be the Guardian of the Candle each day. Their task is to light the candle and as they do so, if they wish, to perform a short dedication. At the close of the day, the candle is extinguished. The Guardian decides each day how the closure will be performed.

Once the candle has been lit, it is then ceremonially passed round the group. On the first day the participants were invited to share their names. At the Centre the task now takes a different form which is repeated on a daily basis. As the candle is passed from person to person, the group is invited to place any items of business on the agenda. When the candle has completed the circle of the group, each business item is then dealt with. The items can vary from the day's timetable to how to work the showers. It is a time for business matters not for personal sharing about issues which might arise in the work. When the business agenda has been dealt with and any staff announcements have been made, the candle may be passed around again, this time for the sharing of any feelings or personal images the group would like to share.

Before closing the first Candle Ceremony at the Centre the group uses the percussive instruments I have previously laid out on the cloth to create a sound improvisation which will ventilate all the feelings concerning the day's events: leaving home, the long journey, the arrival and settling in, the first meal, the expectations of the event. All these are themes to be shared in our first creative event on the edges of Dartmoor.

The Night Walk

The first experience involves the group taking a walk down the narrow Devon road into a darkened valley lane that follows a noisy stream. The lane is quite dark and only moonlight occasionally filters through the trees that make an umbrella over the road. The group has been asked not to talk unless it is absolutely necessary, to stay together, to experience being with others but also individual, to focus on the sensations of the countryside in the still of the night and only to use their torches or the whistles we had issued if they needed to. The walk lasts about an hour and makes a complete circle back to the Centre. Before returning indoors we stay silently outside, looking into the night, across the valley with mist and the light of the moon dancing on the landscape of mist, cloud, trees and rising hills.

The Candle Ceremony

The experience of the Night Walk closes indoors, with the Candle Ceremony. Each person is given the opportunity to share, as the candle is passed round the circle, how the walk has touched them. Finally, the candle is passed round as an act of closure of the first day. The group is invited to share anything from the day's events. This is followed by the Guardian of the Candle proposing how we should blow out the candle and end the first part of our journey – our arrival in Devon.

DAY TWO: EARTH

The Candle Ceremony

Each day begins with the group meeting around the ceremonial cloth and the Candle Ceremony takes place. After the business agendas have been dealt with, the theme of the day is introduced; on the first day the theme is 'earth'. I explain that as well as 'meeting' the earth directly, I will be employing the theme in terms of each individual 'earthing' themselves in their own physical body so that they can perceive the world from the port-holes of their senses. This leads to the first exercise, indoors, which is concerned with awakening the body to the perceptions of the senses.

Sensory experiences

The work begins with simple movement activities, walking around the room and limbering-up actions, what Mary O'Donnell Fulkerson (1977) called 'easy actions', before going on to exercises based upon the Laboratory Theatre's 'exercises plastiques' (Grotowski 1968).

The group is then asked to find a place to be still and to balance the alignment of their body, then with their eyes closed, to focus on each body part, to contact the sensory impressions in the 'here-and-now', simply to apprehend what they can feel. Experiments are then made, still with the eyes closed with the body in motion, starting with simple steps forward and backward, standing on one leg, jumping on the spot, sitting down and getting up while focusing, with the eyes closed, on their senses. These exercises are then followed with blind walking with a sighted guide leading to a more elaborate 'trust run' theatre exercise where, with your eyes closed you run across the space to be safely stopped by a partner who calls out *'and stop'*.

The development of this body/sensory work involves a contact improvisation I only facilitate if I feel a group can contain the processes of disorientation and tactile intimacy involved. Therefore, it is an exercise I would only structure for an out-patient or training group. The 'experience' begins with the group being asked to lie on the floor, to be aware of breathing, to breathe deeply and to watch what effect this has on sensory information, then to roll over, to stop, breathe deeply, but while breathing to be very aware of the sense impressions coming from all parts of the body. Using this process of rolling and stopping, rolling and stopping, I ask them to continue carefully around the space and to explore all that they find. If during the course of the activity they come across others they are to make real contact with them as if they are feeling the human form for the first time, to carefully, creatively, investigate and make contact, without intruding. To make the exploration like a dance, a *contact improvisation*, I put on some gentle but rhythmic music to inspire these first *meetings*. When it is time to close the exercise I ask them to find each other and, while holding hands in a long line, help each other to their feet. I lead them slowly around the space, then, with care for their safety, outside, and close the first experience of practical work with asking them to feel the sun on their bodies, warming them and nurturing them with its energy, then to shade their eyes from the sun and open them and silently to see, hear, smell, feel and taste what they can receive from the immediate world.

Produce of nature

To close the first session I ask each member of the group to collect a 'produce of nature' and, without showing it to anyone else, bring it inside. For this exercise the group members sit around the ceremonial cloth and one at a time take turns to sit in the centre with their eyes closed while someone else places into their open hands their 'produce of nature'. The person in the centre, using only his or her senses, has to guess what he or she is holding. Finally, the candle is replaced in the centre of the circle, passed round the group, and each client is invited to share his or her experience of the first session.

Trek to the woods

The afternoon session is designed to extend the morning's preparatory work on the *senses* and will involve directly working and making contact with 'the earth'. It begins with kitting-up in outdoor clothing and making sure everyone has his/her waterproofs, emergency whistle and knows how to use it. We then begin our walk in silence (agreeing to speak only if it is absolutely necessary), to the large woods where we will spend the afternoon working outside. It is about two miles.

The Earth Ritual

On arrival in the valley bottom we first dig out of the ground a shallow hollow with our bare hands, making real contact with the earth. We sit round the 'hollow' and pass the loose earth round the group, ceremoniously feeling it and watching it pass round the circle. As the earth is passed a second time from person to person we make statements as to what 'the earth' means to each of us.

A part of the Earth Ritual is for the group members to discover a piece of the earth's *produce* which will symbolise their *Instrument of Power*. I ask each member of the group to think in what way the 'earth' has previously inspired them and what piece of produce could represent this for them, to go off into the woods and to spend some time alone, to be with the Earth in their own way, but when they return to bring a piece of produce as a talisman, to represent their Instrument of Power, something from nature they could take home with them as a reminder of how 'the earth' has the possibility to inspire them. When it is time to return to the hollow I will beat a drum. The group members disperse, for about 30 minutes, to be with the Earth in their own way.

On return the produce that represents their Instrument of Power is laid in the hollow. For a moment's meditation, the group lies down on the ground, first with their eyes closed, then with their eyes open, looking up through the tree branches at the sky above. I ask them to have a sense of the Earth beneath, gravity pressing them down and belonging to the Earth, being part of the Earth. To close the Earth Ritual I ask them to breathe deeply and to exhale six times together, building their energy together and on the seventh breath, to let a sound echo round the valley – as their 'Earth Cry'.

The return

On the way back from the valley the group members participate in a number of activities that have been prepared in the morning session. They are encouraged to walk for a period of time as though 'blind', finding their way along the path, that dips and turns, by listening through their senses. This is then contrasted by walking with the eyes closed with a sighted partner, who guides only by touch – over an extended period. Finally, they move as a group, holding on to each other, with eyes closed, being guided by the leader at the front – again over an extended period. To close this experience I ask the group to drop hands, lead each person some distance from one another and then ask them to use sounds as a way of finding their way to each other. When they have clustered together, using humming as a starting point, they develop the note into their 'Song of the Woods'. From here the group walks quietly the mile along the Devon lanes back to the Centre for the evening meal and a well-earned break.

The Ceremony of the Instrument of Power

The evening session takes place on the open moor just before dusk and nightfall. The event is concerned with ritualising in a natural stone circle the receiving of positive healing energies symbolised by their objects from 'the earth'. This is the first contact with the open expanse of Dartmoor. Silently, they walk out onto the moor to the stone circle. Here, each participant devises his or her own ritual employing the following framework.

The first *initiate* chooses someone from the group to enter the stone circle to be their helper. The initiate will then choose a particular place in the circle where their ritual is to be located. The initiate then gives his/her Instrument of Power to the helper and instructs the helper *how*, and with *what words* the helper is to speak and how they are to give them the Instrument of Power. For example, the initiate might wish to be approached across the circle and receive the Instrument of Power while kneeling with the Helper saying, 'Carol I give you this *stone from the Earth* to be your Instrument of Power which will help you express your angry feelings with your partner.' The helper is given these actions and words and then follows the initiate's instructions exactly. Once the initiate's ritual has been completed, the initiate and the helper then join the group clustered outside the stone circle, who have been observing the ritual as witnesses. The initiate's final duty is to choose the next member of the group who will take the role of initiate.

Earth Walk

The final action of the Earth Ritual involves the group members being invited to take a barefoot walk around the perimeter of the stone circle, one at a time, and while doing so meditating on ways they could use their Instrument of Power to find the courage to fulfil their needs in everyday life.

Dusk is falling; it is time to leave the moor to the ponies and sheep, to the night . . . sometimes there is a spectacular sunset. . . . The group members during this experience have taken their first steps into the wilderness and breathed into their bodies the vitality that Dartmoor has to offer. Tomorrow they will return.

DAY THREE: AIR

I explain that yesterday we had prepared 'the body' and then moved outside to explore the body's relationship with the Earth. Today we will be extending the work by using the body to interact with the environment through the Air we take into the body and the air we breathe out from the body. Therefore, the work indoors will be concerned with exploring and expanding our capacities to breathe and using the breath to interact with the world.

Voice work

The Grotowski Laboratory Theatre states that to work with the voice you must first work with the body to open the physical energies which will give the voice its resonance, depth and power (Grotowski 1968). So we begin with a limber-up developing the 'exercises plastiques' that were introduced yesterday. The group members begin by focusing on the energy they experience in their bodies and using this as the dynamic to develop movement using the 'Details and Elements' of the physical exercises to animate their inner life (see Grotowski 1968). To add to this awareness of their inner dynamic I ask them to concentrate on how they are breathing. This is evolved in a number of ways, one of which is for the group members to work with the exercises while singing aloud a song they all know and to observe the breaks for breath, how deeply they are breathing and in what way the form of an exercise affects how they exhale the breath.

The limber-up with a song is how the group make the transition from body work to vocal work. The voice work involves first technically making experiments with expanding the depth of breath by taking it deep into the torso and expanding the ribs at the side, and going on to explore the energies of the body by expressing it through the vocal range of the voice. This means first introducing the group to the body resonators before employing them with images to give expression to energies held in the body.

I find as a dramatherapist that using the voice to release unconscious issues into consciousness is a very powerful tool. Therefore, it is important for the therapist to teach clients the *form* of an exercise with images that are not emotive before encouraging its use with affective material. In so doing, the client is learning what will become a ritual process, a scaffolding that is safe for them to invest with the chaos of emotional life. A teacher of mine, Paul Rebillot, advocates in the process of a transformation ritual, to 'trust' the body to know the way to healing (Rebillot 1993). I would agree with this but also emphasise that it is important first to write into what Grotowski (1968) calls 'the body memory' the journey you wish to take. It then becomes available to you as an unconscious pattern in those moments when your concentration is engaged with emotive images. At this phase of the project, during the voice work, I am concerned therefore with first teaching a form of voice work which will externalise interior energies with images that have no personal affective contents; second, preparing the clients through breath and voice work with expressive resources they might draw on in later *organic improvisations*.

The Voice Cluster

An 'organic improvisation' is what might be called an open-ended event, where those taking part agree to a particular frame of reference. In para-theatrical work this involves using theatre forms of expression – body, voice, interplay, interaction – to animate here-and-now perceptions. To teach the possibilities of this kind of improvisation we close the indoor work with a structure I call the Voice Cluster. This experience involves the group forming a cluster of upright bodies in the centre of the space. From humming a shared note, this slowly evolves into open sounds that become the song of the group. This is a process that has to be taught, for rather than making open sounds, often group members will start to make sounds that are moulded in the voice box rather than natural sounds. Another difficulty which has to be overcome is if the group try to consciously guide the sounds towards melodies they with to impose. Once the group has discovered the mechanics of the experience, then the Voice Cluster can become its own ritual for containing and expressing the unconscious voice of the group, where ventilation of individual issues can be invisibly expressed, and support can be experienced in a collective way.

The Expedition

In para-theatrical work, where a group primarily evolves experiences outdoors, the 'Expedition' is one of the central ways that The Laboratory Theatre help the participants *disarm*, to be open and present rather than hiding behind a whole arsenal of roles, social rituals and personal games. This 'culturalisation', Grotowski states, becomes like a dead skin that hardens and dictates behaviour between people (for a more detailed examination of 'disarming' see Mitchell 1992; Kumiega 1987). The aim of para-theatrical work is to develop the circumstances in which an individual can 're-educate the self' (Grotowski 1980), to create the conditions where a participant can be open and present, to *meet* and *respond* rather than to act and dictate or to be endlessly searching for non-existent 'goals'. In so doing, Grotowski maintains, we 'liberate energies' and experience the 'fullness' of our being. The purpose of the Expedition is to use the process of travelling over a natural terrain to awaken the senses, to use the inspiration of nature to work its magical power on the psyche.

The Expedition on Dartmoor takes about three hours and takes place in silence. The group is asked only to speak if it is vitally necessary. The reason for this is explained:

> Each person will experience the journey in their own unique way. At times it will be delightful, at other times hard. It is important for each person to stay with his/her own process whatever that process is and not have the intensity of it either contaminated or directed by someone else's point of view. By staying silent each participant will see, hear, feel, taste and touch his/her own associations rather than fragmenting them by continually sharing what he/she is

perceiving. If the intensity of the experience is too alarming or some other difficulty arises then we ask you first to approach the staff or, in cases of emergency, to attract attention by using your whistle.

The staff will be strategically positioned, one leading, guiding the way, one in the middle and one at the rear keeping an eye on the tail-enders. The group is also asked not to crowd one another physically during the journey, but also not to lose sight of one another. Before we depart we discuss the dangers of walking in the wilderness, how the weather can change quickly, how disorienting the distances can be and how rough the terrain can become. They are encouraged to breathe in the Air and allow the Elements to inspire their journey.

The Expedition begins at the stone circle where the previous evening the group members ritualised the receiving of their Instruments of Power. From there, the group travel within sight of the edges of the moor to a large outcrop of rock called Kes Tor. Weather conditions will dictate how near or how far from the edges of the moor the group's path will take. Often the wind is very strong, and it it's a head wind, driving into your face, progress can be difficult. If it's from behind, the journey can be easier. Rain can come at any time and, when mixed with the wind, even a light shower can necessitate full waterproofs and make the going much tougher.

The Ceremony of Wishes

Dartmoor has many legends and folk tales; one involves Kes Tor. It states that if you can climb to the top of the Tor, when the wind makes it difficult to stand, stand upright with your arms out-stretched, call out your wishes without being tumbled over – your boon will be granted! In the Venture Project I use this folk legend to furnish the Ceremony of Wishes. For reasons of safety the group members climb Kes Tor with a partner and stand together, making their 'wish'. The Ceremony is optional, those who prefer not to participate are not forced to do so. After the Ceremony, we close with the Earth Cry together on the summit of Kes Tor. This is often one of the highlights of the project for some of the clients, where they 'meet' the wind and use their own 'air' to reclaim their own power. Before leaving the open moor we eat our snack lunch in the lee of Kes Tor.

Ritual of Air

Before we walk the valley path back to the road and the Centre, we have to cross the river by a narrow wooden bridge. Here the Ritual of Air takes place. Each member of the group is invited to cross the bridge with his/her eyes closed and to imagine that in so doing he/she is taking into their body the air of Dartmoor which will inspire him/her towards changing something they would like to change in life. But for this to happen they must first take their courage in hand, be aware what they wish to change, and walk across the bridge.

The process of 'ritual' in para-theatre

For a long time when I was studying drama I wondered about the mechanics of the ritual process but have discovered that, like drama itself, it can be said to be the framing of a life experience. Give an everyday action a 'sacred' intention and you have a ritual process. This is not quite true. For an act of life to transform into a ritual process, not only must it be framed in a particular way but involve an obstacle that requires an act of courage from the initiate, a moment of risk where consciousness, by surmounting the obstacle, enters into what both Eliade (1958) and Turner (1982) have called 'liminal time', a space between, where concrete thinking is loosened, because the initiate is totally absorbed with the action of the ritual process. In primitive societies, the 'liminal' time was often achieved because the ritual contained harsh and painful elements which, through the nature of the pain, engaged the initiate with the present. In so doing, the initiate let go of a particular image, surrendering to the immediacy of the present action which, at its close, again grounded the initiate in his or her everyday consciousness but with a changed perception. The change had taken place because the initiate believed that the symbolic action of the ritual would bring this to pass.

Therefore it might be said that a ritual is a framed act of life that the initiate invests consciously with a particular meaning. This particular meaning is separated out. For example, 'I want to be able to express my anger.' The initiate agrees with the 'as if' action: 'If I cross this bridge with my eyes closed, this very act will move me towards what I want to be able to do.' Then in the action of crossing the bridge, attention is focused towards overcoming the obstacle 'keeping balance, not letting the sound of crashing water overwhelm me and tempt me to open my eyes, not falling off the bridge, the bridge's length seeming endless', then arriving and remembering that the reason for the trial was to have the courage to express anger. Here a possibility has been carved into the synapses of the mind through a process of experiencing. It is via this symbolic process of 'experiencing' that the potentiality for change, the potentiality for healing can take place. For, as Jung reminds us, the psyche will accept symbolic material, and it is this which is at the very heart of therapeutic process – it is this that is at the centre of ritual. However, we must remember, as Paul Rebillot (1993) reminds us, 'the ritual is not the change itself, but the inner preparation for change'.

The close of Day Three

By the time the group members return to the Centre everyone is tired; they have been out in the elements for five hours. Now is a time for rest, sleep, tea, a hot shower and supper, after supper, the Candle Ceremony and the sharing of the day's events. The rest of the evening is free. For most client groups this means a visit to the local hostelry! In para-theatrical work such a trip would not take place. In a dramatherapy group, over an intense time period and after a hard day's work I feel it's important to have a break at the mid-point of the project.

DAY FOUR: FIRE

Exploring the inner fire

The session begins around the central cloth. Laid out on the cloth are a number of different percussive instruments, around the edge some candles and candle-holders. The first task of the group members involves lighting their candle and securing it in a candle-holder (to symbolise the need for care and safety when working with fire).

The group discusses how fire could be likened to anger and aggression, how it could flicker into life or flare up, be useful or cause damage. To illustrate this the group members use the percussive instruments and begin to investigate how, through making sounds, they could impersonate creatively the inner fire of anger, rage and aggression. The result of this 'organic improvisation' is a 'drumming circle' experimenting through the use of percussive instruments with ways of ventilating aggression.

The Power Animal

Each person lies down on the floor and through a process of visualisation explores the animal kingdom to find an animal he/she admires for the way it expresses its aggression. From visualising it, they begin to find in their body the form, the physicality of that animal, to express in gesture and motion the power of the animal as they move on-the-spot with their eyes close (I accompany their work with a rhythmic drum beat). I ask them to discover a repeatable movement, as their animal, and to use sound to express the vitality of the animal's inner fire. This part of the exercise closes with the group members making personal sculpts of their animals. These are then shared in partners: first by showing their final sculpts and then moulding their partners in the sculpt. The partner exercise closes with each partner sharing the qualities they admire in the way their animal expresses its aggression. We then come back to the large group and share round the group the animal they have been working with and what the essence of the animals' 'inner fire' can inspire in their own ways of dealing with anger.

The Fire Dance

To close the morning session we create our own 'fire dance' using the processes we have been working with. Depending on the group we either create masks depicting our 'power animals' – that will be worn in the dance – or I ask the group to make a picture that will be hung on the wall. The picture in some way depicts the essence of the 'power animal'. Then, using the percussive instruments to create rhythms, the masks and the spirit of the animals, we being to devise the 'Fire Dance'. To get this going I take a directive role side-coaching from within the dance, calling out the movements or modelling the actions of the dance, while encouraging them to embody through the moves the characters of their 'power animals'. The aim of the 'Fire Dance' is to offer a creative and physical form to ventilate any feelings that the morning's work has put them in touch with. I encourage strong physical actions, once the form of the dance has been learnt, closing with a gradual letting go of the 'power animal'. We close the session with the sharing of any feelings and by extinguishing the candles that had been lit at the start of the session.

The Give-away

The afternoon session takes place outside in the woods where the Earth Ritual took place. The experience is based on an American Indian 'Give-away Ceremony'. The group is asked to collect 'dead' wood and to build a cairn in the centre of a clearing and to invest the 'dead' wood with parts of themselves, parts they would like to let go of – thus creating a psychological attachment to the wood. Once the cairn has been built, I intensify the experience by asking the group members to search for dry dead wood and to bring a small bundle to the cairn and to invest their bundles of dry wood with specific aspects of themselves they would like to 'let go'. When the wood has been collected I ask them to join up with two others and make a small fire in a safe place, once the fire is burning to watch the flames and see if any meaningful pictures arise for them. Once the exercise is complete we return to the Centre for tea.

The Fire Ritual

The afternoon, in some ways, has been a preparation for the evening session when the group returns to the cairn for the 'Fire Ritual'. This first involves lighting a barbecue and cooking some food, preparing hot drinks, some soup and tea, while the sun is going down. The cairn is fired and using the percussive instruments we drum the flames to life and with the help of our 'power animals', the steps of the Fire Dance we had created earlier, devise further elaborations around the fire.

Vigil

When the sun has set, the only light comes from the burning cairn, or the moon, bathing the valley in shadowy light. In this setting those group members who wish to take part in the next experience are invited to do so. The experience involves leaving the fire and walking into the wood until they can no longer see the fire. The task for those who go into the shadows will be to take some ashes from the cairn and bury them in the wood. Once this act has been completed they are to wait in the dark and listen to the night until they feel ready to return to the fire. (Each person who leaves the fire takes a torch and whistle with him/her in case of emergency.) The signal to return to the fire will be the sound of drumming made by those who prefer to stay near the smouldering fire. On their return, they join the Drumming Circle until the whole group has returned.

The Circle of Stories

The group members sit round the fire and share a personal true story that they have never told before, expressing their wounds and receiving support from the group. The story-telling closes with the group huddling round the embers of the cairn and then as a group stamping-out the dying fire and finally sprinkling water and then earth over the soil where their cairn has been.

Walk by Fire

Before the fire has been put out each person lights a wax taper. These are now used, with the moon to help us, to see our way, with all our equipment, out of the wooded valley and back to the mini-bus. In this manner we return to the Centre and close the night's activities.

DAY FIVE: WATER

Walking the Water

The group travels to Fernworthy Forest to begin the experience of Water. Here, the group follows a stream from the reservoir, through the forest to the open moor. The stream is followed until it joins a small river. The group now follow this river downstream. We enter the river and jump from rock to rock. We walk in the water itself. Then in pairs, with one partner guiding the other with their eyes closed, we make our way down the river – at a certain stage the partners swap.

The next stage of the experience is an invitation to those in the group who wish to go one step further: a rope is laid along the river over and around rocks, in and out of the water, over some distance. Individually, with their eyes closed, clients enter the river holding only the sash-line to guide their journey down river. Apart from the cord they are alone with the river – unless they choose to open their eyes. When they reach the end of their journey, which leads them on to a bank, each person is met and led (still with the eyes closed) to the remainder of the group. First they are wrapped in blankets and have their feet dried, given hot tea (from a flask prepared for the occasion) and finally cradled and hummed to by the group. When they are ready, they open their eyes and reflect on the journey they have made. The group then ready themselves for the next person who is to 'walk the water'. Once all who wish to participate in this 'ordeal' have done so, the group makes its way back to Fernworthy Reservoir for a picnic lunch.

Lydford Gorge

The afternoon session begins the gradual process of re-entry into the everyday world by visiting a natural beauty spot cared for by the National Trust – Lydford Gorge. Here, the group members will not only be 'meeting' nature as they walk down the deep Gorge cut out by the river through the ages, but also come into contact with the general public. After four days away from the 'buzz' of daily life, mixing with people again, for the first time, and watching the exchanges people make with each other can itself be illuminating.

The trek along the Gorge is done together in silence. We are a group amongst others. I ask the group members not to go out of their way to make contact with the public, but if greeted by them to be appropriate without losing an awareness of the experience. The Gorge is in a deep valley which is approached via a path that winds along the top through a wooded landscape, the crashing flow of the river over the rocks out of sight below an ever-present reminder of the theme of Water. There are two main features: at the start White Lady Waterfall and at the end the Devil's Cauldron; between them the path follows the river upstream around huge rocks, sometimes elevated above the river ten to fifteen feet, with precarious ledges, slippery with water trickling down the rock-face that towers above. Ever present is the crashing or ebbing of the flowing river. The journey from the elegance of the waterfall takes about one hour to the Devil's Cauldron. This is a pool of swirling water in a deep rocky cave which has to be approached on specially hung planks above the swirling water; the sound of water in the cave is deafening but can be wondrous to behold.

For clients who have a fear of water or heights this experience may be too alarming and they may choose to remain with a member of staff at the café at the entrance to the Gorge. At the close of the experience the group returns to the Centre for the evening meal before the final activity of the day.

The Ceremony of Purification

The final experience takes place at dusk on the open moor and involves using water to symbolise a process of healing. It begins with a walk in silence to the river where this 'healing ritual' will start. On the journey the group members are asked to meditate on what they would like to let go of in themselves or integrate in a new way. At the river, focusing on this image, they cross the river to a small island where they are asked to find a stone that can symbolise this part of themselves and to return to the group with it. When everyone has collected his or her stone the group makes the short journey to the stone circle – where the ceremony of the Instrument of Power took place. As a group they enter the stone circle and make an inner circle of stones. Each person in the group is invited to describe his or her stone and share its personal meaning. The group then returns to the stream and searches in the stream for a second stone to represent a new possibility. Once more we return to the stone circle and each person exchanges the first stone for the second one. This is accomplished by each person entering the stone circle and first throwing his or her first stone as far as they can onto the moor, anointing the second stone and making a statement to the group concerning how she/he will make a practical step in his or her life to realise the stone's symbolic meaning.

We close the ceremony with the Voice Cluster, creating a group sound in the stone circle on Dartmoor. When the 'song' is finished, as at the close of the first full day, we leave the moor to the night.

DAY SIX: THE FINAL DAY

The last full day continues the process of re-entering the everyday world begun the previous day, by having a structure where the clients can choose the events of the day. In the evening, the group will meet to prepare and take part in the Closing Ritual, an entertainment that looks back at the significant moments of the project, but the day is for them to decide what takes place. At the closing Candle Ceremony of the previous day, I began to gather possible *propositions* from the group as to what they might do – shopping, sight-seeing, swimming or revisiting a Dartmoor location. At that time nothing was decided, simply suggestions made that could simmer over night. At the Candle Ceremony in the morning the decisions are made.

The group's proposals

On most occasions these involve a shopping expedition to one of the local towns, a picnic lunch on the moor followed by a visit to the sea or to one of the other sights of Dartmoor. Sometimes the group splits up, with one group staying at the Centre while another goes out to a particular location; as long as there is staff to cover such eventualities, it is possible to meet such propositions. More often than not the group wants to stay together and activities are decided upon which incorporate everyone's needs.

The Closing Ritual

This event takes place after the evening meal on the final day and for the most part is devised by the group members. They are asked to prepare an organic improvisation which will illustrate the highs and lows of the entire project, to incorporate into the work the five elements and to give voice to how they might use what they have gained from the work in their daily lives. It may take place in the Centre or at one of the locations the group has been to during its stay. The aim of the Closing Ritual is to re-enact important and vital moments of their stay in dramatic terms; how they choose to do this, in what style or mood is up to the group members. Often different group members will approach the event in different ways and their contributions will reflect their personalities. Poems are read, parody and comic turns take their place alongside the moments of deep illumination, sharing and sadness that the project has come to an end.

The Ritual usually concludes with another journey, to the pub! Here we celebrate informally the closing of the week on Dartmoor.

DAY SEVEN: THE HOMEWARD JOURNEY

The Candle Circle

The group meets formally for the last time. If the Closing Ritual has not dealt with sharing the positives and negatives of the week's experience or the making of personal statements of how they might practically employ the experience of the week in their daily lives, they are asked to do so as the candle is passed round.

The business of the day is concerned with how we will clean the Centre, pack the mini-bus and make our journey home.

CONCLUSION

To close this account I would like to note that on certain occasions a drama-therapy group using a para-theatrical model for groupwork has first worked indoors within their Community for six months and then spent a long weekend outdoors. Such a group employs the format of work I have described elsewhere (Mitchell 1992) for the period of time it meets on a weekly basis prior to using some of the structures and processes I have described above. The advantage of a group meeting prior to going away is that the group members know each other well before going away. The disadvantage might be that it excludes certain people who can't attend the weekly group by leaving their homes and families for a long weekend and that it gives less time for the group to work together in the chosen outdoor location.

NOTE

1 This chapter is a companion to Mitchell (1992) which illustrated in what ways para-theatre can be employed dramatherapeutically in closed out-patient groups.

REFERENCES

Eliade, M. (1958) *Rites and Symbols of Initiation*, New York, Harper Torchbooks.
Grotowski, J. (1968) *Towards a Poor Theatre*, New York, Simon & Schuster.
Grotowski, J. (1980) *The Laboratory Theatre: 20 years after: A Working Hypothesis*, Warsaw, Polish Perspectives.
Kumiega, J. (1987) *The Theatre of Grotowski*, London and New York, Methuen.
Mitchell, S. (1992) 'Therapeutic theatre: a para-theatrical model of dramatherapy', in S. Jennings (ed.) *Dramatherapy Theory and Practice 2*, London, Routledge.

O'Donnell Fulkerson, M. (1977) *Language of the Axis*, Dartington Theatre Papers, First Series No. 12.

Rebillot, P. (1993) *The Call to Adventure: Bringing the Hero's Journey to Daily Life*, New York: HarperCollins.

Turner, V. (1982) *From Ritual to Theatre*, New York, Performing Arts Journal Publishing.

Chapter 10

What is dramatherapy?

Interviews with pioneers and practitioners

Sue Jennings

INTRODUCTION

This chapter consists of interviews with major innovators in dramatherapy – Gordon Wiseman, Robert Landy, Mooli Lahad and Pamela Mond – and looks at how they came into the field in the first place, and the thinking and experience behind the application of their methods. I first interviewed Gordon Wiseman, who has a long history of working in this area. Gordon and I first worked together in 1966 when we took the Remedial Drama Group to hospitals, children's homes and special schools. Coming from a theatre background, Gordon was initially interested in translating the theatre experience into direct work with children, especially in his theatre-in-education work. Robert Landy is the major pioneer of drama therapy (two words in USA) in America. He started off in the theatre but also as a teacher, so has always had a practical approach as well as an academic one. Mooli Lahad started as a psychologist, but became involved in drama and play therapy very quickly. He has developed an important assessment method using fairy tales. Pamela Mond graduated in dramatherapy in Israel and achieved a distinction for her innovative research with the siblings of children with severe learning difficulties.

All the people I interviewed have been innovators themselves, both in the early development of dramatherapy and, more recently, in the new generation.

INTERVIEW WITH GORDON WISEMAN

Gordon Wiseman was a pioneer in both Theatre-in-Education (TIE) and Drama-therapy when both were breaking new ground in the 1960s. His particular specialism was the bridge-building between TIE, people with special needs in schools and dramatherapy. He is now a freelance dramatherapist, who works in hospitals, schools and theatre companies. He is Consultant to South Manchester College for a new dramatherapy training programme in the northwest, as well as a tutor and advisor to the Institute of Dramatherapy.

SJ   As one of the founders of dramatherapy, would you like to look back at the steps that took you there?

GW   I was originally going to go and study Law at Glasgow University, but I then decided that I was going to go to drama school as I'd got so interested in this whole area of creativity. I applied to the Royal Scottish Academy of Music and Drama and I got in, for which I was highly delighted. Drama school was a whole new ball-game for me: instead of being repressive and controlling like my secondary school, it encouraged my creativity; it encouraged me to explore myself, my thoughts, my feelings, my emotions, to translate them objectively and to present and share areas with other people as an actor, as a performer.

    I was lucky enough, after drama school, to go straight into repertory theatre, and I went to the Belgrade Theatre, and there, for a while, the business of theatre was enthralling – the rehearsal process, the excitement of 'a part', looking at situations, looking at interaction, looking at human behaviour, trying to make sense of it, trying to bring that into your character – all those areas were very exciting, and indeed the structure within that which is the structure of the play. But I found that after a while, for me, something was missing because although I loved this research and rehearsal and exploratory process, the process of the rehearsal, once it came to performance, after the initial 'buzz' of acclaim from your audience, and once you'd established the basic technique to put across the part you were playing within the structure, it became static, and although there was that lovely sort of interplay with the audience, it didn't go further than that, and for me there was just something missing and I didn't know what it was.

    And then, by accident, I happened to meet the very first Theatre-in-Education company in the country – The Belgrade Theatre-in-Education (TIE) in Coventry. They'd been going for about six months and were interested in evolving new forms of theatre, but they were actually going back to very old forms of theatre; however in Britain at that time they were considered new forms – forms of theatre which had been introduced by great pioneers such as Brian Way and Peter Slade. The TIE Company wanted to develop a way of working in which the audience became part of the play structure: in other words, the audience could participate in the piece of work. So they evolved what has now become known as Theatre-in-Education: a structure in which the actors took on roles within a story-line – and that could be a traditional legend such as Jason and the Golden Fleece or it could be a documentary such as the Tay Bridge Disaster – these are early pieces that I was involved with; or it could be some social issue such as noise, pollution and so on. The kids would be themselves, the actors would be in-role, and the actors would interact with the kids and challenge them to explore those different areas.

    I was asked to join when one of the company members left. Initially, I was very scared because I'd never worked in that way before and I hadn't worked with young people before. I joined the company and suddenly that final link that I'd been looking for was there. It was a sharing process, a two-way process that, as a performer, as a creative person, you could create something, share it out with an audience or a group, and they bounced it back and, within role, you had to then bounce back again; and so the two-way interactive process was in play. This was very exciting.

I also started to run young people's workshops and explored the areas of improvisation and theatre games, using all the things I'd learned at drama school. A very significant thing happened while I was working for the TIE company: we'd advised on some projects specifically for quite a wide range of special schools – both those with young people with severe learning disabilities and those with emotional problems. And it was noted that when we went into the dramatic structure, these young people became 'engaged'. I believe passionately that creativity allows us to explore our positive potential: it doesn't look for the bad areas within us and therefore label us, it looks for the positive areas and encourages those.

One classic incident was with a young lad who was terrified of heights, and he wouldn't even in the junior classes step on and off a tiny bench. In a dramatic structure about a ship, someone said, 'Oh, there's an island over there, climb up the rigging and find out if it's there.' This young lad suddenly zooms up the wall-bars, right up to the top, and looks through an imaginary telescope towards this imaginary island and then comes running down again and says, 'Yes, there's land ahead.' That young lad had never got off the ground more than half an inch in his entire school career.

There was the young girl who hadn't spoken for six months in a special needs group in a special school, dramatising in a context where she had to help a character through a difficult situation: suddenly, she spoke – she gave advice.

These weren't miracles – these people tapped into something that motivated them; their spontaneity was encouraged and they were released for a moment from whatever was blocking them.

There was then, of course, a lot of hard work to reinforce that, to encourage and develop. That first tiny step forward was vitally important. Teachers and group workers were often amazed at some of the things that happened within those special education projects.

But then, I think probably the most significant part of my development happened. I went to a party and I met you, Sue Jennings, and I remember we happened to bump into each other. It was all a bit crowded and we just started chatting about drama, theatre, areas in common, and you told me about some of the work you'd been doing abroad in large hospitals like Wittekindshof in Germany. I was very interested. I said, 'Well, I've been doing some similar work' and I explained some of the work I'd been doing in Theatre-in-Education and in special schools, and immediately there was a synthesis of ideas and practice.

And so, well, for me the rest is history: we got together and we worked together in those early days, going abroad, working with a range of severe disabilities and remedial and hospitalised groups, exploring the use of drama structures, creative work with 'the horrible labels of the disadvantaged' – that was the biggest step forward for me. So that's how I came from the theatre into therapy.

SJ I think, one thing you've always been clear about: however much reading you do and however much thinking you do, you're not a person to write articles or record your experience. So, I'd be interested for you now to develop your own philosophy of drama-theatre-therapy.

GW Yes, it's very much about using drama and theatre to encourage creativity, a spontaneous energy, but also to enable us to look at areas of importance and help us to sort out who we are, where we are, perhaps even why we are, and enable us to use all of that growth, all of that learning, all of that knowledge to develop forward as human beings, and as human beings to share with each other and work co-operatively, as opposed to being individualistic and being competitive and closing ourselves off.

SJ But then we do that in theatre as well?

GW In the theatre people have an experience together, they all perceive, feel, think, observe different things throughout that experience, but at least they have a *common core* that they can then discuss, agree, disagree. But in dramatherapy they've had a *collective communal experience* – this experience goes way back to ancient times when people would sit round a fire and would tell stories, or people would celebrate together a birth, a death, a getting-together for partnership; depending on the culture, they would get together to worship the rising of the sun, the rain coming in the rain forests so necessary for life's preservation – it goes back as far as that.

The whole area of dramatherapy is about encouraging people to work practically together – to explore together their creativity, their energy, their problems, their aims, their joys – all those areas that are integral to us as human beings, and – you can hear the ghost of Augusto Boal[1] here!– there's only one area that I've found, in therapy, that does that so well, and that is the area of dramatherapy, which is why I'm very proud to have been part of it from the early beginnings.

SJ Quite apart from the healing process you've talked about and the shared experience, also there is a political dimension to dramatherapy: you talk about competitiveness and individualism and passivity in society don't you? Would you like to talk a bit about that?

GW This is where my respect for a ghost of Boal comes in, and his development of political theatre or *politicised theatre*. I've always been interested in that, right from the days of Theatre-in-Education, which not only explored myth, legend and fantasy, but also explored issues of immediate concern. Boal would say that theatre helps us to learn about ourselves and helps us to make decisions for ourselves, decisions that are going to enable us to function well within the world.

Now I believe that an absolutely essential factor of dramatherapy is the exploration, the creativity, the sharing of experiences. But that is only a part of it; the second part is using what we've learned in order to progress as human beings in this world and indeed help to change this world. I think Theatre-in-Education and dramatherapy are quite subversive: they challenge the status quo, particularly areas of the status quo which are oppressive, or unjust, or unfair. Dramatherapy has to be concerned with issues of gender, sexism, racism, and it has to be concerned with areas of political ideology in that we want to make this a better world. We're facing immense problems as we hurtle towards the twenty-first century: we see breakdown in communications; at the same time we see some areas of the world opening up. We have the whole awareness now of the planet, the limited lifespan, and we have to look at conservation, not destruction. Dramatherapy has to look at how we can learn to grow and develop positively together and to make this world a better place, and also to have a better quality of life for ourselves.

INTERVIEW WITH ROBERT LANDY

Professor Robert Landy is Director of the MA Drama Therapy programme at New York University and author of numerous publications on theory and practice in dramatherapy. He is the new Editor-in-Chief of the Arts in Psychotherapy Journal *and in 1992 was made an Overseas Fellow of the Institute of Dramatherapy.*

SJ   Now, Robert, I'm really interested in you reflecting back on that process of where you came into dramatherapy and where you are with it now.

RL   Well, I guess I started by accident in the mid-1960s, because I was working in a school for emotionally disturbed adolescents and I was hired as an English teacher – English teacher by day and actor by night. I realised that I couldn't teach reading and writing and interpreting Wordsworth's poetry to kids who were severely hyperactive or severely withdrawn, and there was nothing I could do that could reach some of them. So, purely as a method of survival, I turned to the thing that I knew best and that was acting. I attended a theatre workshop at a weekend and then I would take some of the ideas and try them out the next week in class. I discovered that the theatre was opening up not only interest in the students, it was calming down the hyperactive, it was speeding up the withdrawn and it was also exciting my own interest in a way that heretofore was lacking. So, we – the students – were interested in doing plays, and we started doing plays and we did a very bizarre production of *Godot* in 1968 with people who had a great understanding of what it means to wait and for nothing to happen and the wordgames to be played and that kind of thing. I was there at one school for about four years, and over that time I developed a very, very deep connection with my students. I continued my theatre studies and theatre performance. I was involved in experimental theatre forms, and the students were very interested in playing around with these ideas. I was working in ritual theatre and theatre that explores *the darker parts of the psyche and the archetypal demonic parts* – that really resonated what these kids were going through. So, that was the start of it for me.

SJ   Who at that time would you say were the greatest influences in terms of actors or theatre writers?

RL   Well at that time I was working with members of the Living Theatre and the Open Theatre, so my influences very much came from them. Certainly, Joe Chaikin, who started the Open Theatre in the early 1960s was very important to me, as was the Bread and Puppet Theatre run by Peter Schuman who's still very active. Peter Schuman came to our school for a week and did a series of workshops with severe emotionally disturbed students. He wasn't particularly interested in working with emotional disturbance, he just performed the kind of theatre that was very primal, that was non-verbal. It was a theatre of giant puppets and a theatre of ritual, it was a theatre of very slow motion and it was theatre that did something quite extraordinary: at the end of every performance and every workshop of the Bread and Puppet Theatre, the actors took loaves of bread baked by Peter Schuman himself, broke it into little pieces and distributed a piece of bread to every person in the audience of the workshop. And my students were very impressed by this. The thought that one would come to the theatre to not only be nourished through the senses but also to be nourished with food. That image stuck with me throughout, and I thought if you can do that for the theatre, if you can feed people in every possible way, then this is for me. And, over a number of years, I found that my interest in more conventional and now even experimental forms of theatre waned to the point that I became only interested in the therapy. When I say it waned, I mean it waned in the sense of being a witness to theatre, being an audience member. Over the years I found going to theatre a very frustrating experience, very empty, very false, and I found that what actors do is not enough for me. You know about the professional theatre: you have to present yourself in a certain way to get a certain role, and it's one of the most competitive and, in some ways, mean-spirited professions around. Theatre then becomes something about rejection and acceptance – gratification of sometimes very narcissistic tendencies – and I found that in working in dramatherapy that wasn't the case: theatre didn't have to be anything, you didn't have to fit into any role, you could be in fact any role that you needed to be or wanted to be. That's what excited me about dramatherapy; so over the years in the 1960s, 1970s, 1980s, I began to play around with some of these ideas. Around the late 1970s I immersed myself even more into theatre performance and began directing plays and began writing plays, and when I directed I found myself drawn mostly to the theatre of Bertolt Brecht and the epic theatre style. This paved the way for me for the later work that I did with projective techniques and dramatherapy. The theatre of Brecht appealed to me because it was a theatre of reflection: like the Bread and Puppet Theatre, the actors were hidden, the personality wasn't important, *it was the persona that became important, the archetype.* I was very impressed by the ideas of people like Gordon Craig; you know, the theatre of marionettes, the theatre without actors, without personality, where images and giant puppets prevailed.

SJ   And, of course, that's something also of Artaud – those amazing images of the 'Theatre of the Sun', the 'Theatre of the Moon'.

RL   Exactly, and you know in many ways it came out of the ideas of the Aegean and even earlier than that, the more I studied theatre: I realised that it was very much Ancient Greek theatre as well – the actors would be on stilts and would have giant masks and it was the great image of the theatre that really prevailed. So, that's what impressed me about theatre, and as I got on with this work with various groups of emotionally disturbed people, drug-addicted people, elderly people, physically disabled people and so forth, I just began to try out these ideas in a lot of places. In those years, that is in the 1960s and 1970s, I worked mostly with remedial educational settings or in institutional settings. Again, I began to experiment with puppets and masks and moved away from texts, because again I was interested in the archetype, the image.

SJ   How did you use masks?

RL   Well, I think in the beginning . . . one of my students had talent, and taught me how to make masks on one's face and also using a mould. My first use of masks wasn't in the theatre, it was in photography. I began to take pictures and I found out that when I made a mask on my face, it looked a lot like me, but it also wasn't me at the same time. I wondered what would happen if I were to put myself on other people, put my face on other people, that is: if I could see myself as a woman, if I could see myself as an old person, if I could see myself as a young child again, if I could see myself as a severely physically disabled person.

So – you see some of the pictures here, we can't show them on tape – of people in my family, friends, people I'd meet in the street. I'd say, 'Do you mind wearing this mask and posing for me?' as I took the pictures, and, something quite extraordinary happened: I realised that the image of myself was so multiplied, I wondered 'Is there a central Robert Landy, or is there just a series of extensions of myself that could be found in everybody that I met?' And I thought of the concept of one of the early sociologists, Charles Cooley, of 'the looking-glass self', and he said that I am a self, I know who I am by virtue of looking in the mirror: that is, all other people in my social world and what they look like back, is a sense of what I am. At that time I was introduced to the whole world of symbolic interaction which looked at the sense of other people becoming mirrors for us. It was a simple leap from photography back to the theatre, and I began playing with these ideas in the theatre and eventually in dramatherapy.

So, the mask work – one day I said to a group of people I was working with, 'How about after you make your mask, you give your mask a name and you put that mask on somebody else in the group, and take the mask home and put it on your father, put it on your mother, put it on your baby sister and so forth.' People began to go through the same process that I had done.

In the late 1970s I began to work at New York University: I was hired to, in part, develop a dramatherapy programme. At that time there was no such thing as an organised profession or certainly an academic profession of dramatherapy. I knew about psychodrama and I had started to study psychodrama out in California with a Moreno disciple called Yablonski. It was very exciting, but in some ways it really frightened me: it was too powerful in a way that was very different from the mask work; it was too direct, there wasn't enough safety, there wasn't enough distance, there wasn't enough room to reflect. Actually, I wrote a play around that time. I was teaching in the university and was not granted my tenure, so I wrote a play called *Kill the Chairman* where the central character is up for tenure in the Theatre Department, and he has to do some performance in order to prove that he's worthy of tenure. He chooses a psychodramatic performance where he will cast the protagonist as the chairman of the Theatre Department and do this psychodrama and, of course, the idea of the play is that in fact he kills the chairman and the chairman winds up killing him by refusing him tenure because he's been so exposed. It's a sort of play within the play.

SJ   So, you actually set up a piece of healing theatre for yourself?

RL   Yes exactly. Yes . . .

SJ   Did it work? Was it healing?

RL   Eventually it did. At the time there was too much unresolved feeling going on with me around the loss of that job, which turned out to be a blessing in disguise. The double irony was that the Theatre Department in California didn't want me to develop any dramatherapy; they were very frightened by the idea, so there was no way that, had I stayed, I could have developed my ideas. So, by killing off the chairman – maybe the chairman within my head – I allowed myself to move onto greener pastures. The greener pastures in academia became New York University which indeed hired me to develop dramatherapy as an acceptable academic profession in the United States, and it was the first time that was done.

When I came to NYU in 1979, we already had art therapy, dance therapy and music therapy, and they were very much in process. I got excited about dramatherapy and began to develop courses and curricula. I found my colleagues becoming very nervous and very frightened: they wanted me to teach acting and directing and play-writing, and dramatherapy was really slowed down. I was on such a fast track with this that I couldn't stop, and I just kept going and going until, several years later, the curriculum was pretty much full-blown. I continued my experimentation with masks and puppets and with many other kinds of projective techniques – video, make-up, storywork and so forth – and, as the years went by, I found myself moving away from theatre. Nevertheless, I found myself embracing more of the ideas of Peter Schuman, Joe Chaikin, Bertolt Brecht, Peter Brook to some extent and, of course, Artaud behind that.

Now, in some ways, I'm in a different place. There's a point of saturation that I've reached in relationship to the field of dramatherapy – especially in this country, in America – because it hasn't grown very much at all. It's grown very much in New York in terms of the programme here at NYU and there's another excellent programme in San Francisco that's called the California Institute for Integral Studies, but it hasn't grown anywhere else; there's a certain stagnation.

SJ   Why do you think that is?

RL   I don't quite understand. It could simply be that, in the last ten years, universities in this country have been in financial trouble, and the obvious place to cut back is in the arts; dramatherapy seems a 'fringe of a fringe'. I think the real reason is that there are not enough articulate spokespeople around, even though we've gone through several generations – maybe if a lot of people had stayed in the field and found a voice to spread the word . . . ? I think part of my frustration here has been that colleagues are few and far between. I have a very strong relationship with David Johnson who's a major figure in the field – with René Eumenah who is also a strong figure, and a couple of others – but, you see how hard it is: I can't even name five or six people. I have contact with you, Sue, and with Alida Gersie and a couple of others in Europe who have really kept me going. We don't see each other often, but I read all your writings as they come out and we do stay in touch.

SJ   How much is that to do with what I call the loneliness of the pioneer, that in a sense you were there, up front, breaking new ground as I was in England, knocking on doors, pushing? And the students coming after you now are the sort of first generation and second generation of drama-therapists. So, I suppose I'm not surprised that it feels a lonely field, but maybe you're also saying that it's not growing.

RL   Yes, I feel that. I'm in a position where I read papers as the editor of *The Arts in Psychotherapy*, and it's shocking to me to see how few papers come in in the field of dramatherapy. The ones that do are either, you know, directly inspired by, let's say, people like yourself or Dave Johnson or some of the work that I do, or else they're unacceptable as publishable papers. There are very few new ideas that are coming out, and it discourages me. I don't quite know why.

SJ   What would you like to happen, in an ideal world?

RL   Well, I feel that in some ways the dramatic world view is a very powerful one; whether it's dramatherapy we're speaking of, or theatre or educational drama or improvisation. The dramatic world view is an extraordinarily rich one that most people reject in their adolescence when they become more concerned with how they appear to other people and get into their stages of greatest conformity.

To articulate what I mean by the dramatic world view, it's very simple: it's one where one recognises that there are two realities – one the reality of the everyday, and the other the reality of the imagination – that clash, that intersect in some ways. In drama, we are constantly moving in and out of role, which means moving in and out of one reality and into another, and it is that in-between space where the greatest possibilities could grow and occur. To me, that applies to drama on all levels, including the play. I think what discourages me is that very few people even relate to that under-standing of drama – what it is and what it can do and what its possibilities are. I think that's happening very much in theatre as well, because if you look at theatre for example in New York, you find a Broadway that is so based on very big money: I'm not even talking about the commercial Broadway that I remember of twenty years ago, but a situation where a non-musical play is almost assured of certain death. The off-Broadway movement is affected by the same economic background as Broadway. So . . . there's no growth there and there's no recognition of what the dramatic world-view means. It's the same with drama in education and drama-therapy. So, on that level I feel saddened.

What I'd like to see happen is that people are educated in their families and in their schools and in their communities, as to the value of fiction, as to the value of pretend, as to the value of moving in and out of different states of reality, as to the value of choice, as to the value of ritual, as to the value of symbol, as to the value of metaphor, as to the value of non-quantifiable phenomena, as to the value of non-positivistic phenomena, as to the value of non-scientific phenomena. To do that, of course, would be a major revolution in our culture I think, but maybe small revolutions will take place among people who have a vision that perhaps they're a little bit out of step with others in their culture: teachers who are parents, who are healers, perhaps.

SJ   Could we perhaps end by you talking a little bit about your new work, your original research in terms of taxonomy of roles. Quite apart from your dramatherapy pioneering, you've contributed original thinking that's a major influence in the dramatherapy field.

RL   I moved from thinking about the process of distancing – really, via Brecht – and how that helps one explore the relationship between being in-role and being out-of-role, and the relationship between feeling and thinking as internal states, back to theatre. Even though I haven't performed or directed or written for a while, I needed to get back to theatre in some way, I needed to understand historically what theatre has essentially provided for humanity, I needed to say – if any theory within dramatherapy makes sense, it's got to be based on a deep understanding of what theatre *is*, how it has worked through the centuries and why it has survived as an art form.

I began to ask myself a question: What is essential to all theatrical activities? and I answered it for myself. There are two essential media: one is role and one is story, and without role and story, theatre cannot occur. With anything else, such as scenery and lighting and themes and conflicts – if you take any of those things away, you still might have theatre. If you take the role away and you take the story away, you have no theatre – postmodern forms notwithstanding – because postmodern forms of theatre have done away with story, but they haven't done away with role.

My essential concern is with role, and I began an extensive reading of theatre from the early Greek plays right up to the postmodern forms. At the same time, I am doing clinical work with fairly 'normal' neurotic populations. I am discovering that certain repeated types of role come out in the dramatherapy work. *The most noticeable ones are to do with victims and survivors*: is there a connection between the roles that I'm seeing clinically and the roles that have been repeated over the centuries in theatre? Look at all the fools, look at all the victims, look at all the heroes, look at all the villains and so forth. I did an extensive analysis of theatrical plays and I counted up the roles, the repeated roles, and I found that there were *eighty-four roles in world drama repeated over and over again*. If a role is repeated throughout genres, throughout history, many times, I said: this is an archetypal role. So, I came up with this taxonomy – a way of systematising the repeated role patterns throughout history and very much in keeping in some ways with the Jungian archetypical system. I call this the theatrical archetype system and, in carrying those role types with the ones that came up clinically in dramatherapy, I thought maybe there's a way to make better sense of the dramatherapy in terms of diagnosis, treatment and evaluation, using some kind of a theatrical model.

So, I asked myself: how am I going to do this, how am I going to make the connection? I thought, well, what do playwrights need to know about roles? Each role seems to have certain qualities. Whether it's a physical quality, the first thing an actor does is ask: how do I use my body to enter into this role? Is this person big, fat, tall, skinny? How does he move, how does she feel about her body, what happens when this person puts on clothes, and so forth? So, there are physical qualities of roles.

How does the character think? We have mental qualities of roles. How does the character feel from moment to moment, and so forth? What kind of spiritual quality is in the body of this character? So qualities seemed to be very important. And I thought that would be important also in making sense of the dramatherapy.

Certainly, style is important. In what style do we create the character? Here my distancing model comes back, because this is another way of talking about distance because *style can be representational – true to life – or presentational, non-reality-based human beings.* To me, the presentational style has to do with the primacy of role.

Of course, it's highly emotional. Greek culture is a very 'feeling' culture; however, Greek drama is presented in a very stylised way and the actors are presentional in style. So this interesting paradox got me thinking: what is it about style that leads to a basic presentation of feeling – versus thought, versus a paradoxical relationship of feeling or thought? So, style is very important.

Quality is very important, style is very important, and then also the question: what is the function of a role within a given scene, a given play or, bringing it back to everyday life, to one's given life?

An actor must understand his or her motivation, his or her reason for playing a scene, what he or she wants out of that particular scene – as does a human being in everyday life.

This was basically my role model: looking at role types, deciding on the quality, the function, the style – and bringing it back to everyday life. We play roles very quickly in everyday life; they come and go, they flit in and out, and we have very little opportunity to reflect upon them or to make sense of them or to modify them in some way. *What if, in the process of therapy we could slow down the everyday life process and just say let's look at the victim part of ourself?* Let's explore it in some depth. Let's look at its qualities. Let's look at what is wanted in the scenario that is our life. Let's look at the ways we stylise that victim; the ways we stop feeling when we are the victim and so forth, and what happens when we create another role that perhaps is the opposite of the victim or perhaps an extension (or sub-quality) of the victim, such as the martyr – the part of us that says I will suffer for the sins of my mother or the sins of the world and I will take this and suffer quietly and so forth.

In creating this large system, very much based on theatre, and making the assumption that I have a way to understand the process of dramatherapy based in the art form – and that is also true of other psychological models such as the Jungian archetypal model – gives dramatherapy a way of making sense of behaviour on three levels: in theatre, in everyday life and in the dramatherapeutic process of healing as one reflects upon one's role. So, in a nutshell, that is the system that I've been working on for some years and which culminates in *Heroes and Fools, Victims and Survivors: the Study of Role and Everyday Life Theatre and Therapy*.

SJ   It's interesting that you've turned back to the theatre to investigate this role model rather than going into role from a psychological point of view and I think perhaps the greatest contribution that people like yourself could make to dramatherapy is to stay within the art form. This isn't to say that the other disciplines don't inform the dramatherapist, but if drama and theatre are truly a therapeutic form, then they are of themselves – it is the art that is the healing process; we may be informed through psychology or psychoanalysis. It is interesting that in dramatherapy's growth, both in the States and in the UK, we have had to go to the doors of the clinic and back again; we have had to take on psychoanalysis, and then have the courage to let it go and say that *dramatherapy isn't a way of doing role-play psychoanalytically*.

RL   Right exactly. Now you see in this country maybe one of the reasons that the field hasn't grown enough in my opinion is because some of the more interesting people in dramatherapy are psychoanalytically trained and see themselves as first and foremost as psychoanalysts, like Eleanor Irwin and a colleague of hers named Elaine Porter. I have tremendous respect for Eleanor Irwin, she's published some interesting articles and does marvellous work with children, but in my opinion she hasn't taken a step which I feel is a necessary step beyond that psychoanalytic model, which in some ways is limiting because it doesn't ultimately go into the heart of theatre art.

I'd like to say in closing that you and I have spent some time talking about Shakespeare and his relationship with drama as a whole and dramatherapy as a specific, and one of the examples I've given in my book is the example of Hamlet's dilemma which is expressed best in his famous soliloquy: 'To be or not to be' – his dilemma of being and not being – and I think of the question, 'To be or not to be?' It's usually said in the theatre as a statement, not a question, but it is a question: To be or not to be? – *That* is the question.

Now, if there's a question, there needs to be an answer. To be or not to be? That is the question, and the answer is: to be *and* not to be. That is the answer – it isn't one or the other. Either one is in-role or one is not in-role; either one is alive or one is dead, either one is mother or one is daughter. The dramatic answer is that one is mother *and* daughter at the same time, one is alive *and* dead at the same time, one is de-roled *and* en-roled at the same time. There is a profound connection between the two realities, the two parts of ourselves, that coexist and that is the *ultimate exploration*.

INTERVIEW WITH MOOLI LAHAD

Dr Mooli Lahad is Leader of the Crisis Intervention Programme in Upper Galilee and Director of the Dramatherapy Training Programme at Tel Hai College. His research into evaluation methods and the application of BASIC Ph (see Chapter 11 this volume) in work with children is well known in the Post Traumatic Stress Disorder field. In 1992 he was made an Overseas Fellow of the Institute of Dramatherapy.

This interview, with Mooli Lahad, took place in rather difficult circumstances. It should have been done by me in England, but Mooli was the victim of a near fatal accident. Pamela Mond, a dramatherapy graduate, agreed to do the interview for me.

PM   What's your definition of dramatherapy?

ML   Dramatherapy for me is the combination of multi-modal, the multi-modality of the arts, that manifests itself in the dramatic act. By that I mean that dramatherapy, unlike the other arts therapies, enables both the therapist and his or her clients to be able to move through different mediums and explore different areas, and use the 'dramatic part' as the climax or the turning point of things. The dramatherapeutic process, in my view, brings about the resolution of inner conflicts or unfinished businesses or issues that have already been dealt with in other (arts) therapies. I'll explain: I'm not undermining other arts therapies; what I suggest is that dramatherapy uses the other arts as the warm-ups or, as I would say, 'stations', where things can happen and therapy can take place. But the fact of the enactment, the very physical enactment, the taking up, or taking on, of a role, the negotiation with others, the role-playing with others, I think brings it a further step ahead – it mobilises. I believe in the multi-modality of human beings, that's why I say dramatherapy is, to my understanding, the only multi-modality or multi-model technique of the arts therapies. The rest may use several modalities, but the only one that has a multi-modality is the dramatherapy, because it uses all of these processes.

Now, the drama, the enactment, the action – which is the translation of drama – is the accumulation of the process and, when you want to go deeper and mobilise more energies and help deeper processes to take place, my understanding is then you are using the dramatic techniques. The *inner drama* happens all the time in all the therapies, but the *actual drama* is unique to dramatherapy (or to a therapy that has drama integrated into the process). That's where I see the difference.

May I make it even clearer. Sue Jennings uses movement, embodiment, right from the beginning. I use the movement and the enactment and the drama towards the end of the therapy. *Embodiment is non-verbal movement, whereas enactment is verbal movement.* In that respect I believe that we don't differ so much, but I feel that, starting with adults, with more passive approaches such as colours, paints, writing, talking, playing, in a very moderate way, is less threatening and invites more material. Then, when the enactment comes, when the dramatic act takes place, I believe more stuff touches people and they are more ready to look into their material.

The one thing that I want to say in this moment is also the difference I see between psychodrama and dramatherapy. I think that the ability of dramatherapy to use a remote story, a metaphoric story, a metaphor as such that it's not just a story, opens up more pathways for many people. Now, I feel that psychodrama is very useful with dramatherapy, but it's always a matter of the choice of the therapist – should he or she move into the identification of the figures or the roles, or stay with the metaphor? I believe that this is one of the advantages of dramatherapy: that we can heal without identifying *the* thing – through the distancing. There is no need to ask the question, 'What does it mean to you in your life?' all the time, and sometimes there is no need for it at all; whereas it is impossible in psychodrama not to ask, 'What does it mean to you in your life?', because psychodrama, after all, is your life enactment in many ways. But *the* process at the end of the day is identifying roles in your life, events in your life, and replaying them. This whole phenomena of drama has so many doors, windows, gates, for many people to enter: it is the unique thing about dramatherapy.

So, if I may sum it up, dramatherapy for me is the ability to invite a variety of people with very little declared talent in any of the arts to enter into the creative arts therapy process and, by that, heal themselves. I personally think that creativity *is* the source of life: the ability to play, the ability to use humour, colours, stories – that is the flame of life. Once you get in touch with that, I think you help the person to heal.

PM   Let me ask you now then, what do you think of the advantages of dramatherapy with children in trouble?

ML   My definition of a child in trouble is a child that doesn't believe his or her own senses. Now, we have at least five senses (although some people say that we have a sixth one, or even seven, I don't know), but five for sure. A child who's in trouble will deny the fact that she or he is able to use some or all of their senses because it's for their own good not to believe in what they see. So they close off from the world and start believing terrible things about themselves – a terrible thing that they might have heard from parents or other adults or other people – and internalise those beliefs and start to believe that they are not lovable and that they are stupid and that they are bad, evil or crooked, or whatever you want to say – worthless.

Now, let's go back to your question. Again, if dramatherapy in a clinical approach is multi-modal, by opening up for a child so many pathways, slowly it brings about a belief for the child that he or she can trust their senses, that they can play, or play with small figures in the sand, or they can play the drum, or they can roll on the floor – all these are a mixture of psychological or psychic and physiological phenomena or experiences. And, with the therapeutic atmosphere of acceptance, and I would even say love (which is a different matter: what do I mean by love in that respect? – a lot of respect and concern), the child again is opened up with many pathways. I think that one of the main problems for children, as much as for adults in trouble, is that they think that there is only one solution to their problem, or that there is only one way in life that they can go to. Now again, dramatherapy, being the multi-modal approach, is enabling them to see that there are many roads to take, 'Million Ways to Go' as the song goes – you know the film? – it's about a young boy and an old woman and there she sings for him that when you want to be high, be high, and when you want to be low, be low, because there are a million ways to go; you know that there are. This is the belief that the troubled person doesn't have. Working with suicidal adolescents, I can tell you that they don't even believe that there is *one* way. In fact, I think that their only solution is taking their own lives.

Now, the dramatherapeutic process is also how you think. We think about the role, we think about a role, not only in the sense of the part in the act or in the play, but the role a person will take in the normal or abnormal sequence of development: what is the metaphor here? Is it an animus or anima story, and so on? Just as a psychoanalyst thinks psychoanalytically, a dramatherapist needs to think dramatherapeutically.

PM   Are there areas in dramatherapy that you think are neglected?

ML   Most of my work is with children and adolescents and child-abuse which is pushed very much under the carpet by society. There is a need to work with these families and with children. Again, I think of dramatherapy as a tool to learn new roles, new encounters, new abilities to make contact, through the metaphor – stories, drama or otherwise.

Other areas that I can see, are the elderly. I think that with the lifespan that has been so extended in recent years, there is a great need to enter into work with elderly people and, slowly slowly they feel less worthless and more and more worth – can I say that? And I think that dramatherapy, reminiscence therapy, these approaches, the creativity that comes with it, is a very useful approach. I've never come across any other group as successful in my very long experience as a supervisor and therapist. A group with the elderly is always successful. *I don't recall one dramatic failure, either for myself or for my supervisee.*

PM   Did you find it always easy to 'get' to the groups?

ML   No, no. Once you work with them, it's very rewarding and it's usually very . . . I'm using the word 'successful' because you can see the change in the mood so dramatically from passivity, greyness, dullness, emptiness, to light in the eyes, enthusiasm, rhythm and movement, real movement, dancing, singing, flying hands, life – it's a vivid change. I think that Sue can tell you that that's her experience with people with severe learning disability, but I don't have any experience with this group. And of course, the groups that you're working with are very neglected; those who are, as I could say, at the 'second circle' of the problem, not those who are personally being victimised or are victims of any phenomena, but those who are surrounding them, such as their families, are very neglected.

PM   Mooli, thank you. Before we finish, is there anything else you want to say?

ML   Yes, I think that dramatherapy is lacking theory: we are moving towards that era where we have brilliant ideas, vast experience, and there is a need now to conceptualise it into a more theoretical approach. There is Sue Jennings's approach and Robert Landy's approach and Mooli Lahad's approach. There is a need of some sort of umbrella approach or theory of what is dramatherapy, because we have concepts, artists, enactments, but basically it is still *an approach*, it is not a theory, it's a model. So there is a need to move from experience and models, to theory. I think dramatherapists need to go through more supervision and to *establish their self-definition*; yet, as someone who works closely with other therapists.

I also think that there is a great need for us to publicise what dramatherapy is all about. People are very interested in it, yet do not know what it is – it sounds more like magic to them – and they often don't know the difference between psychodrama, creative drama and dramatherapy. This could be the beginning of theory, just the definition. . . .

INTERVIEW WITH PAMELA MOND

Pamela Mond graduated in drama in the UK before settling in Israel. She was one of the first dramatherapists to graduate in Israel, receiving special merit for her research on dramatherapy applied with healthy siblings of people with learning disabilities. She now works at Safed Hospital with people with mental health problems and tutors on the dramatherapy training programme. She was interviewed by her husband, Peter.

Q   Who or what is a dramatherapist?

PM   Before I can begin to look for my own definition of a dramatherapist (and each time I've tried to do so in the past it's come out differently!), I feel the need to be able to relate to being able to say, 'I, am, a dramatherapist.'

I would like to clarify that further and say that I'd been a dramatherapist '*in utero*' for many years and neither the pregnancy nor the birth was easy.

I graduated from the New College of Speech and Drama in London in 1971 and shortly after, moved to live in Israel. For seven years before I began my dramatherapy training, I worked in a variety of ways using drama and movement as a 'therapeutic' means towards communication. I worked with 'normal' children, producing end-of-school plays, running drama and movement story hours, and I also worked with many 'special' education populations whilst working for School Psychological Services in special education kindergartens and in Safed's Child Development Centre where children who were mentally retarded or emotionally or physically disabled were assigned to me.

I developed my own style of working which might at one time have been described as 'movement work' and at another time was very 'dramatic' in its approach. I used every type of material that was available for 'play' purposes. The child gave a 'clue' and I helped develop the idea into something 'playable' and then passed it back to him or her for 'working on'. This seemed to be successful – the kids loved it, the staff were anxious to pass me more and more cases – but strangely, I became less confident and began to have questions and doubts about what I was doing and whether I was qualified to be doing it. Also, I never quite knew what to call myself. I wasn't a 'teacher' any longer, nor an actor and I had no training as a therapist, yet was often introduced as one and this frightened and embarrassed me. So who was I . . .?

I could compare my life and my work at that time to a very complicated, many-pieced jigsaw puzzle. All the pieces promised to be there, just waiting to be worked on and sorted out into a scene. But the picture on the lid which is usually available for copying purposes, wasn't clear enough to be used. Well, some of the puzzle's pieces fitted into place quite easily; in fact, somewhere, joined together already in the box. However, the puzzle got progressively more difficult to work on and though I sensed and believed that it would eventually come together, I began to lose confidence in doing it.

Just around this time, it looked as though 'a Puzzle Instruction Booklet' might become available, as Tel Hai College in Northern Galilee under the auspices of Dr Sue Jennings and Dr Mooli Lahad started Israel's very first ever three-year dramatherapy training programme. I 'went for it' – admittedly it wasn't quite that simple – no blueprint presented on a platter!

I had to write and rewrite those instructions again and again for myself, but the staff were there as guides and the fumbling in the dark and chaos were done with a very supportive peer group.

So, my jigsaw puzzle began to take shape and a lot of it got done during my training. Today, I don't need the 'picture' in order to continue working on the puzzle – in fact, it is of course much more exciting without one! When a new area of the puzzle gets done – and it can drop into place whilst I'm working with a client or during a supervision session, or whilst making a review of a group with a co-therapist or my student – the thrill is enormous, very exciting and so creative. I often get the motivation to go to work on the puzzle and try to reveal a hidden scene after an argument, whilst watching my children play or fight, before or after a meeting with my own Jungian therapist and at many many other moments in my life – the puzzle gets worked on almost continually. So, although it is not yet finished, may never be, and even though the picture isn't clear, I do know one important thing and that is that *this* puzzle has a name, my name – 'Pamela – the Dramatherapist'.

So, now on to a more 'definite definition'. A 'dramatherapist' can be anyone who believes in the powers and strength of the drama and uses it in all its forms in their work. A dramatherapist takes 'a prompt' from the client, 'plays' with it and then gives it back for his or her 'action'. A good dramatherapy training is an important requisite which helps the dramatherapist to know when 'to let go' or when 'to stay with it'. She/he is someone who continues to learn and receive supervision and, by the way, I strongly suspect that she/he also believes in and very much enjoys being a dramatherapist.

Q   What is dramatherapy?

PM   Towards my search in finding a definition of 'dramatherapy', I would like to share with you the comments of some of my clients about their experiences of working within the dramatherapy medium. First, there was a 12-year-old boy with whom I worked during his 5-week stay on the orthopaedic ward in Safed's general hospital after a traumatic road accident; this is what he said:

'Dramatherapy is about touching and playing with objects, drawing and telling stories and making up plays about them. This lets you collect up and get out the frightening feelings from inside you and doing all this helps you to be calm.'

'Something else too', he added, 'I can't explain it, but it's got to do with something here', he said, as he patted the area around his heart. (Sounds quite like Sue's EPR Paradigm to me!)

The 'mother' of a sick baby who worked with me dramatherapeutically, told me after she'd done work on a collage around the subject of the hospitalisation:

'It helped me to face the ugly things – things which became much less fearful after I'd allowed them to surface and to put some order and perspective back into my life which had seemed to be standing still . . .'

Personally, I would like to suggest that dramatherapy has something to do with accompanying and being accompanied on journeys and meetings. Journeys into the familiar and unfamiliar, meetings with the known and unknown – fearful and wonderful places within our conscious and sub-conscious minds – and inside our souls. Dramatherapy might be called 'The Creative Travellers' Guide to Good Health'.

Q   Which areas are most neglected?

PM   Working a lot with sick and disabled people, I also get to meet some of their healthy siblings and parents and learn about the burdens they carry because of their family's disabled member. I was able to create dramatherapy groups for 'Healthy Sibs' where many personal difficulties were examined around the issues of anger, fear, guilt, feelings of over-involvement and responsibility and their social difficulties. The sibs' work on their personal issues was very much hampered because of the lack of knowledge and understanding from their friends and the community at large. The lack of sensitivity towards disabled people and their families creates endless additional problems of shame, guilt and loneliness for other family members. Just the stares, whispers and finger-pointing, to name but a few, cause them tremendous pain.

So, I would like to see dramatherapy used in schools and community centres and all sorts of in-training institutes with 'healthy' populations, to work around the many and varied issues of disability.

Last year, with the backing of the Ministry of Education and the interest and encouragement of the staff on the children's ward in the local general hospital, I created a new work position for myself – a hospital dramatherapist working on a Crisis Intervention Programme. I use dramatherapy with hospitalised children and/or their parents, helping them to cope with the fears, pressures and regressions surrounding the very fact of being hospitalised. This work has proved successful and we are developing it all the time. However, it is still very new and not yet widely recognised. I think that with some publication of case studies, so creating a wider awareness of how dramatherapy can help patients and their families and the contribution it makes towards helping nursing and other staff, more dramatherapists would be employed.

CONCLUSION

It is interesting to see how the above interviews – although very different in some ways – bring together some similar issues. People see dramatherapy as affecting not just individuals but society itself and that its application should be with family and community groups – not just the 'identified patient'. All of the interviewees have had more than one profession before the 'theatre of healing' came to represent a strong part of their lives.

Mooli Lahad is right – we do need a strong body of theory, and perhaps Robert Landy's new book is the first step. I'm investigating bodies again, so between us we may be able to offer some more signposts on the dramatherapy journey.

NOTE

1 Augusto Boal challenges assumptions about theatre and society through his work on 'Theatre of the Oppressed'. See also Chapter 1.

REFERENCES

Boal, A. (1979) *Theatre of the Oppressed*, London, Pluto Press.

Boal, A. (1992) *Games for Actors and Non-Actors*, trans. A. Jackson, London, Routledge.

Lahad, M. (1988) (ed.) *Community Stress Prevention*, Kiriat Shmona, CSPC.

Lahad, M. (1992) 'Storymaking: an assessment method', in S. Jennings (ed.) *Dramatherapy Theory and Practice 2*, London, Routledge.

Landy, R. (1983) 'The use of distancing in dramatherapy', in *The Arts in Psychotherapy*, 10.

Landy, R. (1986) *Drama Therapy: Concepts and Practices*, Springfield, IL, Charles C. Thomas.

Landy, R. (1992) 'One-on-one: the role of the dramatherapist working with individuals', in S. Jennings (ed.) *Dramatherapy Theory and Practice 2*, London, Routledge.

Landy, R. (1993) *Heroes and Fools, Victims and Survivors: a Study of Role in Theatre, Everyday Life and Therapy*, New York, Guilford Press.

Mond, P. (forthcoming) *Dramatherapy with Healthy Siblings of Children with Learning Disabilities*.

Chapter 11

Evaluation and assessment in dramatherapy

Brenda Meldrum

INTRODUCTION

Research and evaluation in dramatherapy has not until recently had a high profile. However, there is now a thriving Arts Therapies Research Committee, which holds annual conferences to which the Research Committee of the British Association for Dramatherapists sends delegates and submits papers. However, I think it is fair to say that dramatherapy professionals have seen no urgency to research into and evaluate their practice and publish the results. For example, in the training programmes, there is no module specifically dealing with research methodology, although tutors are careful to teach trainees the importance of assessing clients for individual and group dramatherapy. This may well be because there is no recognised research methodology for dramatherapy and while the Journal of the British Association for Dramatherapists, *Dramatherapy*, publishes articles on theory and practice, papers describing or evaluating research methodology are few. In this chapter, I shall be reporting on some of the empirical research and the methodologies used in papers and books published in Britain.

In these days of business plans, audits and budgets, dramatherapists are being asked increasingly to provide assessments and evaluations of their work with clients. As 40 per cent of full members work in the National Health Service this is a very important area for dramatherapists to look at their own practice. As part of my research for the writing of this chapter, I approached dramatherapists who are working in the National Health Service and asked if they would tell me what assessments and evaluations they carry out as part of their work programmes. Formal assessment and evaluation has given rise to many mixed feelings from those I contacted.

Dramatherapists are encouraged to have supervision throughout their working life, and most bring their practice to their supervision sessions. Many review clients for feedback before they are discharged in more or less formal ways. Some are resistant to what they call 'scientific' assessment and are impatient with what one has called 'politically motivated' evaluations. Others, however, recognise that this is the way that practice is going in the health services and yet others welcome some formal assessment of their work.

One person working as an occupational therapist and dramatherapist wrote:

> There is, I must admit, a somewhat indignant (and possibly defensive) part of me that finds this whole subject of evaluation and assessment very difficult indeed. It all seems too scientific, empirical and reductive. Most freelance therapists I've spoken to or worked with, seem to operate a very open-ended approach based on the premise that the client evaluates for himself when the desired goal is achieved. In the NHS, where I have always worked, different professions and services emphasise evaluation and assessment to varying degrees, although it is generally true to say it is coming in more and more, with ideas such as 'outcome' becoming as significant as 'throughput'. It is also part of the new 'consumer' ethic, with efforts being made to ensure that clients are fully assessed in order that the most relevant/suitable therapeutic approach is offered. For me personally there is something very central to this about whether therapy is 'done to' the person (in which case you can assess/evaluate the approach) or whether it is something which isn't quite so simple to pin down and quantify. I tend towards the latter view, but I work in an agency that asks me to assess and evaluate.

The problem with testing and evaluation is that it is hard (and some people believe it to be impossible), to think of them in parallel with therapy. To be a good therapist, it is important to try and give your client unconditional positive regard; testing and evaluation, on the other hand, may require judgements; many of our clients are coming to therapists for help because they have been judged and controlled and mistreated all their lives. Roger Grainger, a dramatherapist who has conducted research with thought-disordered clients, argues (personal communication) that an 'Us and Them' mentality just would not be *dramatherapy*. The harder he tried to use dramatherapy itself as a means of assessing individual clients, the more the evaluation got in the way of the therapeutic process. So in a sense, it was better to use an orthodox empirical test, which the clients and he could see as being separate from the dramatherapy process. Then, when a client asks him: 'Are we being tested?' he can with a clear conscience say: 'Yes.'

The dilemma, however, still exists. If the therapist conducts 'before the session' and 'after the session' tests, or examinations of states of mind, or asks the person to fill in a grid, then the dramatherapy *is* part of the assessment procedure, even when it is not videotaped or observed or recorded electronically or by notes. Informed consent of the client to any assessment and evaluation is as important in dramatherapy as it is in psychology. Clients who have agreed to assessment and evaluation, and have answered questions about their states of mind before the dramatherapy session, know quite well that when they are asked how they feel after the session, the effects of the dramatherapy work on them are being evaluated and they may well feel that they themselves are being evaluated. It is a very difficult area indeed, and one can readily understand the resistances of many dramatherapists to the whole subject of assessment and evaluation. That is why it is so important to bring the debate into the open and to find a *dramatherapeutic* way of assessment and evaluation.

This chapter will look at both published and unpublished research, assessment and evaluation projects; I have not looked at dramatherapy research in Europe, Australasia or the United States. I shall examine some of the ways dramatherapists make assessments of clients in dramatherapy practice; I shall then look at evaluation and assessment in current work, and I shall mention research programmes which are in the planning stage. I shall present some research instruments which dramatherapists and arts therapists might find interesting and useful in their work.

ASSESSMENT IN DRAMATHERAPY

In this section I shall first be looking at the ways in which dramatherapists assess their clients for group or individual work and some of the techniques they use. Mooli Lahad, Alida Gersie and Ann Cattanach use story-making techniques to assess the problem areas their clients present. Through the medium of the story that the person tells in their assessment sessions, these therapists discover not only how the client is coping with distress and trauma, but also, and what is perhaps more important, what language he or she is using.

Secondly, I shall be looking at ways in which dramatherapists working in the National Health Service are coping with the requirements of managers to assess clients' suitability for dramatherapy. Steve Mitchell, Steve Nash and Martin Gill have devised various ways of responding to referrals; I briefly discuss Mitchell's initial response; Nash and Gill have given details of how their structured assessments proceed and these are described in this section.

Assessment by story-making

Mooli Lahad's use of story-making to assess the way people cope with stress

Mooli Lahad (1992), Israeli dramatherapist and psychologist, uses story-making in the assessment of individuals coping with stress. His research has shown him that people differ as to their coping styles; some will use a cognitive-behavioural approach, searching for information and then acting upon it; others will use an affective, emotional approach, expressing themselves by demonstrating their reactions or channelling them into creative activity; others will seek the support of groups by taking a social role; a fourth type will use their creative imaginations to obscure the brutal facts of the traumatic event; a fifth type will rely on their beliefs – religious, political, ethical – and their values to guide them; and yet others will react and cope by using their bodies in physical expression, movement and activity.

Using these six groups and their different coping styles in reaction to stress, Lahad has coined an acronym: BASIC Ph.

These are the six dimensions that underlie the client's coping styles:

B   is a reliance on Beliefs and Values,
A   is the expression of Affect,
S   is the Social mode,
I   is the Imaginative way,
C   is the Cognitive response,

Ph is the Physical and active coping strategy.

The problem, as Lahad sees it, is to find a shared language with the client. What is usual in therapy, Lahad has observed, is that the client starts talking the therapist's language not his or her own, because that is what the client thinks the therapist wants. And yet, therapy has been operating for over a hundred years, and Lahad believes that we should by now know that there is a different language to be used for each person. His assessment tool is the therapeutic technique of bibliotherapy: the use of story and story-telling in order to assist the person reach self-awareness and to improve internal and external communication. His instrument is called 'Six-piece story-making (6-PSM)' (see Lahad 1992). It gives the therapist a quick assessment of the client's coping modes, with the objective of helping the therapist reach an understanding of the client's 'internal language'. Lahad trains students and workers in the use of the BASIC Ph as an instrument, via a story-making technique. Central to Lahad's bibliotherapeutic approach is the Jungian notion that in fairy tales the world over we may best study the comparative anatomy of the psyche. Lahad asks each client to tell a story in a structured way.

The clients divide a sheet of paper into six sections; in section one they are asked to draw the main character and where that character lives; the second picture will be the mission or task the character has to fulfil; in the third picture the clients draw the person or thing that will help the character; in the fourth picture clients are asked to draw the obstacle that stands in the way of the character carrying out the mission or task; in the fifth picture they draw how the character copes with the obstacle and in the sixth section they are asked to draw what happened then: does it end or does it continue?

The theory suggests that these six elements are always represented in fairy tales and Lahad's assumption is

> that by telling a projected story based on elements of fairytale or myth, I may be able to see the way the self projects itself in organised reality in order to meet the world.
>
> (Lahad 1992: 157)

Each picture gives the therapist insight into the coping modes of the client. The whole story is analysed using the BASIC Ph into the different coping modes. Readers interested in this exciting methodology will find it useful to refer to Lahad's chapter in Jennings (1992). Using this structured story-making, a client's coping resources and conflict areas can be located and crisis intervention programmes planned accordingly.

Alida Gersie's use of story structures for assessment

Gersie (1990, 1991) argues that myths and traditional stories embody essential human experiences which transcend race, culture and time. If we allow these myths and tales to resonate with our personal experiences, we are in touch with the experience of the human race. A myth that survives throughout the ages bears witness to the universality of its themes. In her books, she tells many lovely and unusual stories from different cultures and times and she provides each story with a working structure to be followed by therapists and counsellors. When the worker or therapist is utterly familiar with the traditional story she is to tell her group, then the images in the story will be transmitted to the clients who will then work with the story according to the structure supplied by Gersie.

A powerful way of assessing clients and their particular difficulties is to ask them to make their own stories. Gersie suggests a methodology similar to that of Lahad's; clients are asked to draw or tell or act out a six-part structured story. Gersie's six structures are:

1 the landscape,
2 the character,
3 the dwelling place,
4 the obstacle,
5 the helpmate,
6 the resolution.

Her structure is more flexible than the BASIC Ph; depending on the client you may start the story with the landscape and then come to the character. The client may show some resistance or blocking at some part of the story and the therapist's aim is to help the client discover the cause of this resistance. Picture 5, the helpmate, is the most likely healing place for the client and if her story shows that the helpmate is not being utilised, then the therapist knows that this may be the area on which to work. Similarly, if the obstacle is overpowering the character, then this is a good start for therapy. The aim of the therapist is to help clients solve their problems for themselves. The process of working with the story is first, to help the clients find the ability to soothe themselves; second, to help them find the confidence to trust another person; and, third, to generate an experience where play and the unknown becomes inviting.

Ann Cattanach's assessment from play therapy

In her work with children and young people who are referred to her because they have been physically, emotionally or sexually abused, Cattanach (1992; see also Chapter 8 this volume) stresses the function of play. In her work play *is* the healing process and her function as therapist is to help the person play. Play has a developmental progress from embodiment, through projection into enactment. It is important to see at what developmental stage the person is at the moment; if the child is operating only in the sensory embodiment mode, then the therapist stays with him or her; the therapist's function initially is to make an assessment of the meaning things have for the child. As part of her initial assessments, Cattanach uses an instrument called the Shield, which I am including here as, in my view, it is a useful tool for all types of client.

At the first or second interview, Cattanach tells the child that she has some questions she would like to ask and also that she wants to get to know him or her better and so they are going to draw a personal shield, which will be the child's own story. She herself draws a shield on a piece of paper and divides it into six sections, while the child copies her. She asks the child to draw the first thing that comes to mind; her intention is to stress that the child should answer from the way he or she feels now.

1st section   What is the best thing that has ever happened to you?

2nd section   What is the best thing that has happened to your family – any family? (Some children have had the experience of being in several families.)

3rd section   What is the worst thing that has happened to you?

4th section   What do you want most from other people, *not* your family, but people of your own age? (Cattanach then lists a number of possibilities: love, sex, money, toys, friendship, things, help, etc., making sure that she says both 'love' and 'sex' separately.)

5th section   Say you were really ill and you had a year to live and all the money you want, what would you do for that year?

6th section   You are dead; it is your funeral and people are there and they are all remembering you; what three things would you *like* people to say about you? They don't have to be true. Just write down three words. (If the child cannot write, Cattanach writes in the words for him.)

Therapist and child talk about the story in the shield, with Cattanach giving continual reinforcement to the child. If he says that nothing good has ever happened to him (section 1), the therapist will prompt until something good is remembered; the family section (section 2) is often illuminating and gives clues as to the child's experiences; section 3, the worst thing, may not be the abuse the child has suffered, but may be something apparently trivial like: 'The teacher told me off.' Cattanach's experience is that the more severe the level of abuse, the more trivial this answer tends to be. The therapist then has to tread very carefully indeed. Many children say that they want money most (section 4), because they are not attached to another person. It is important to reinforce the child at this point, so that one does not appear judgemental. Most children are not as sensitive to the notion of death (section 5) as adults, but if the therapist feels uncomfortable about using the phrase 'a year to live', then he or she may rephrase this section. What is interesting is that responses seem to divide people into those who choose fight and those who go for flight. Some people respond by saying that they will stay at home and make life better and others say that they will go around the world and see as much as they can. Section 6 tells the therapist how the child would like to be seen: loving, funny, clever and so on. Using the shield story helps to break the ice and gives the therapist information. With children it is a start in achieving some self-esteem, as the therapist constantly reinforces that this is the child's shield, that it is important because it is his or her own; and because it was drawn by him or her, it is good and she likes it.

Assessment of clients by dramatherapists working in the NHS

Steve Mitchell (see Chapters 3 and 9 this volume), working as a dramatherapist in an Occupational Therapy Unit attached to a National Health Service hospital in the northwest, has clients referred to him from psychiatrists or GPs. When a client is referred, Mitchell reads the referral letter carefully, and when he meets the client he tells them honestly that he has read the referral letter, but asks them to tell him what *they* would like to say. He then writes an open letter to the referee saying:

X has presented herself for dramatherapy. She has given me your name as her general practitioner or psychiatrist. I am intending to conduct an assessment and in view of the possibility of my working with this client, if there is any information which you would like to share with me regarding this client, I should be very grateful if you would write to me. Unless I hear from you, I shall be seeing her on a given day.

It is Mitchell's practice to assess clients using various dramatherapeutic techniques, such as asking them to draw a life-map showing the most important milestones along the way, in order to see what is important to them. The map becomes a basis for discussion before areas of mutual interest are examined.

Working in the Midlands, Steve Nash's initial assessment with the client defines a simple life-history. There are then two options: either he allows the work to develop in partnership with the client, or he takes a problem-oriented approach, working with a behavioural psychotherapist.

If he takes the latter option, the initial assessment is more structured. The client is given a full individual interview, where a complete personal, social and family history is elicited. At this interview, the client makes two (or more) *specific* problem statements, illustrating his or her experience of the problems and how these affect him or her. Next, the client scores the extent to which the problems affect each of five 'life areas', such as home management, work, family relationships and so on. At this point, a relative or friend might also score the individual on these points as well. The client then undertakes a two-week programme of groups and individual sessions, leading to further assessments. After these assessments, specific targets of achievable, measurable activities or behaviours are defined. The client then scores what he or she thinks the chances of achieving the targets might be. The follow-up includes re-scoring life areas and targets.

Martin Gill, a dramatherapist working with a colleague and two music therapists in Wales, has a potential client group of 1000 county-wide. Recently, he has had face-to-face meetings with the Care/Budget Manager which are the starting point before meeting new clients. Jointly, the Care Manager and the dramatherapist are designing the first stages of a database of client needs, whose categories are age groups, sex, interests, mental health and family needs. Clients are sorted into groups in order to design services around a 'needs-led approach'. One such group has been established which is a Women's Group for clients of a certain age, with a particular interest living in a particular area.

The idea is that, because the Care Managers are involved in the early stages of identifying needs, then it is anticipated that it will simply be a matter of informing them when suitable client groups are formed from their case load. This system is in its very early stages at the moment and it is yet to be seen how it works in practice.

Gill and the arts therapy team have compiled the following 'Areas of Need Schedule', which may be appropriate for some clients and not for others:

1 Creative and expressive drama/movement projects, such as visiting specialist artists, dance teachers, etc., could offer a creative outlet for participants.
2 Communication projects, such as therapy programmes addressing individual needs through a collaboration of drama/movement and speech therapy to enable the person to communicate more effectively.
3 Role development: helping the clients develop and explore new roles to enhance and extend their ability to respond more effectively to new situations.
4 People who challenge services: helping the client develop trust by improving group interaction skills and later on roles for normal living.
5 Therapy/counselling: a series of treatment-based interventions to enable clients to develop new perceptions about themselves or others. The aim is to enhance social involvement or deal with here-and-now life problems, or bereavement, past trauma, abuse and so on.
6 Family support work: supporting holistically by offering parent support groups or sessions for individual family members or carers who experience problems in relation to the person with a mental handicap.
7 Special and complex needs: the service offers a creative contribution to a team approach in addressing some of the needs of people who have special and complex needs such as those who are partially sighted or who have a hearing disability. Such work includes assisting in designing service plans for individuals.
8 Training: many of the skills of dramatherapy can be of use to other professionals and group leaders. Courses are designed to meet different needs.

Stage 1 This schedule of possible needs is discussed with the Care Manager.
Stage 2 After meeting the client, the dramatherapist identifies a number of possible needs from the Schedule as they may apply to the particular person. The dramatherapist writes to the Care Manager after a weekly multi-disciplinary discussion to suggest the particular areas of need the group has identified. For example, one client may need therapy/ counselling (number 5 on the schedule) and also role development (number 3).

Stage 3 The client is referred to the dramatherapist who works with the person. The dramatherapist reports to the Care Manager the client's behaviour, communication, the level of interaction, and identifies the client's skills and abilities. From these reports the care management team makes recommendations for a care plan and the group to which the client is assigned. Alternatively, the client may be referred to another service or psychotherapist.

RESEARCH AND EVALUATION IN DRAMATHERAPY

In this section I shall first look at four published research papers. Fontana and Valente's (1989; Valente and Fontana 1990) study looks at the attitudes and practice of dramatherapists. I have included their research because of its intrinsic interest to dramatherapy even though it is not directly dealing with research into practice with clients. In his research with thought-disordered adults, Grainger (1990, 1992) used Kelly's Personal Construct Theory (Kelly 1955), over-riding the widespread and, as he proved, erroneous belief that dramatherapy was too dangerous to be used with psychotic people, because drama, by its nature, asks people to leave everyday reality and enter dramatic reality. Jones's (1993) work with autistic adults was part of a wide-ranging theoretical study into the acquisi-tion of meaning in dramatherapy from the point of view of the client as active witness. I shall be reporting on the research work only, which was an imaginative synthesis of the dramatherapeutic with the psychological. I shall then consider a pilot research study which I undertook (Meldrum 1993) to investigate the use of New Paradigm Research (Reason 1988) in dramatherapy. New Paradigm Research, with its rejection of mechanistic old paradigm notions of the person as 'organism' or 'subject' in the hands of the all-knowing scientific 'researcher', seems to many to be the way psychotherapeutic research should go. I am sure this is so; but I am including my report because I found the methodology so difficult in practice. Last, I report on Myra Kersner's (1990) investigations into the usefulness of questionnaires as an appropriate tool in arts therapies generally, and dramatherapy in particular. This sane and helpful article gives dramatherapists a logical procedure of enquiry before they embark on designing a questionnaire for their clients.

In the second part of this section, 'Current research and evaluation', I shall look at research and evaluation projects which are in their initial stages. When I wrote to the dramatheraperists to ask about their practice I wished to find out the answers to the following questions: What is the current practice of drama-therapists with individuals and with groups? How do dramatherapists evaluate and assess in ongoing practice? I have divided their responses between their evaluation of their work with individuals, and their work with groups. I must emphasise that I am giving summaries of work in progress; this is not published research and much of it is both speculative and innovative – a response from a few brave dramatherapists to their changing work demands.

Published research papers

David Fontana and Lucilia Valente's survey data

Valente and Fontana (1990) report on research with the Department of Education at the University of Wales, Cardiff, into the nature and practice of dramatherapy as recorded from interviews with twenty leading dramatherapists.

Semi-structured interviews with a sample of leading dramatherapists were recorded with the results fed into an item bank of 354 statements, which were grouped into twelve categories of concern, five related to dramatherapy theory and seven related to practice. From the analysis of these interviews, a detailed questionnaire on the theory and practice of dramatherapy was circulated to all registered dramatherapists and dramatherapy students in Britain. The aim of the research was to provide a comprehensive study of the use of drama in therapy.

What is of interest to this chapter, however, was a report the authors made in 1989 entitled: 'Monitoring client behaviour as a guide to progress' – a kind of behavioural model of dramatherapy. This model, they suggest, is primarily descriptive rather than explanatory. The model is atheoretical, in the sense that it arises from interview data from the leading dramatherapists, without a prior conceptual hypothesis which the authors were testing. The model 'started to emerge', they say, as a result of their finding that these twenty leading drama-therapists collectively regard 'dramatherapy as firmly action-based'. This they see as the major distinction between dramatherapy and other psychotherapeutic disciplines. There is no mention, however, that the drama itself is the action component of dramatherapy. Therapy progresses through action and

> although it may at times embrace introspection and the verbal accounts clients give of themselves, if it ceases to involve the client at key points in doing, then it ceases in any direct sense to be dramatherapy.
>
> (Fontana and Valente 1989)

Behaviour, then, is the most important aspect of dramatherapy and of their model which the authors describe as a four-stage sequence of diagnosis, defining therapeutic objectives, process and assessment of outcome.

The authors suggest that the behavioural model can be used to demonstrate to 'sceptics the "scientific" plausibility of what the dramatherapist is trying to do'. By calling theirs a 'behavioural model', the authors are aware that this could imply a theoretical association with 'behaviourism', which they deny. They claim to see behaviourism for

> what it is – namely a useful tool, and provided we don't make the mistake of seeing behaviourism as in any sense the last word on human psychology, or as negating the insights provided by psychodynamic, cognitive, humanistic and other psychological approaches, it can be of undoubted help to us and it is strictly in this limited sense that we employ the term behaviourism in this paper.
>
> (Fontana and Valente 1989)

Unfortunately, behaviourism does do just that – it does negate insights provided by psychodynamic, cognitive, humanistic and other psychological approaches and as such is rejected by many psychologists and psychotherapists (see for example Pilgrim 1990) on the grounds that it is mechanistic and denies the fundamentally humanistic nature of psychology and psychotherapy. I take it that the authors mean that some of the techniques used in the clinical practice of behaviour modification have relevance for dramatherapy. However, an examination of the methodologies of new paradigm research (Reason and Rowan 1981; Reason 1988) would give many researchers courage to take up arms against mechanistic and positivistic old research paradigms of which behaviourism is the most notorious, and embrace new paradigm, humanistic and holistic approaches. Dramatherapy, in my view, does not need to lie down with such an uncomfortable bedfellow as behaviourism, no matter how persuasive he appears to be!

It will, however, be most interesting to read the results of their comprehensive research into the attitudes and practice of dramatherapists, which they hope to be able to extend to the Continent, Israel and the United States.

Roger Grainger's research with thought-disordered adults

Grainger (1990, 1992) reports on a research project of ten sessions involving a cross-section of clients attending a psychiatric day-hospital using the psychologist George Kelly's personal construct system (Kelly 1955); there were twelve clients in the research group.

Kelly did not believe in the Cartesian duality of the mind/body split. Theoretically the person is an integrated, indivisible whole, but people do not necessarily see or construe themselves in that way. A fierce opponent of the use of the medical model in psychological disorders, Kelly suggests the concept of *functioning* is a much more helpful one. A person who is functioning fully is one who is able to construe the world in such a way that his or her predictions are validated. Kelly said that we all encounter the world 'as if' we were scientists; that is to say, we have theories about events and why things occur; we make hypotheses about what will happen and we put these predictions to the test to see whether our thoughts are validated or not. 'Viewing all behaviour "as if" it were an experiment is one of Kelly's unique contributions to our understanding of the person' (Fransella 1990: 128).

The psychology of personal constructs suggests that we understand ourselves and others in psychological terms and that we can study the personal constructs we have each developed to predict events in the personal world. Thus, if we can discover the client's personal construct system, then we are able to understand better his or her reaction to life events. If the person's hypotheses, constructs or predictions are continually invalidated by experience, then he or she may well construct him or herself by saying: 'I have a problem', or they may try and 'make' things work out in such a way that their predictions are validated.

What was so brave of Grainger was that he was using personal construct psychology with thought-disordered people, using dramatherapeutic techniques which directly involve the person in playing 'as if I were someone else' and – fundamentally – the ability to take the role of the other and to see oneself and one's behaviour both subjectively and objectively.

People with the thought disorders labelled schizophrenic have difficulty with *differences*, Grainger says. To ask the questions: 'How do I know who I am?' and 'Who or what are you?' is fundamental to the establishment of 'me/not-me', which is a distinction made in very early childhood.

> Existential conclusions about identity which others take for granted as part of the given structure of reality are, for them [schizophrenics], perpetually under review, so that there is no stable or reliable basis, background, or framework, for the natural process of ordering and re-ordering conclusions about what is actually happening at any given time.
> (Grainger 1992: 168)

The thought-disordered person does not appear to share the same meanings as the other person as to what is happening around him or her. Communication has broken down as if there were too much noise in the system for the person to make a distinction between what is real and what is imagined. But Grainger believes wholeheartedly in the therapeutic nature of drama and the efficacy of drama-therapy so that

> cognitive clarity is communicable through dramatic experience. I maintain that dramatherapy establishes or validates a certain way of thinking about personal reality which is essential for relationship; one which is not salient in schizoid people who are suffering from thought-disorder.
> (Grainger 1992: 169)

Personal construct theory is valuable because it starts from the premise that what people think of themselves is important. Kelly is reported to have said that if his work were known for only one thing, then he would like to be remembered for saying: if you do not know what is wrong with a person, then ask him and he may tell you. Personal construct theory deals with the here-and-now of the client's immediate experience.

Grainger used Bannister and Fransella's Grid Test of Schizophrenic Thought Disorder (1966) and after ten dramatherapy sessions he found a heightened degree of cognitive clarity among those who scored lowest. All of the ten sessions involved 'putting oneself in another's place', leading to the use of role-reversal techniques to explore the experience of the other person. Grainger reports improvement in insight and awareness, but most important of all

> was the experience of meaningful change within the process of therapy. This was revealed in the expansion and deepening of imaginative awareness within the group as the sessions became more difficult – that is, more emotionally demanding and cognitively challenging. So far as the therapeutic process itself was concerned, this was 'new paradigm research' – that is, research *with* rather than

into – concerned with experiencing the nature of a shared event. In this, the attempt to measure outcomes was always secondary to the celebration of change.

(Grainger 1992: 177)

Phil Jones's research with autistic adults

In his chapter 'The active witness: the acquisition of meaning in dramatherapy' (1993) Phil Jones defines the active witness as the audience member to others and to oneself in dramatherapy. He sees both aspects as being of equal importance. With his colleague, Rosemary Sanctuary, an experimental psychologist, he worked with three young adults diagnosed as autistic. Jones's major aim was to find a model with which to establish a language to make a synthesis of theatre and therapy, but the specific aims of the work were to increase the clients' range and frequency of interactions with others through the use of puppetry and improvisation. It was decided to use the medium of puppetry 'to enable clients to become involved with the "small actors" they created, becoming audience-participants or active witnesses to themselves'.

The therapists used puppets as a projective technique, in the hope that the clients would use dramatic distance by being both separate and yet identified with their puppet representations, so that interpersonal interaction, which they found difficult in real life, might be possible if they became audiences of representations of themselves. This interesting and imaginative research used a dramatherapy design together with an instrument developed by Sanctuary (1984) from Parten's study of young children (1927, cited in Irwin and Bushwell 1980). Clients were videotaped in different situations and from these films the following behavioural categories were developed: stereotyped; withdrawn; solitary; responsive; aggressive; initiated; helping; and parallel activity. The latter three areas had not previously been observed in the clients' behaviour. A continuum was drawn from 'withdrawn' to 'active and pro-social behaviours and interactions' which was time-sampled two weeks before, during and immediately after the dramatherapy intervention, with a follow-up two weeks later.

The dramatherapy group met once a week for nine weeks during which time they made the puppets, followed by an intensive period of nine sessions over two weeks in which they engaged in free play, structured activity, video playback and role-play using the puppets. Jones reports that during the introductory period, when the puppets were being made, clients were able to identify their own and would verbally identify other clients' puppets using the clients' names. Within the intensive sessions, clients showed evidence of the ability to project themselves into their puppet actors by moving towards each other and with their puppet greeting another puppet and developing relationships between them. The therapists found that, whilst there was considerable change during the sessions, there was less change in observation periods outside the sessions.

The research showed, however, that during the period of active witnessing, the change of behaviour predicted by the model was effected; furthermore, the research project enabled a synthesis of theatre and therapeutic language.

Brenda Meldrum's pilot study using new paradigm research

In my chapter 'On "being the thing I am": an enquiry into the therapeutic aspects of Shakespeare's *As You Like It* ' (1993) I report on a pilot study using new paradigm research techniques (Reason 1988) to explore the therapeutic qualities of working on the text using techniques from drama and dramatherapy. The two dramatherapeutic models underlying the research plan were the Embodiment–Projection–Role model (EPR) of Sue Jennings (1991) and the Role Generation model of Robert Landy (1986).

New paradigm research methods require a non-directive approach, allowing for co-operative venture, with all group members contributing to the direction of the research. The minimum requirements of such co-operative ventures are:

1 that the involvement of all participants shall be openly negotiated;
2 that all the members should contribute to the creative thinking; and
3 that relationships should aim at being authentically collaborative.

The group met for eight 2-hour sessions and used the text of *As You Like It* to explore the overall question: is the nature of the theatre process intrinsically therapeutic?

This was a pilot study and it was successful in that theatre and drama-therapeutic techniques were used effectively together and in interaction in each session. Each session used Jennings's EPR model and the quality of the work supported the efficacy of this model. Landy's role generation model was fruit-fully expanded to bring the emotional to bear on the social roles in the text. But I found difficulties in using the new paradigm research techniques.

Theatre models of dramatherapy think of the therapist as an empathic director (Mitchell 1990), but the new paradigm research model suggests that 'if the facilitators get stuck in their role as facilitators, then they will no longer be participating members of the enquiry group' (Reason 1988: 31). I was stuck in the role of facilitator, not because I wanted to be but because the group wanted me to be. While it could be argued that this is my projection and that I could not bear to give up control, it was a matter that was discussed exhaustively within the group! My aim was to pass the facilitation over to group members and to become an ordinary group member but, as Reason admits, this is easier said than done. Having said that, there was considerably more discussion and analysis between group members than is usual in my experience and to this extent new paradigm research methods were useful.

I have to admit that this pilot model was not expanded into further research, because I found that this aspect of new paradigm research did not fit in with the work that I wanted to do on a theatrical model of dramatherapy, which requires an empathic director or facilitator. But I reflect that that is the purpose of pilot research projects – to show you what is feasible and what methodology is not appropriate to the research you wish to do.

Myra Kersner's investigation into the usefulness of questionnaires in arts therapy research

Kersner (1990) reviews the literature on the pros and cons of using questionnaire data in sociological, marketing and psychological research and considers their usefulness to arts therapy and dramatherapy research. Questionnaires may prove useful in certain instances to ascertain clients' perception of their own level of function and to express their feelings and views as to the setting, the therapists, the therapy itself and future directions of the sessions. Completing the questionnaire is in itself a learning experience (Cohen and Manion 1980) as it allows people to engage and reflect on the specific issues in therapy.

Because each research study and client group presents its own particular challenges and problems, a pilot study in advance of the main programme is able to pinpoint inadequacies in the design. In setting up the study, the researchers must be clear about their primary aims and secondary objectives by asking themselves questions such as: What do I need or want to know? Will that question give me the kind of response I need? and so on. Kersner gives suggestions as to the appropriate wording of the questionnaire, which ideally should avoid the use of relative terms such as 'well' or 'better' and undefined concepts such as 'often' or 'regularly'. Questions should be written to capture and hold the interest of the client and not antagonise, irritate, embarrass or intimidate.

Researchers should consider carefully the order in which they present the questions to avoid a mind set and the format and the design of the questionnaire itself should be inviting, with clear instructions for completion. Kersner concludes:

> Although questionnaires are based on the more traditional research paradigm, they do provide an important source of data collection which may have a place in arts therapies research, providing that their limitations are recognised and that they are always used appropriately. It is up to us to find innovative ways of making them work.
>
> (1990: 95)

Current research and evaluation

When working with individuals, Steve Nash (a dramatherapist working in an NHS hospital in the northeast) allows the client/therapist interaction determine the pace and duration of the dramatherapy sessions. Nash evaluates the progress of the work by observing changes and by asking the client to make her own evaluation. Working with groups, Nash uses adaptations of psychological measures which allow the client and therapist to evaluate and correlate their perceptions of the dramatherapy sessions.

Sylvia Wheadon (a dramatherapist in a day hospital for the elderly in the southwest) uses several structured methods to assess and evaluate her work; but because she is uncertain whether progress can be attributed to the dramatherapy process or to other important variables, she is working with a clinical psychologist on the design of an instrument to control for the other variables and assess the dramatherapy alone.

Brenda Meldrum presents a rating scale (Table 11.2), which is quickly completed and which can give the therapist a rough measure of change in the client's emotional state, involvement, disclosure and outward appearance.

Working with individuals

Steve Nash, when he works with clients on an individual basis, tries to assist them identify some very basic needs that do not happen in their life now, and which they want to see taking place; similarly, he helps them identify some patterns that are happening in their lives now that they would like to see stop. Another way of putting it is to ask them if in a year's time they were to look back on their work with him what areas of change would indicate that the therapy was successful. This, Nash says, is straightforward if the person is able to identify their needs, which, of course, is not always the case. However, as the work develops, at his instigation or at the client's instigation, they have a conversation about where the work is going or needs to go.

At some point, either by mutual decision or because of the pressure of external events, the work is closed and client and therapist assess together the progress of the work in terms of basic observational changes on the therapist's part and input from the client. Variables such as improved sleeping patterns and increased social life are examined, but the focus has moved from an examination of 'symptoms' to an assessment of feelings of awareness and insight. Clients are contacted after a year to see if they felt the work was successful and to talk of changes in their lives.

Working with groups

Steve Nash, working with groups, uses two sets of measures: a Dramatherapy Group Evaluation Form (Table 11.1), using and adapting some of the therapeutic factors outlined by Bloch *et al.* (1979), and a Life Area Profile.

Nash believes that the Dramatherapy Group Evaluation Form has a lot of promise. The procedure is as follows:

1 Clients identify key events in the group.
2 Clients tick 4 of the statements that describe possible benefits of the group. Each statement corresponds to one of the categories Yalom (1985) has identified as a curative factor in group psychotherapy, for example: vicarious learning: 'learning from watching someone else's work'; universality: 'realising that I wasn't the only one', etc.
3 Meanwhile facilitators guess for each client what they will indicate as the key event on their form.
4 Differences and similarities between client and facilitator evaluations are noted.

Table 11.1 Dramatherapy group evaluation form

Part one: What you got out of the group

Look through the following list of statements very carefully. USE UP TO FIVE TICKS to indicate the most important statements for you. You are free to tick less than 5 statements but PLEASE DO NOT TICK MORE THAN 5.

(a) Being able to release feelings and openly show my emotions to the group.
(b) Being able to share personal problems and private fears with the group.
(c) Exploring new ways of relating to other people.
(d) Learning that my problems are not unique.
(e) Feeling that I was accepted and supported by other members of the group.
(f) Recognising that I can offer help and support to someone else.
(g) Receiving useful information or advice from either the therapist or other patients.
(h) Understanding my own behaviour in a new or different way.
(i) Benefiting from seeing someone else's behaviour in the group.
(j) Feeling hopeful that the group can help me and/or others.

Part two: Key event

Please describe below what you would choose as the most significant event during the group as a whole.
What took place? Who else was involved? What was your reaction? Why is this so important?

Part three: How would you change the group?

(a) What would you have liked 'more of' in the group?
(b) What would you have liked 'less of' in the group?
(c) What would you choose to remain the same about the group?

Part four: Advice to others

What advice would you give to someone else joining the group? Why?

Part five: The venue and setting

How satisfied were you with:
(a) the venue,
(b) the time,
(c) the number of sessions?

Part six

Any other comments?

Source: Steve Nash, dramatherapist

The second measure used by Steve Nash is the Life Area Profile which is more behavioural in nature and refers to a closed two-week assessment programme he helped set up for day-patients which included individual and group work and sometimes included dramatherapy sessions.

The formulation is written after the initial interview, which was mentioned above. The Life Area Profile involves the client (and perhaps an important 'other') in trying to state, on a scale of 0–4, how seriously specific problems affect her or his functioning in a particular life area. The divisions into work, home management, social leisure, private leisure, self-care and family and relationships are fairly standard in psychiatry, although the 'family and relationships' area is the most difficult usually to try and reduce to a single, simple number. The Life Area Profile can be repeated after the given intervention and again at follow-up. The client is also asked to fill in Problem Definition sheets whose aim is to try to objectify and make measurable personal distress and symptoms. The third part of the process is Target Setting, which is carried out after initial work has begun. Nash reports that this approach, while useful for some clients, causes problems for others, who find the process of putting a number on their distress very intimidating. Also, the procedure, with some clients more than others, was very time consuming.

Sylvia Wheadon, a Clinical Manager and head dramatherapist working in a day-hospital with elderly patients with mental health problems, structures her groups by measuring attendance, measuring mood before and after the group session, through discussion with the clients and using sculpts to determine progress. Wheadon finds the assessment difficult because she asks herself: is perceived progress due to the various dramatherapeutic techniques or are other factors involved? She has identified possible variables which might contribute to progress such as the time of day, that is to say some times of day seem more therapeutic than others. Is it because clients are invited to the day-hospital? Is it because they are collected by a hospital driver who treats them with kindness and respect? Is it because of the journey to the hospital which allows them to go out and be in a different environment? Is it because of meeting other clients with similar problems? Or is it because of the dramatherapy itself or a combination of several of these variables? In order to try and find out, she is working with a clinical psychologist to form an instrument to be given to clients at the start and the end of the sessions.

Brenda Meldrum devised a rating scale for use with any type of clients in order to make a very rough assessment, not for predictive purposes but as a measure of change. When I was working in a closed forensic psychiatric unit, I wanted some way of observing alteration and change over the weeks. I devised this scale which, like many rating scales, is a list of subjective judgements, after reading Cox (1986), from whom I adapted the Level of Disclosure Scale. Ideally, two people should rate clients on any observational scale and agreements and disagreements should be noted and discussed, but I was on my own and I felt the need of an instrument to help me assess my own process, as well as change in the clients. I present the scale in the hope that it might be useful to others.

Table 11.2 Basic rating scale

Dimension 1: Emotional State Scale

1 Flattened, appears to be very depressed. Tearful in a quiet, helpless way.
2 Able to express the feeling of depression, but able to involve her/himself in the session. Some preoccupation.
3 Neither depressed nor elated.
4 Appropriately cheerful and active.
5 'High'; hyperactive, elated, over-reacts.

Dimension 2: Level of Involvement Scale

1 Almost no involvement; just moving through; withdrawn.
2 Very little spontaneous involvement.
3 Calmly involved.
4 Active involvement and engagement with drama.
5 Hyperactive: throwing self into drama.

Dimension 3: Emotional/Affective Disclosure

1 None – both in appearance and active denial.
2 Disclosure of a very superficial nature.
3 Disclosure of a personal nature but not of an emotional nature.
4 Disclosure of an emotional affective nature within an appropriate context.
5 Disclosures of an emotional and affective nature – spilling out.

Dimension 4: Appearance

1 Very poor standard of cleanliness. Clothes in a real mess. Unbathed.
2 Unkempt: clothes not too clean, uncared-for appearance.
3 'Ordinary' clothes. Clean. No special effort.
4 Clean, cared-for appearance: appropriate.
5 Obsessively concerned with appearance.

Source: Brenda Meldrum, dramatherapist

Immediately after the dramatherapy session, I scored each client on each of the four dimensions. When I wrote my report on the clients I used the results to supplement my written statements. The figures from these scales are readily presented in graph form and by the simple method of physically imposing one graph profile over the other it is possible to see how one dimension may affect the other. For example, with one client I found more of a correlation between her Level of Involvement and Affective Disclosure profiles, than with her Emotional State profile. This suggested to me that this client both wanted to involve herself in the drama and needed to talk about her feelings, whatever her emotional state, and my notes of the sessions reflected this judgement. I also use this instrument with individuals, and I find it helpful as a clarification of the therapeutic process.

Dramatherapy research in the planning stage

Here I report briefly on just three research projects that are in their initial stages at the moment, to give some idea of the range of dramatherapeutic work in progress.

Maggie Young, an occupational therapist and dramatherapist, is currently doing an MA and for her dissertation she will be working with a group of women with bulimia using psychological instruments as part of the assessment procedure, such as an Eating Disorders Inventory; a Locus of Control questionnaire; a Family Environment Scale and a Self-rating Scale for Bulimia. These measures will be scored at the start and at the end of twenty weeks to measure change. The aim is to identify shared goals of treatment at the initial assessment and also to identify goals that are not shared between therapist and client. At the end of the twenty-week treatment session, there will be a client and therapist evaluation of progress or lack of progress.

Ditty Doktor, convenor of the Dramatherapy Research Committee, has registered for a PhD looking at 'Cultural and ritual processes in arts therapies healing', the first stage of which will be a comparative study of different arts therapies. The second stage will look at their application with clients from different cultural backgrounds.

Lorraine Fox, working in a National Health Service Hospital in Scotland, is currently engaged in research into evaluative instruments, which she hopes will be adaptable for dramatherapists in the NHS who work in care teams where audits, assessments, evaluations and budgets are called for by hospital management.

CONCLUSION

I do not myself believe that dramatherapists have to prove, or even suggest, that dramatherapy practice is in any way 'scientific', because it is not and never will be, nor should it be. However, we live and work in the 'real' world of market forces, consumer-led service, throughputs, evaluations, assessments, budgets, audits and so on and so on. Unless we are to be marginalised in the National Health Service, dramatherapists would do well to face these issues and workplace requirements in a truly *dramatherapeutic way*. That is to say, we should address research, evaluation and assessment creatively, realistically and with as much objectivity as we can muster to find tools and instruments as suited to our therapeutic practice as we can make them. From the research projects I have presented in this chapter, some dramatherapists are joining with psychologists in very fruitful ways and others are using their own adaptations of psychotherapeutic and psychological instruments to help them evaluate their practice. With the advent of MA research degree courses in dramatherapy, many more students will be addressing these difficult areas and the training should reflect methodological concerns. In *Daughter of Copper Woman,* Anne Cameron (1981) tells the story of Sisiutl, the fearsome monster of the sea, who is terrifying and fearful. 'When you see Sisiutl the terrifying, though you be frightened, stand firm. There is no shame in being frightened' (p. 36).

Finally, I should like to express my gratitude to all those who have helped me with this chapter, some giving considerable time to write about their practice in detail.

REFERENCES

Bannister, D. and Fransella, F. (1966) 'A grid test of schizophrenic thought disorder', *British Journal of Social and Clinical Psychology,* 5, 95–102.

Bloch, S., Reibstein, J., Crouch, E., Holroyd, P. and Thement, J. (1979) 'A method for the study of therapeutic factors in group psychotherapy', *British Journal of Psychology,* 134, 257–63.

Cameron, A. (1981) *Daughter of Copper Woman,* London, The Women's Press.

Cattanach, A. (1992) *Play Therapy with Abused Children,* London, Jessica Kingsley.

Cohen, L. and Manion, L. (1980) *Research Methods in Education,* London, Routledge & Kegan Paul.

Cox, M. (1986) *Coding the Therapeutic Process: Emblems of Encounter,* London, Pergamon Press.

Fontana, D. and Valente, L. (1989) 'Monitoring client behaviour as a guide to progress', *Dramatherapy,* 12(1).

Fransella, F. (1990) 'Personal construct therapy', in Windy Dryden (ed.) *Individual Therapy: a Handbook,* Milton Keynes, Open University Press.

Gersie, A. (1991) *Storymaking in Bereavement: Dragons Fight in the Meadow,* London, Jessica Kingsley.

Gersie, A. and King, N. (1990) *Storymaking in Education and Therapy,* London, Jessica Kingsley.

Grainger, R. (1990) *Drama and Healing: the Roots of Dramatherapy,* London, Jessica Kingsley.

Grainger, R. (1992) 'Dramatherapy and thought disorder', in Sue Jennings (ed.) *Dramatherapy Theory and Practice 2,* London, Routledge.

Irwin, D. and Bushwell, M. (1980) *Observational Strategies for Child Study,* New York, Holt, Rinehart & Winston.

Jennings, S. (1991) 'Theatre art: the heart of dramatherapy', *Dramatherapy,* 14(1), 4–7.

Jones, P. (1993) 'The active witness: the acquisition of meaning in dramatherapy', in H. Payne (ed.) *One River, Many Currents,* London, Jessica Kingsley.

Kelly, G. (1955) *The Psychology of Personal Constructs,* New York, Norton.

Kersner, M. (1990) 'Are questionnaires a useful tool for arts therapies research?', in M. Kersner (ed.) *The Art of Research,* Proceedings of the Second Arts Therapies Research Conference, April.

Lahad, M. (1992) 'Storymaking: an assessment method of coping with stress: six-piece storymaking and BASIC Ph', in Sue Jennings (ed.) *Dramatherapy Theory and Practice 2,* London, Routledge.

Landy, R. (1986) *Drama Therapy: Concepts and Practices,* Springfield, IL, Charles C. Thomas.

Meldrum, B. (1993) 'On "being the thing I am": an enquiry into the therapeutic aspects of Shakespeare's *As You Like it* ', in H. Payne (ed.) *One River, Many Currents,* London, Jessica Kingsley.

Mitchell, S. (1990) 'The theatre of Peter Brook as a model for dramatherapy', *Dramatherapy*, 13(1).

Pilgrim, D. (1990) 'British psychotherapy in context', in Windy Dryden (ed.) *Individual Therapy*, Milton Keynes, Open University Press.

Reason, P. (ed.) (1988) *Human Enquiry in Action: Developments in New Paradigm Research*, London, Sage.

Reason, P. and Rowan, J. (1981) *Human Enquiry: a Sourcebook of New Paradigm Research*, Chichester, John Wiley.

Sanctuary, R. (1984) 'Role play with puppets for social skills training', unpublished report for London University.

Valente, L. and Fontana, D. (1990) 'Research on the use of drama in therapy', in M. Kersner (ed.) *The Art of Research*, Proceedings of the Second Arts Therapies Research Conference, April.

Yalom, R. (1985) *The Theory and Practice of Group Psychotherapy: 3rd edn*, New York, Basic Books.

Epilogue

Sue Jennings

This book has taken the reader on a rich and varied journey through the exciting world of dramatherapy. It has taken us through the history and establishment of dramatherapy, the training programmes, the central concern with the nature of role, as well as the importance of evaluation and research. It has taken us into the world of the newborn and children through dramatic development and play; and it looks at application in various contexts of people with mental health problems as well as people with learning disabilities. A feature of many of the chapters has been the 'space between' or the interface: between play therapy and drama-therapy, between psychodrama and dramatherapy, between ritual theatre and healing, and between the life-size and the larger-than-life. Dramatherapists work at the interface, the space between themselves and their clients, which is a space of dramatic reality, a symbolic and ritualised space where change and transition, through masques and masks, can take place.

It is important that dramatherapists continue to address the way forward in their work and make attempts to develop a language of dramatherapy that is not shrouded in mystery but is readily available to clients, managers, families and non-specialists alike. Practitioners need to address their practice through research and assessment as well as written publications, and to continue to find new forms and structures, new rituals and games. Dramatherapy must continue to respond to the need of the society within which it is placed, as society grows and develops in unexpected ways. We need to continue the dialogue with the other arts therapies in art, music, dance-movement and play and to make sure that the end of this century can be heralded by a creative entry into the next.

Where there is no vision, the people perish.

(Proverbs 29: 18)

Our revels now are ended. These our actors,
As I foretold you, were all spirits, and
Are melted into air, into thin air.

(*The Tempest* IV. i. 147–9)

Appendix 1

What is dramatherapy?

Dramatherapy is an artistic therapy based on theatre art and applied in clinical and social settings, with both individuals and groups.

Dramatherapy assumes that people are intrinsically 'dramatic' in their development; the early manifestations of dramatic principles are observed in the first three months of life.

Dramatherapy methods include movement, mime, voice-work, dramatic play, drama-games, role-play, scripts, masks, myths and stories.

Dramatherapy theory is based primarily on theatre theory, play and role theories, and developmental drama (EPR); it is also informed by developmental psychology, Jungian archetypal psychology, object-relations, and group dynamics and processes.

Dramatherapy aims to:

- promote the healing intrinsic to theatre art;
- focus on healthy aspects of the person;
- develop latent creative drama;
- encourage intuition, metaphor, dramatic imagination;
- practise life and social skills through dramatisation;
- stimulate communication through voice and drama;
- enable working through of issues in 'dramatic distance';
- maximise personal growth and social developmental drama.

Dramatherapists are trained at a postgraduate level for 3 to 4 years in drama-therapy theory, method and practice, theatre art and technique, clinical theory and pathology. Trainee dramatherapists carry out supervised clinical placements as well as experiencing their own extended personal therapy.

Dramatherapy complements other forms of therapeutic intervention and reinforces artistic, therapeutic and learning processes. The dramatherapy process moves from everyday reality into dramatic reality and includes both 'ritual and risk'. The dramatherapy process expands rather than reduces a person's experience of themselves and the world and its necessary limits.

Dramatherapy is an art and a craft, applied in the service of prevention, growth, therapy and enrichment. Dramatherapy may be applied in psychological and social models, but it is unique in its capacity to enter the mythic and the ritual and therefore the metaphysical.

The Institute of Dramatherapy
30 June 1993

Appendix 2

Codes of Practice and Ethics

The Institute of Dramatherapy applies the following Codes of Practice and Ethics to its training and therapeutic staff, registered trainees in dramatherapy and play therapy, and visiting staff.

CODE OF PRACTICE

Registered dramatherapists agree to:

Observe the Code of Ethics of the Institute of Dramatherapy.

Establish a clear contract with the client/patient based on open information regarding fees and qualifications. Where possible this contract should be confirmed in writing.

Ensure that the client/patient fully understands the nature of dramatherapy or play therapy (that it allows touch and noise, for example).

Encourage a client/patient to seek medical help where appropriate, and seek the client/patient's consent to inform the GP that the client/patient is receiving dramatherapy or play therapy (either individually or in groups).

Ensure that the methods used are appropriate for age, gender and limitations of the client/patient and that at no time should a client/patient be made to look foolish.

Protect the client/patient from any behaviours that may be misconstrued, and not enter into a sexual relationship with a client/patient, or indeed a social relationship before or after therapy.

Ensure that the workspace is appropriate for the nature of the work in relation to comfort, lighting and heating and that it ensures privacy.

Keep appropriate records of clinical therapy and material to be presented at supervision.

Monitor their own practice and teaching, and seek professional/personal support where appropriate.

Undergo regular supervision and consultation; continue creative development through workshops and theatre visits; take out professional indemnity for their practice.

Maintain respect for colleagues in similar professions and encourage open dialogue on theory and practice.

Inform the Institute of Dramatherapy of any conviction or lawsuit.

CODE OF ETHICS

Registered dramatherapists agree to the following parameters:

The interests of the client/patient are put first.

The client/patient is given full instruction as to the nature of the treatment undertaken so that informed decisions may be made.

The client/patient is not abused in any way, either financially, sexually or socially. The dramatherapy or play therapy so offered does not impose particular values, beliefs or ideology.

The dramatherapy or play therapy does not present material that is inappropriate to client/patient needs or that in any way undermines a client/patient's self-esteem and confidence.

The confidential nature of the treatment situation is clearly understood, i.e. whether material is confidential to the team or to the individual therapist. The exception to this is if the safety of the client/patient or others is threatened. The client/patient can be informed that confidentiality may be broken under these circumstances.

While engaged in the work of the Institute, either in teaching or in therapy, they will monitor their own professional competence and undertake such re-training and personal therapy as is necessary.

They will have regular supervision and consultation in relation to teaching and therapeutic practice.

Any research undertaken with students or the client/patient conforms to the Tokyo Convention of 1975.

They do not act in any way to bring the Institute of Dramatherapy into disrespect.

Appendix 3

Dramatherapy training

The British Association for Dramatherapy validates appropriate dramatherapy training courses which are taught at postgraduate level and lead to full membership of the Association.

Dramatherapy courses are taught at the following colleges in the United Kingdom:

The Institute of Dramatherapy at Roehampton
The Roehampton Institute

The School of Art and Design
The University of Hertfordshire

The University of Ripon and York St John

South Devon College

City College, Manchester

St Margaret's College, Edinburgh

The Institute of Dramatherapy and the University of Hertfordshire also offer MAs in Dramatherapy. All the colleges offer a variety of short courses and summer schools.

The addresses of all these courses are available in the Dramatherapy Information Pack, available (price £3) from:

The British Association for Dramatherapists
5 Sunnydale Villas
Durlston Road
Swanage
Dorset BH19 2HY

Overseas Dramatherapy Training
The Greek Institute of Dramatherapy
Arradou 55A
Ilissia 15772
Athens
Greece

Dramatherapy Diploma Course
Tel Hai Regional College
Upper Galilee 12210
Israel

Drama Therapy Programme
New York University
35 West 4th Street, Suite 675B
New York 10012-1172
USA

Drama Therapy Programme
California Institute of Integral Studies
765 Ashbury Street
San Francisco
CA 94117
USA

The British Association for Dramatherapists

The British Association for Dramatherapists is the professional body which represents dramatherapists and their professional practice. It is formally constituted with officers and an Executive Committee. It has the legal status of a non-profit-making company, limited by guarantee, although it is currently working towards applying for charitable status. Through the work of its executive officers, sub-committees and individual members, it represents dramatherapists' interests in numerous ways, for example, with employing authorities, government departments, professional bodies and the media. In recent years the Association has been liaising and negotiating with the following organisations (amongst others):

- United Kingdom Standing Conference on Psychotherapy (UKSCP)
- Standing Committee for Arts Therapies Professions (SCATP)
- Department of Health (DoH)
- Department of Education and Science (DES)
- National Joint Council for Local Authorities (NJCLA)
- Council for Professions Supplementary to Medicine (CPSM)
- Various Trade Unions
- British Psychodrama Association
- Colleges offering Training in Dramatherapy

The Executive Committee also receives regular feedback from dramatherapist representatives on the Arts Therapies Research Committee and the organisation for Arts Therapists in Prisons. Recent notable achievements have included official recognition by the Whitley Council (giving set pay and conditions for NHS-employed dramatherapists), establishing a Code of Practice, agreeing mandatory supervision for newly qualified dramatherapists and successfully accomplishing the first stage of our application for registration with the CPSM.

The Association publishes the journal of *Dramatherapy* three times a year and a quarterly newsletter keeps members up to date on developments as well as also providing a forum for debate and information. The Annual National Conference and AGM attracts dramatherapists, related practitioners and other participants from all over the United Kingdom, Europe and the USA.

In this way the Association, via its Executive Committee, facilitates the systematic growth and overall professional development of dramatherapy in the country.

MEMBERSHIP OF THE BRITISH ASSOCIATION FOR DRAMATHERAPISTS

For individuals, the following categories are available:

Full   for all practising, qualified dramatherapists,
Associate   for people with an interest in dramatherapy,
Student   for those in training on a recognised dramatherapy course.

Library membership is available for organisations that wish to subscribe.

All enquiries: The British Association for Dramatherapists (BADth)
5 Sunnydale Villas
Durlston Road
Swanage
Dorset BH19 2HY

Appendix 5

Bibliography

Andersen-Warren, M. (1992) Private Correspondence with S. Mitchell for 'Therapeutic Theatre Project'.

Antinucci-Mark, G. (1986) 'Some thoughts on the similarities between psychotherapy and theatre scenarios', *British Journal of Psychotherapy*, 3(1).

Arieti, S. (1976) *Creativity: the Magic Synthesis*, New York, Basic Books.

Artaud, A. (1964) *Oeuvres Complètes IV–V*, Paris, Gallimard.

Artaud, A. (1970) *The Theatre and its Double*, London, John Calder.

Bannister, D. and Fransella, F. (1966) 'A grid test of schizophrenic thought disorder', *British Journal of Social and Clinical Psychology*, 5, 95–102.

Barker, C. (1977) *Theatre Games*, London, Methuen.

Bettelheim, B. (1978) *The Uses of Enchantment*, Harmondsworth, Penguin.

Bloch, S. (1982) *What is Psychotherapy?*, Oxford, Oxford University Press.

Bloch, S., Reibstein, J., Crouch, E., Holroyd, P. and Thement, J. (1979) 'A method for the study of therapeutic factors in group psychotherapy', *British Journal of Psychology*, 134, 257–63.

Boal, A. (1992) *Games for Actors and Non-Actors* (trans. A. Jackson), London, Routledge.

Bowlby, J. (1988) *A Secure Base: Clinical Applications of Attachment Theory*, London, Routledge.

British Association for Dramatherapists (1991) Membership List and Code of Practice, London, BADth.

Brook, P. (1988) *The Shifting Point*, London, Methuen.

Cameron, A. (1981) *Daughter of Copper Woman*, London, The Women's Press.

Campbell, J. (1973) *Myths to Live By*, New York, Bantam.

Campbell, J. (1990) *The Power of Myth*, New York, Doubleday.

Castellani, V. (1990) 'Drama and Aristotle', in J. Redmond (ed.) *Themes in Drama 12: Drama and Philosophy*, Cambridge, Cambridge University Press.

Cattanach, A. (1992) *Play Therapy with Abused Children*, London, Jessica Kingsley.

Cattanach, A. (1992) *Drama for People with Special Needs*, London, A. & C. Black.

Chesner, A. (forthcoming) *Dramatherapy and Learning Disabilities*, London, Jessica Kingsley.

Cohen, L. and Manion, L. (1980) *Research Methods in Education*, London, Routledge & Kegan Paul.

Courtney, R. (1985) 'The dramatic metaphor and learning', in J. Kase-Polisini (ed.) *Creative Drama in a Developmental Context*, Lanham, University Press of America.

Cox, M. (1986) *Coding the Therapeutic Process: Emblems of Encounter*, London, Pergamon Press.

Cox, M. (ed.) (1992) *Shakespeare Comes to Broadmoor*, London, Jessica Kingsley.

Cox, M. and Theilgaard, A. (1987) *Mutative Metaphors in Psychotherapy*, London, Tavistock.

Doktor, D. (1992) 'Dramatherapy a psychotherapy?', *Dramatherapy*, 14(2): 9–11.

Dunn, J. (1988) *The Beginnings of Social Understanding*, Oxford, Basil Blackwell.

Eliade, M. (1958) *Rites and Symbols of Initiation*, New York, Harper Torchbooks.

Ellis, N. (trans.) (1988) *Awakening Osiris*, Grand Rapids, Phanes Press.

Erikson, E. (1965) *Childhood and Society*, Harmondsworth, Penguin.

Fontana, D. and Valente, L. (1989) 'Monitoring client behaviour as a guide to progress', *Dramatherapy*, 12(1).

Foulkes, S.H. (1990) *Selected Papers*, London, Karnac.

Fox, J. (1987) *The Essential Moreno*, New York, Springer.

Fransella, F. (1990) 'Personal construct therapy', in Windy Dryden (ed.) *Individual Therapy: a Handbook*, Milton Keynes, Open University Press.

Fransella, F. and Dalton, P. (1990) *Personal Construct Counselling in Action*, London, Sage.

Gersie, A. (1987) 'Dramatherapy and play', in S. Jennings (ed.) *Dramatherapy Theory and Practice 1*, London, Routledge.

Gersie, A. (1991) *Storymaking in Bereavement: Dragons Fight in the Meadow*, London, Jessica Kingsley.

Gersie, A. (1992) *Earthtales: Storytelling in Times of Change*, London, Green Print.

Gersie, A. and King, N. (1990) *Storymaking in Education and Therapy*, London, Jessica Kingsley.

Goffman, E. (1959) *The Presentation of the Self in Everyday Life*, New York, Doubleday.

Goffman, E. (1972) *Encounters*, Harmondsworth, Penguin Books.

Goffman, E. (1974) *Frame Analysis*, Cambridge, MA, Harvard University Press.

Goldman, E.E. and Morrison, D.S. (1984) *Psychodrama: Experience and Process*, Dubuque, IO, Kendall/Hunt.

Grainger, R. (1990) *Drama and Healing: the Roots of Dramatherapy*, London, Jessica Kingsley.

Grainger, R. (1992) 'Dramatherapy and thought disorder', in S. Jennings (ed.) *Dramatherapy Theory and Practice 2*, London, Routledge.

Grotowski, J. (1968) *Towards a Poor Theatre*, New York, Simon & Schuster.

Halprin, A. (1976) 'Theatre and therapy workshop', *The Drama Review* (March).

Hampson, S. (1986) 'Sex roles and personality', in D. Hargreaves and A.M. Colley (eds) *The Psychology of Sex Roles*, London, Harper & Row.

Hampson, S. (1988) *The Construction of Personality: an Introduction*, London, Routledge.

Hillman, J. (1983) *Healing Fiction*, New York, Station Hill.

Holmes, J. and Lindley, R. (1991) *The Values of Psychotherapy*, Oxford, Oxford University Press.

Holmes, P. (1992) *The Inner World Outside*, London, Routledge.

Horwood, T. (1992) 'BADTh and the humanistic and integrative group of the UKSCP', *Dramatherapy Newsletter* (Summer), p. 6.

Huizinga, J. (1955) *Homo Ludens*, Boston, Beacon Press.

Irwin, E.C. (1979) 'Drama therapy with handicapped', in A. Shaw and C.J. Stevens (eds) *Drama, Theatre and the Handicapped*, Washington, DC, American Theatre Association.

Jenkyns, M. (1992) 'The warm up', Teaching notes, Dramatherapy Course, St Albans.

Jenkyns, M. and Barham, M. (1991) *BADth Application to Join the Council for Professions Supplementary to Medicine, on Behalf of the Profession of Dramatherapy*, London, BADth.

Jennings, S. (1973) *Remedial Drama*, London, Pitman.

Jennings, S. (1986) *Creative Drama in Groupwork*, Winslow Press.

Jennings, S. (1986) 'The loneliness of the long distance therapist', Paper from *The Annual Forum*, Axbridge, The Champernowne Trust.

Jennings, S. (ed.) (1987) *Dramatherapy Theory and Practice 1*, London, Routledge.

Jennings, S. (1990) *Dramatherapy with Families, Groups and Individuals* (also trans. into Danish), London and New York, Jessica Kingsley.

Jennings, S. (1991) 'Theatre art: the heart of dramatherapy', *Dramatherapy*, 14(1), 4–7.

Jennings, S. (1992) 'The nature and scope of dramatherapy: theatre of healing', in M. Cox (ed.) *Shakespeare Comes to Broadmoor*, London, Jessica Kingsley.

Jennings, S. (ed.) (1992) *Dramatherapy Theory and Practice 2*, London, Routledge.

Jennings, S. (1993) *Introduction to Dramatherapy*, London, Jessica Kingsley.

Jennings, S. (forthcoming) *Shakespeare's Theatre of Healing*.

Jennings, S. (forthcoming) *The Greek Theatre of Healing*.

Jennings, S. and Minde, A. (1993) *Dramatherapy and Art Therapy*, London, Jessica Kingsley.

Johnson, L. and O'Neill, C. (eds) (1984) *Dorothy Heathcote: Collected Writings on Education and Drama*, London, Hutchinson.

Jones, P. (1991) 'Dramatherapy: five core processes', *Dramatherapy*, 14(1).

Jones, P. (1993) 'The active witness: the acquisition of meaning in dramatherapy', in H. Payne (ed.) *One River, Many Currents*, London, Jessica Kingsley.

Kelly, G. (1955) *The Psychology of Personal Constructs*, New York, Norton.

Kersner, M. (1990) 'Are questionnaires a useful tool for arts therapies research?', in M. Kersner (ed.) *The Art of Research*, Proceedings of the Second Arts Therapies Research Conference, City University, London (April).

Kumiega, J. (1987) *The Theatre of Grotowski*, London and New York, Methuen.

Lahad, M. (1992) 'Storymaking: an assessment method for coping with stress. Six-piece storymaking and the BASIC Ph', in S. Jennings (ed.) *Dramatherapy Theory and Practice 2*, London, Routledge.

Landy, R. (1986) *Drama Therapy: Concepts and Practices*, Springfield, IL, Charles C. Thomas.

Landy, R. (1990) 'A role model of dramatherapy', Keynote speech to the Conference of the British Association for Dramatherapists, Newcastle.

Landy, R. (1991) 'The dramatic basis of role theory', *The Arts in Psychotherapy*, 19, 29–41.

Landy, R. (1992) 'One-on-one: the role of the dramatherapist working with individuals', in S. Jennings (ed.) *Dramatherapy Theory and Practice 2*, London, Routledge.

Landy, R. (1992) 'A taxonomy of roles: a blueprint for the possibilities of being', *The Arts in Psychotherapy*, 18(5), 419–31.

Landy, R. (1992) 'The case of Hansel and Gretel', *The Arts in Psychotherapy*, 19, 231–41.

Landy, R. (1992) 'The dramatherapy role method', *Dramatherapy*, 14(1), 7–15.

Langer, S. (1953) *Feeling and Form*, London, Routledge & Kegan Paul.

Langley, D. (1989) 'The relationship between psychodrama and dramatherapy', in P. Jones (ed.) *Dramatherapy: State of the Art*, Papers presented at 2-day conference held by the Division of Arts and Psychology, Hertfordshire College of Art and Design.

Langley, D. and Langley, G. (1983) *Dramatherapy and Psychiatry*, London, Croom Helm.

Lewis, G. (1980) *Day of Shining Red*, Cambridge, Cambridge University Press.

Lewis, I.M. (1986) *Religion in Context: Cults and Charisma*, Cambridge, Cambridge University Press.

McDougall, J. (1989) *Theatres of the Body*, London, Free Association Press.

Marrone, M. (1991) Address to the Institute of Dramatherapy, London.

Maslow, A. (1970) *Motivation and Personality*, New York, Harper & Row.

Maslow, A. (1971) *The Farther Reaches of Human Nature*, London, Pelican.

Mead, G.H. (1934) *Mind, Self and Society*, C.W. Morris (ed.), Chicago, IL, University of Chicago Press.

Meldrum, B. (1993) 'On "being the thing I am": an enquiry into the therapeutic aspects of Shakespeare's *As You Like It*', in H. Payne (ed.) *One River, Many Currents*, London, Jessica Kingsley.

Meldrum, B. (1993) 'A theatrical model of dramatherapy', *Dramatherapy*, 14(2):10–13.

Mitchell, S. (1990) 'The theatre of Peter Brook as a model for dramatherapy', *Dramatherapy*, 13(1).

Mitchell, S. (1992) 'Therapeutic theatre: a para-theatrical model of dramatherapy', in S. Jennings (ed.) *Dramatherapy Theory and Practice 2*, London, Routledge.

Mitchell, S. (1992) 'The similarities and differences between the theatre director and the dramatherapist', Keynote speech at the Shakespeare symposium, Stratford-upon-Avon.

Neelands, J. (1990) *Structuring Drama Work: a Handbook of Available Forms in Theatre and Drama*, T. Goode (ed.), Cambridge, Cambridge University Press.

O'Donnell Fulkerson, M. (1977) *Language of the Axis*, Dartington Theatre Papers, First Series No. 12.

O'Neill, C. and Lambert, A. (1982) *Drama Structures*, London, Hutchinson.

Opie, I. and Opie, P. (1992) *I Saw Esau*, London, Walker Books.

Ouspensky, P.D. (1977) *In Search of the Miraculous*, London, Routledge & Kegan Paul.

Parkin, D. (1985) 'Reason, emotion and the embodiment of power', in J. Overing (ed.) *Reason and Morality*, ASA Monograph 24, London, Tavistock.

Parten, M. (1927) cited in D. Irwin and M. Bushwell, *Observational Strategies for Child Study* (1980), New York, Holt, Rinehart & Winston.

Piaget, J. (1962) *Play, Dreams and Imitation in Childhood*, New York, Norton.

Pilgrim, D. (1990) 'British psychotherapy in context', in Windy Dryden (ed.) *Individual Therapy*, Milton Keynes, Open University Press.

Read Johnson, D. (1982) 'Developmental approaches in drama', *The Arts in Psychotherapy*, 9, 183–90.

Read Johnson, D. (1992) 'The dramatherapist "in-role"', in S. Jennings (ed.) *Dramatherapy Theory and Practice 2*, London, Routledge.

Reason, P. (ed.) (1988) *Human Enquiry in Action: Developments in New Paradigm Research*, London, Sage.

Reason, P. and Rowan, J. (1981) *Human Enquiry: a Sourcebook of New Paradigm Research*, Chichester, John Wiley.

Rebillot, P. (1993) *The Call to Adventure: Bringing the Hero's Journey to Daily Life*, New York, HarperCollins.

Rebillot, P. and Kay, M. (1979) 'A trilogy of transformation', *Pilgrimage*, 7(1).

Rees, E. (1992) *Christian Symbols, Ancient Roots*, London, Jessica Kingsley.

Roose-Evans, J. (1989) *Experimental Theatre from Stanislavski to Peter Brook*, London, Routledge. [This book is the only published account of Anna Halprin's work, although individual commentaries can be found in *The Drama Review*, 1960–1979.]

Roth, G. (1989) *Maps to Ecstasy*, San Rafael, CA, New World Publishing.

Rycroft, C. (1985) *Psycho-analysis and Beyond*, London, Hogarth.

Salmon, P. (1985) *Living in Time*, London, Dent.

Sanctuary, R. (1984) 'Role play with puppets for social skills training', unpublished report for London University.

Schechner, R. and Appel, W. (eds) (1990) *By Means of Performance*, Cambridge, Cambridge University Press.

Schwartzman, H.B. (1978) *Transformations: the Anthropology of Children's Play*, New York, Plenum Press.

Sellin, E. (1986) *The Dramatic Concepts of Antonin Artaud*, Chicago, IL, University of Chicago Press.

Shaffer, R. (1989) 'Early social development', in A. Slater and G. Bremner (eds) *Infant Development*, London, Lawrence Erlbaum.

Sinason, V. (1992) *Mental Handicap and the Human Condition*, London, Free Association Press.

Stern, D. (1985) *The First Relationship: Infant and Mother*, London, Fontana.

Turner, V. (1982) *From Ritual to Theatre*, New York, Performing Arts Journal Publishing.

Valente, L. and Fontana, D. (1990) 'Research on the use of drama in therapy', in. M. Kersner (ed.) *The Art of Research*, Proceedings of the Second Arts Therapies Research Conference (April).

Van Gennep, A. (1960) *The Rites of Passage*, London, Routledge & Kegan Paul.

Watts, A. (1973) *Psychotherapy East and West*, Harmondsworth, Pelican.

Watts, A. (1973) *The Book on the Taboo against Knowing Who You Are*, London, Abacus.

Watts, A. (1976) *Nature, Man and Woman*, London, Abacus.

Watts, A. (1976) *The Wisdom of Insecurity*, London, Rider.

Wickham, G. (1985) *A History of the Theatre*, Oxford, Phaidon.

Williams, A. (1989) *The Passionate Technique*, London, Tavistock/Routledge.

Wilshire, B. (1982) *Role Playing and Identity: the Limits of Theater as Metaphor*, Bloomington, IN, Indiana University Press.

Wilson, C. (1986) *G.I. Gurdjieff: the War Against Sleep*, Wellingborough, Aquarian Press.

Winnicott, D.W. (1974) *Playing and Reality*, London, Pelican.

Yalom, I. (1985) *The Theory and Practice of Group Psychotherapy* (3rd edn), New York, Basic Books.

Yalom, I. (1990) *Existential Psychotherapy*, New York, Basic Books.

Yalom, I. (1991) *Love's Executioner*, London, Penguin Books.

Name index

Subject index

abstract communication 64
abstraction from reality 34
Absurd, Theatre of the 102, 103
abuse by directors 52, 53
abused people: play therapy 191–3; regressive play 135; sexually abused 48, 141, 142, 181
achievement 67
acting in everyday life 2–3
actions: as basis of dramatherapy 196; easy 151; initiation of 33; and responses 81
active coping strategies 190
actors and observers 83–4
actors' roles in theatre 15, 78–9, 84–5
acute patients 45–8
aesthetic distance 85–6
affect see emotion
air rituals 154–8
altered states of consciousness 4
analytic psychodrama 119
Ancient Greek theatre see Greek theatre
anger 69
animals, identification with 159
anthropological approach to dramatherapy 25
appearance of client 205
archetypes, theatrical 88–91, 177
Areas of Need Schedule 194
articulacy 100
arts: decline of 94–5; multimodality of 179, 181
Arts Therapies Research Committee 187, 216
assassination of the self 86
assessment in dramatherapy 187–208
attachment 82, 84
audiences 2

authority as theme in clients' stories 69–70
autistic adults 199
autonomy and development 32, 100
auxiliary egos 120
awareness continuum 55

Balinese theatre 102, 103, 104
ball/name game 63
BASIC Ph 23, 189–90
beanbags 60
beginning of dramatherapy sessions 37–8, 46, 61, 63–5, 150–1
behavioural models of dramatherapy 196–7
behaviourism 196–7
being and doing 78–9, 85
Belgrade Theatre in Education (TIE) 167, 168, 170
belief systems 121, 122
beliefs and coping strategies 190
biological roles 77, 83
body: awareness of 105, 126, 155; boundaries of 142; in drama 115; and mind 91, 100, 115, 197
boundaries: of behaviour 138; of body 142; of spaces 136–7
Bread and Puppet Theatre 171
breathing exercises 46, 105, 155
British Association for Dramatherapists (BADth) 16–17, 19–20, 187, 216–17

Cambodian theatre 103
Care Managers in NHS 194
carer–client interactions 62
Central School of Speech and Drama 20, 215
ceremony see ritual
chairs in studio 60

5–6, 117–18, 176; solar drama 103, 104, 108, 109–10, 172; sound in 104, 105; space in 104, 116; story in 176; therapeutic 23–4; *see also* theatre
dramatherapists 21–2; interviews with 166–86; relations with clients 15–16, 54–5, 61, 76, 130–1, 201–2; role in client's story 25; roles 25, 43, 45, 47, 49, 75, 76, 90, 131; *see also* therapists
dramatherapy: definitions of 14–19, 114–15, 166–86, 210–11; history 12–14; professional position of 19–22; research into 195–206; structure and technique 125–9
Dramatherapy Centre 13
Dramatherapy Group Evaluation Form 202–3
Dramatherapy Venture Project 145–65
dramatic distance 15, 177
dramatic fiction 34–5
dramatic metaphors 31
dramatic play: with children 133–44; and drama 5; groups 140
dramaturgical model of behaviour 75, 77–80
dreams: and drama 116–17; theatre of 49

early experiences: of learning-impaired people 69; *see also* development
earth rituals 151–4
easy actions 151
Edinburgh, Grassmarket Theatre Project 52
education and training in dramatherapy 20–1, 183, 214–15
effigies, larger-than-life 106–12
ego integration in development 33
egos, auxiliary 120
'Egyptian Book of the Dead' 39
elderly people, dramatherapy with 42–4, 181–2
embodiment 126, 180
embodiment play 30, 135, 137
embodiment–projection–role (EPR) 4, 97, 100, 108, 112, 184, 200
emotional stages in development 32–3
emotions: assessment of 205; communication of 16; and coping strategies 190; expansion of 45; and therapy 16
enactment 84, 86, 180
encouragement of clients 67

ending dramatherapy sessions 37–8, 44, 46, 53–4, 61, 71–2, 150, 163–4
engagement 2, 107
environment: of children 36–7; and individual 34
epic metaphors 106
EPR *see* embodiment–projection–role
equipment *see* materials
ethics of dramatherapy 8, 212–13
evaluation in dramatherapy 187–208
'exercises plastiques' 152
expansion of emotions 45
expansive play 139
expectations: clients' 73; of role behaviour 76–80
exploration: in development 30; in play 139; of roles 89–90; of self/space 62
expression in dramatherapy 16
eye contact in dramatherapy 63

facilitative role of therapists 15–16, 23, 200
failure, risk of 53
Fairy Story Method 100
fairy tales *see* traditional stories
familiar space 70–1
family support 63, 185
fantasies, guided 46, 49
feelings 42, 68, 142, 176, 177
fiction, dramatic 34–5
fictional lives 28
fictional present 34, 138–9
fictional roles 140
finishing sessions *see* ending
fire rituals 159–61
flexible play 139
flights of fancy 67
folktales *see* traditional stories
formal operations stage of development 32
fun in dramatherapy 127
functioning, disorders of 197
furniture in studio 60
future and past 34, 42

gender roles 77, 83
generativity in development 33
Gestalt therapy and dramatherapy 25
gestures 81, 104
Grassmarket Theatre Project 52
Greek theatre 172
Grid Test of Schizophrenic Thought Disorder 198

Lightning Source UK Ltd.
Milton Keynes UK
UKHW020745091120
372966UK00010B/224